FRENCH LAW
Its Structure, Sources, and Methodology

René David

Translated by *Michael Kindred*

Louisiana State University Press BATON ROUGE
1972

Under the auspices of
The Louisiana State University Law School
Institute of Civil Law Studies

Originally published in 1960 as *Le droit français: Les données
fondamentales du droit français*
Copyright © 1959, Librairie Générale de Droit et de Jurisprudence
The English translation has been revised by the author to reflect changes
that have occurred since publication of the French edition.
ISBN 0-8071-0248-2
Library of Congress Catalog Card Number 74-181563
Translation copyright © 1972 by Louisiana State University Press
All rights reserved
Manufactured in the United States of America
Printed by Colonial Press Inc., Clinton, Massachusetts
Designed by Dwight Agner

Foreword

The Institute of Civil Law Studies of Louisiana State University Law School was established in 1967, with one of its primary purposes to encourage and facilitate research and publication in the civil law. Works which have already appeared include two volumes by A. N. Yiannopoulos, *The Civil Law of Property* and *Personal Servitudes*; the first volume of a treatise, *Obligations*, by S. Litvinoff; and *Essays on the Civil Law of Obligations*, edited by J. Dainow. In collaboration with the Louisiana State Law Institute, there have appeared the two-volume *Successions and Donations* by Aubry and Rau in the English translation by C. E. Lazarus; and the English translation by J. Mayda of *Prescription*, treatises by Baudry-Lacantinerie and Tissier, Aubry and Rau, and Carbonnier. Other works are in preparation.

In conformity with one of its principal objectives, the Institute of Civil Law Studies is pleased and proud to be able to sponsor the publication of this English edition of René David's *French Law*, translated by Michael Kindred. Professor David is internationally reputed as a foremost scholar and comparatist, and this book contains the distillation of his long experience in describing and explaining the French legal system to students and scholars of other countries. Professor Kindred has made an excellent English translation, which has been read and approved by Professor David to insure that the translation reflects his original meaning. Time will attest to the ultimate significance of this work as a contribution to the civil law and comparative law literature in the English language.

Joseph Dainow
Professor of Law, Louisiana State University
Director, Institute of Civil Law Studies

Preface to the
English Edition

English common law is technically the law developed and applied in English courts, and yet its influence extends far beyond the territorial limits of the British Isles. Almost all countries that once belonged to the British Empire, and most other English-speaking countries as well, modeled their legal systems after the common law of England and continue to draw inspiration and guidance from it. English judicial decisions and legal treatises are often read and referred to outside of England. Professors schooled in English law train lawyers abroad for other countries; and some foreigners still go to England for their legal training, even when they could be admitted to the practice of law in their home countries without being "called to the bar" in England or graduated from an English university.

French law holds a comparable position. It is more than the law applied in France. Like the English common law, French law is the model upon which other countries have built their legal systems. This is true of countries that were once part of the French colonial system and of many others that were never a part of that system. French law books are used in many such countries, particularly in Latin America and the Middle East. These countries often still send their students to be trained in French law schools or hire French law professors to teach in their own national universities. It was precisely for such foreign students, whom I taught when they came to study law and earn a doctorate in law at the University of Paris, that this introduction to French law was prepared.

Several factors help explain the central role of French law within the Romano-Germanic family (as contrasted with the common law family) of legal systems. The most important is no doubt the widespread recognition, use, and prestige of French as a language, which is itself a consequence of France's importance through the centuries as a major political power and, even more crucially, as the center of world culture. One need not emphasize that French was once the language of the aristocracy throughout Europe. It is sufficient to note that today French is the national language, either alone or with another language, of twenty-nine member nations of the United Nations.

On the more strictly legal plane two factors converged to establish the unique importance of French law in the world. One was the Napoleonic codification and the other was the lead France had over other European countries in establishing a democratic political system. These two elements deserve some further elaboration here.

The Napoleonic codification played a crucial role. Legal science had been international for centuries. Universities taught an ideal, theoretical "law," representing the law as enlightened minds knew it ought to be, rather than the "laws" applied in practice in the various European countries. This ideal law had been built upon the foundation of the Roman emperor Justinian's sixth-century compilations of Roman law. It was taught in Latin, the language of religion and science, at universities whose perspective was international regardless of their national location. Enlightened society regarded this utopian law developed in the universities as vastly superior to the customary law actually applied in the courts. The customary law was sometimes vehemently criticized for its diversity and lack of clarity and, increasingly, for its service and support of a social system that seemed indefensible in the age of the Enlightenment.

The French Revolution of 1789 sought a complete renovation of society and undertook to rectify the shortcomings of the legal order. The duality of the law, the disparity between the ideal law and the applied law, would be abolished by raising the latter to the level of the former. This concept inspired the codification, which was initiated at that time and completed after the establishment of the Empire. Five codes were thus enacted in France and proposed for the world. These codes contained clear and systematically presented rules of substantive and procedural law. In the new society they could be both taught in the universities and applied in the courts.

Legal science was thus offered a new framework, which it could not ignore. Although the new codes were initially applicable only in France, they gradually came to supersede the old Roman texts in other countries as well. Increasingly, judges and government officials were urged by people who believed in the principles of the French Revolution to adopt the French code solutions to particular problems. Although the initial introduction of the French codes into a large part of Europe resulted from military conquest, the codes responded to the deepest aspirations of the time and often continued in force after the end of the Napoleonic period. All French political pressure aside, these codes became in the nineteenth century the model for all countries desiring a modern legal system. This was true both in European and Latin American countries where democratic principles prevailed and in those countries of the Orient that thought it necessary or opportune for one reason or another to westernize. Naturally there were variations from country to country, according to decisions of legislatures and courts, but the French codes continued to be the model according to which one discussed modernization of the law at least until 1900, when the German civil code was enacted. As a consequence, Roman law commentaries fell into disuse and French treatises and case reports were consulted in their place. The use of such materials was particularly important in countries which were too small or underdeveloped to create an adequate national body of case law and legal scholarship.

The Napoleonic codification did not deal with all the various kinds of legal problems that exist. It was limited to the relations between individuals (civil and commercial law), criminal law, and the law of procedure; it left aside the law dealing with organization of government and the relations between the government and individuals (constitutional and administrative law). In these areas, therefore, the French codes did not provide a model for other countries. What the Napoleonic codes did not accomplish in this regard, however, occurred during the nineteenth and twentieth centuries as a result in large part of a second factor, namely the comparatively early establishment in France of a democratic political system. French political institutions inspired the respect of freedom-loving men in the many countries that still had authoritarian governments. The way in which governmental action gradually was brought under control and made subservient to the welfare of the people it was supposed to serve brought considerable prestige to French administrative law. In the end, French public law has had as significant an impact as French private law. The first German treatise on administrative law (published in 1886) was a treatise on *French* administrative law.

The purpose of the preceding discussion has been simply to indicate the historical reasons why French law has a unique place and importance at the center of the Romano-Germanic family of legal systems. In no way is it intended to suggest that contemporary French law is superior to any other national law belonging to this family. Even less could one assert that French law constitutes a perfect expression of ideal justice in the contemporary world. Other legal systems have improved upon the French model in many ways; and sweeping reforms are required in French law to deal with the challenges of today's world. Nevertheless, the new developments that have occurred over the past two centuries in the countries of the Romano-Germanic family have been profoundly influenced by French law, and the best way to understand these other legal systems, as well as those of the socialist countries of Eastern Europe, is still to study initially the principles of French law and the way in which French lawyers reason about legal problems.

The primary purpose of this book is to demonstrate what these principles are, how French lawyers reason, and how these principles and ways of thinking differ from those familiar to common lawyers. In addition, it is appropriate here to make a few general remarks about the whole body of legal systems that comprise the Romano-Germanic family.

The first point is that a Frenchman, German, Brazilian, or Iranian does not regard the law as something of interest only to lawyers. The law is not a restricted domain. It is not the business of judges and practitioners alone, because the law is not limited to litigation. The law is seen as a method of social organization, always changing, and is thus of primary interest to statesmen and in fact to all citizens.

It is crucial to remember that for many centuries "the law" as taught in the universities was purely an ideal law. Judges and lawyers were asked to draw inspiration from this ideal, and the leaders of society were asked to adopt the ideal system. While the rules of the ideal law were never entirely adopted, the rules developed by the government and the courts were never regarded by scholars, or by public opinion, as the law. This concept is difficult for the common law lawyer to understand, inasmuch as the common law is tied by definition to the work of the courts. But the concept is essential. It was a central reality in the development of law in the Romano-Germanic family of systems, and is the concept of law held today by jurists in Islamic and Hindu legal systems.

This traditional view of law has not disappeared completely yet in the countries with Romano-Germanic systems. It is significant that in all of these countries it is constantly asserted that judicial opinions are not a source of law. And from this follows the importance of scholarly writing. It is this concept also that dictates that a person who is a law professional must have a university degree. It also explains the phenomenally large number of students in French law schools. Law is not simply a matter for lawyers. French law schools are not, and do not seek to be, professional schools. In addition, law is taught outside of the law schools, in the Institutes of Political Science, schools of government, faculties of economics, and business schools. Politicians and administrators often are, and sometimes are required to be, trained in the law. The approximately 15,000 students who graduate from French law schools each year have no trouble finding employment.

Why is this all so? The reason is that for the French, law is the social science par excellence, an instrument which deals not only with conflicts in society, but which provides for the ordering of relationships within society. As Lenin said, law is politics. This assertion, constantly repeated in socialist countries, is equally true in the countries of the Romano-Germanic family. The only difference—which is of central importance—is that in the materialistic view, politics is sovereign, whereas in the idealistic view that the French hold, politics is subordinate to the concept of justice.

A second characteristic of French law, which is related to the preceding, is that law is primarily regarded as a body of substantive rules of organization and conduct; procedure and the administration of justice take a secondary place.

Initially the English common law consisted of a limited number of procedural actions through which the courts could obtain jurisdiction and on the basis of which they administered justice. What solution would be given at the end of these procedures? Often it was difficult to predict. *Remedies precede rights* is a notion that dominated the common law until recently and continues to have an effect today in common law countries.

In the countries of the European continent, on the other hand, procedure was of less importance. In France it was never necessary to ask what kinds of cases one could take before the royal courts. Nor did one ever ask what form of action should be used to establish jurisdiction and to proceed. Courts had universal jurisdiction and a single, relatively simple procedure. Under these conditions, legal science was able to turn its attention from procedural questions and focus on what substantive rights it was appropriate to accord individuals in the name of justice. The universities ignored procedure, evidence, and problems of the execution of judgments. All of these matters, whose regulation differed from country to country, were regarded as problems of the administration of justice rather than of justice itself, which was the essence of law. Legal science left these problems to practitioners, since they were not truly questions of law.

This is not to say, of course, that procedure played no role in the development of French law. It was only possible to teach law in French universities because a rational court procedure was very early substituted for the nonrational procedures of the Middle Ages. Without this revolution, which occurred at the initiative of the church, the teaching of law would never have gotten beyond the problems of practice, and the universities would have played no role. The procedural system thus adopted on the European continent influenced the development of the law, but very differently from the way procedure influenced the law of England. The absence of forms of action made it possible to consider the law as a whole, as a system. The absence of juries placed power in the hands of jurists, who received their training in the universities. It allowed for progress toward, if not reception of, the ideal law developed from the Roman compilations. The freedom the continental procedure gave judges allowed them to develop the law to meet changing needs, so that there was no need to turn to special courts or rules of "equity"; the English distinction between law and equity has no counterpart in continental legal systems, and it is beyond the comprehension of lawyers in these countries. The institution of the trust, one of the principal products of English equity, is unknown in French law.

This observation brings us to a third broad difference between the legal systems of the Romano-Germanic family and those of the common law family. The Romano-Germanic systems have a completely different structure from the English system and systems modeled on that of England. The structure of the common law has been greatly marked by historical accidents. The distinction between common law and equity is one of these distinctions, and more generally the categories and concepts of the common law are very closely tied to the "forms of action" that previously restricted the growth of the law.

Nothing of this sort happened in France or the other continental countries. The preoccupation with jurisdictional issues and the need to fit problems into narrow, formal procedural categories never was a matter of concern for the jurists who taught law in the universities or the judges who applied and developed it in the courts. In these circumstances considerable progress was made, even before the final achievement of codification, toward organizing the law systematically, explaining it rationally, and articulating the general rules and principles that transcend decisions in individual court cases.

Although continental legal systems are more systematically organized than the common law, it would be a mistake to regard them as the creation of impractical theoreticians. While one school of Roman law scholars, the nineteenth-century pandectists, might be criticized as too oriented toward abstract systems and logic, this criticism cannot be leveled at the earlier schools of Roman law scholars, who collaborated in the development of the system that found its realization in the French Civil Code. Nor is it applicable to the draftsmen of the codes. The universities have always collaborated closely with the courts, and many of our greatest legal scholars are judges. No law teacher was involved in drafting the Civil Code or the other Napoleonic codes, and only three of the twelve men appointed to the commission to revise the Civil Code after the Second World War were law teachers.

French law is not a creation of law professors. Like the common law, it is a judge-made law in its origins. The only difference is that judicial decisions have not been viewed as authoritative in themselves. Their authority arises only after they have received scholarly study, evaluation, and systematization. Legal science has viewed them as an essential, but not the exclusive, source of insights into the kinds of rules required to achieve justice. Scholars try to view judicial decisions in the context of the system as a whole and to distill from them their essence, in the form of more general rules which avoid a detail that may be injurious to the clarity of the law.

The most outstanding characteristic of modern French law, from the common law lawyer's point of view, is the importance it gives to legislation. French law appears to a common law lawyer first and foremost as codified law. The primary source of the law in France appears to be legislation, whereas in common law countries the primary source appears to be case law. There is of course much truth in this observation, but like any generalization it is misleading if not correctly understood. It is essential to understand how legislation is viewed and applied in France.

French law is codified, and legislation occupies a paramount position. While this statement is valid, it is no more true than an assertion that English, American, or Australian law is based upon judicial decisions. In many areas of those legal systems legislation is of great importance, and similarly in France there are areas of the law that consist primarily of judicial decisions. A few of the most important areas where this is true are administrative law, private international law, and noncontractual liability.

Even in the areas where legal rules are legislative in form, French lawyers view them very differently from common law lawyers. A common law lawyer regards a statute as a legislative dictate that must be obeyed as strictly as possible, while a French lawyer has a completely different perspective. He thinks of the codes as a modernized *Corpus Juris Civilis*. Everyone knows how that document was interpreted and distorted over the centuries to develop the kinds of solutions required by a changing society. Now the same kind of effort is required of the courts and scholars with respect to the codes. This effort was not very apparent during the nineteenth century, when the codes were new and their rules generally coincided with lawyers' views of the requirements of justice. But this harmony no longer exists in some areas, and courts and scholars have taken great liberties with the codes. "By the Civil Code, beyond the Civil Code" was the motto provided to jurists in 1900 by Saleilles, who paraphrased Ihering's earlier statement in Germany: "By the Roman law, beyond the Roman law." This formula describes the method of contemporary French jurists.

In a very broad sense, legislation plays the same role in France as judicial decisions play in common law countries. Legislative rules provide the starting point from which lawyers and judges work toward their goal, the most just solution for the problem at hand. Usually the statute provides a clear answer to the problem. In those cases, the statute is strictly applied, more because it is just than because it is a statute. Because of this it often appears that legislation is the law and that the judge's role is simply to apply automatically the ready-made solutions provided by the legislature. Nevertheless, there are a great many cases where the judge's role is far more creative. The legislature sometimes deliberately speaks in very general terms: it has said that divorce can be obtained where there are serious grounds; contracts must be performed in good faith; a person must repair the damage caused another by his fault; the penalty for a crime can be reduced if there are extenuating circumstances; an act of a government official is invalid if in excess of his powers. The legislature, however, has not defined serious grounds or fault, nor explained what is required by good faith nor what constitute extenuating circumstances. Of course statutory law is being applied in all of these cases, but it is essential to recognize that the statute takes on real meaning only as the courts interpret it. The way in which the United States Supreme Court interprets the United States Constitution can give a common law lawyer an idea of how French courts interpret the legislation from which they work. Sometimes statutory rules that are explicit beyond any possibility of interpretation are neutralized and their application avoided by the use of certain supereminent principles of law or morality. The principles that rights are not to be abused, that fraud contaminates anything it touches, that public order must be respected, that citizens must be treated equally in the public sphere, and other principles that dominate our legal order (whether or not they have received legislative expression) are sometimes used, like the *Generalklauseln* (general provisions) in German law, to avoid the application of particular statutory rules.

Thus, the difference between French law and the common law in their treatment of the sources of law is much more a matter of technique than of substance. In common law countries, the basic raw materials are provided by judicial decisions, and the lawyer seeks to use these raw materials to build a just solution for his case, using where necessary the tool of "distinguishing cases." The French jurist, starting from his raw materials of legislatively formulated rules, tries to achieve the same result by using the tool of interpretation.

At one time the legal systems of the common law family and those of the Romano-Germanic family had very basically opposing natures. This was so as long as the common law took a fundamentally procedural approach and the formalistic requirements of this approach kept lawyers from devoting their attention to substantive questions. The contrast between the two families of systems has become less profound as the "forms of action" have disappeared and emphasis has shifted from procedural to substantive problems. Recent legal scholarship in common law countries has attempted, as it has in European countries for centuries, to articulate the law in a rational manner and to improve and modernize it. The difference between the two families of systems today is less one of different conceptions of law and its role in society than it is one of the different techniques utilized to create a social order founded on the same basic premises and directed to the same goals.

Even from the point of view of legal technique the difference between the two legal families has grown less distinct. The importance of judicial decisions, which was obscured for a time by the codification, has again become manifest in contemporary French law. On the other hand, legislation has achieved an increasingly important role in the common law countries, as the notion of a welfare state has come to be regarded as a necessary attribute of a democratic society. The differences that remain in the theory of the sources of law have become more formal than real. The essential difference which persists is in substantive concepts, which are still strongly influenced in common law countries by their historical origin in the old "forms of action."

Basic legal reform is under way today both in common law countries and in those of the Romano-Germanic family. This reform is an essential response to the social upheaval that has been caused by industrial and technological innovation. The law can no longer be regarded simply as a way of resolving disputes between individuals. It has become a tool to be used everywhere in building the new order required by our sense of justice. In building this new order, and particularly in undertaking the essential task of rebuilding an international order, jurists of western countries must act together. French jurists can no longer ignore the common law world, and common law lawyers must come to understand the world of the Romano-Germanic legal systems. It was in this spirit that, when placed in contact with foreign students in France, I came to write this book on the French legal system. I am delighted to see it now translated into English by my young colleague Michael Kindred. I extend my thanks to him and to the Louisiana State University for the support they have given this undertaking.

René David

Translator's Note

Professor David's introduction to French law speaks for itself. I consider it an honor to be permitted to help it speak to a broader audience.

I have tried to translate as directly from the French as possible, in order to maintain the structure and amplitude of the French original, while seeking to lighten the style somewhat to meet the expectations of an English language reading audience. At several points I have included translator's notes in the footnotes to indicate peculiar difficulties of translation. In general, however, it seemed that the text adequately conveyed the author's meaning without further explanation. Thus, such notes have been kept to a minimum.

Contents

PART ONE

The French
Legal Tradition

I   French Law Before Codification

French legal history has been the subject of several excellent studies[1] and these first two chapters are not a condensation of that history. Rather, we wish simply to emphasize a few basic historical facts as background for our discussion of contemporary French law and to present some perspectives that may help explain why French lawyers think as they do.

At the fall of the western Roman Empire, A.D. 476, what is now France was inhabited by Romanized Celts, or Gallo-Romans, and Germanic tribes, the Franks, Burgundians, and Visigoths. Each group had its own law, with the Gallo-Romans living under Roman law and each Germanic tribe under its own customary law.

At that time Roman law had not yet been systematically compiled by Justinian, and its rules were to be found only through imperial Roman statutes, which had been officially collected in the Theodosian Code of A.D. 438, and the many writings of the jurisconsults. The principal source of Roman law in France from its promulgation in 506, however, was the *Lex Romana Visigothorum*, or *Alarician Breviary*. The *Breviary* was an abridgment of Roman scholarly writings and legislation, which was prepared by the Visigothic king Alaric II for those of his subjects who were governed by Roman law. The *Alarician Breviary* remained the main source of information about Roman law in France from the sixth to the twelfth century. Nevertheless, the Roman law actually applied in France during this period deviated from the *Breviary* locally on many points because of special practical needs, the influence of Germanic concepts and, increasingly, as time went on, simple ignorance.

Meanwhile, the Germanic tribes continued to live under their individual customary laws. We know little about these today, but it is certain that they reflected a level of civilization more primitive

---

1. The standard treatise is F. Olivier-Martin's *Histoire du droit français des origines à la Révolution* (1948). Since the 1955 reform of the license in law program, French legal history has been included in the second volume of the treatises, entitled *Histoire des institutions et des faits sociaux*.

than that of the Gallo-Romans. Our principal source of knowledge about these laws derives from those reduced to writing about A.D. 500: the Salic Law, the Ripuarian Law, the Burgundian Law, and the Visigothic Law. Only a small part of the customary law, however, was reduced to writing. The statutes did little but state the amounts of compensation due for various delicts; they did not include any of the other rules basic to Germanic social organization.

This was the primitive foundation from which French law developed. A similar interaction between divergent legal forces took place in Italy and on the Iberian peninsula. The situation was quite different, however, in Germany and England, where Germanic customary law acquired an indisputable predominance. And in the Byzantine Empire, Roman law maintained its earlier importance through the compilations prepared under Justinian and his successors beginning in 530.

A development of great importance took place in France between the sixth and tenth centuries. As a feudal society evolved, the principle that each person is governed by his personal, or tribal, law was replaced by the principle of the territoriality of customary law. The Gallo-Roman and Germanic elements of the population had been living in close proximity. As religious obstacles disappeared [2] and social patterns became more similar, these peoples gradually mixed and intermarried. After three or four centuries, it became virtually impossible to determine the ethnic origin of individuals; and simultaneously it became pointless to try, since the laws of the different groups became intermingled and confused.

Thereafter, customary law was territorial. The customary law of the preponderant ethnic group within a given fief or territory applied to everyone under the authority of the lord or monastery that controlled the area. Since these customary laws were recorded only in peoples' memories, they changed in the course of time, sometimes adopting elements of other laws and sometimes simply evolving to reflect the new concept on which feudal society was based: that both persons and property vary in status and thus in the legal rules by which they are governed.

2. Most of the Germanic tribes originally accepted the Arian heresy, but the Franks were converted by Rome under Clovis and thus were part of the Roman Catholic Church from an early date.

The gradual emergence of regional customary laws from the multiplicity of local laws enables one to draw up a legal map of twelfth-century France. On such a map, the principal distinction is between the Midi, "land of written law," and the North of France, "land of customary law." The Midi, south of a line extending from Geneva to La Rochelle, lived under a single customary law based on Roman law, which, although greatly altered from Roman times, was relatively uniform, stable, comprehensive, and ascertainable. Northern France, on the other hand, lived under a variety of customary laws. Although these laws differed greatly from the primitive customs of the sixth-century Franks and Burgundians, they had developed from them and are therefore called Germanic. These customary laws were still evolving in the twelfth century and were incomplete and often obscure.

The real contrast between northern and southern France, however, was less pronounced than this picture implies. In both areas, canon law influenced important parts of the law and was paramount in others. Specifically, the law of procedure and evidence was significantly reformed in the thirteenth century on the pattern of ecclesiastical court rules, and marriage law everywhere conformed to canon law. Also, Roman law spread into customary law territories, filling in where customary law was incomplete. Thus, contracts, which were not adequately regulated by Germanic laws, were governed throughout France by principles derived from Roman law.

This twelfth-century legal map of France was not significantly altered until the French Revolution. The distinction between provinces of written and of customary law remained fundamental until 1789. Nevertheless, the meaning of the distinction was altered over the centuries by two significant events.

First came the renaissance of Roman legal studies, beginning in the twelfth century. This renaissance never brought about a reception of Roman law in France, and consequently Roman law was never applied in France except as customary law. It was never regarded as having legislative force. In conformity with the dictum "The king reigns supreme in his kingdom," it could not be admitted that rules promulgated by a foreign sovereign were legally binding in France. Still, this renaissance, with which French universities were associated from an early date,[3] did affect the application of Roman law in France. The general Roman customary law of the Midi, which had until then been represented primarily by the *Alarician Breviary,* was gradually replaced by rules based on Justinian's compilations. Moreover, local customary deviations were unable to resist the renewed prestige of Roman law and declined in importance.

The second noteworthy event occurred when the customary laws were reduced to writing in northern France. In order to make the law certain and eliminate recurring problems of proof, Charles VII ordered, in the Ordinance of Montil-lez-Tours of 1454, that the customs of all customary law provinces be reduced to writing. This task was largely completed in the course of the sixteenth century with the compilation in a first edition, and the revision and publication in a second edition, of the principal customary laws: for example, Paris (1510, 1580), Burgundy (1459, 1570, 1576), Brittany (1539, 1580), Normandy (1583), Orleans (1509, 1583), Niverny (1534), and Poitou (1514, 1560). Approximately sixty regional systems, with variations for nearly three hundred local areas departing on some points from the regional systems to which they related, were codified prior to the Revolution.[4]

This development of French law set it apart from other European legal systems. It assured French law an intermediate position between English law on the one hand and other continental legal systems on the other, a position it still retains today. The unity and cohesion of English law were unknown in France. The French monarchy, contending with powerful feudal lords and ruling a country larger and less centralized than England, did not even try to use its courts to create a law common to the entire kingdom. Until the time of the Revolution, there were numerous independent supreme courts (eighteen *parlements* and several *conseils sover-*

3. The University of Paris received official recognition in 1200, when King Philippe-Auguste declared the students and teachers of the *Studium parisinese* subject to the jurisdiction of the ecclesiastical courts. It was also recognized in 1203 and 1206 by a decretal and a bull of Pope Innocent III, who conferred certain privileges upon its teachers and students.

4. Almost all of the written customary laws were conveniently collected by Bourdot de Richebourg in his *Nouveau coutumier général* (4 vols. in-folio; 1724). A map of customary laws was published by Klimrath, *Travaux sur l'histoire du droit français* (2 vols.; 1843).

eigns).[5] France experienced no upheaval similar to that in England which centralized the administration of justice in the Royal Courts at Westminster and created a common law. Customary law varied even within the jursidiction of a single *parlement*.[6]

The diversity in French law was one of the principal reasons for the subsequent resort to codification. Codification provided for France the legal unity that England achieved through its courts. Although prerevolutionary French law lacked unity in comparison with English law, it was more uniform and coherent than other legal systems of continental Europe. The Holy Roman Empire, in particular, is little more than a historical figure of speech. Sovereignty was split up among countless territories; no central authority successfully asserted itself. Laws were diverse in the extreme, and the area of authority of any one customary law was very limited. With no government able to impose a regrouping of laws and to end the anarchy and chaos, a remedy was sought in the reception of Roman law.[7] Paradoxically, after the sixteenth century Germany came to have a legal system more Roman and less Germanic than France. The regrouping of customary laws by the *parlements* of France and their later reduction to writing gave French customary law a cohesion and certainty that enabled it successfully to resist domination by Roman law.[8]

More bound by tradition than English law, more Germanic than German law: so French law appeared on the eve of the Revolution. To complete our picture of the prerevolutionary formation and growth of French law, we must examine the respective roles played by judicial decisions, scholarly writing, and legislation.

Judicial decisions deserve first attention. Custom truly becomes

5. TRANSLATOR'S NOTE: The *parlements* of prerevolutionary France were appellate courts with specified territorial jurisdiction, but they also exercised significant rule-making power. Although the modern legislative branch of government owes a part of its conception to these earlier bodies, it also differs greatly from them, most notably in exercising no judicial function. To avoid confusion, the prerevolutionary institutions will be referred to by the French term *parlement;* the modern legislative branch will be referred to by the English term Parliament.

6. This was particularly true of the *Parlement de Paris,* whose jurisdiction covered an area that included a variety of customary laws and in which even the written law was applied.

7. This reception occurred also in Alsace, which was part of the Holy Roman Empire until the Treaty of Westphalia (1648).

8. J. P. Dawson, *The Oracles of the Law* (1967).

law only as it is recognized and enforced by the courts. This is universally true, but was particularly so in prerevolutionary France, where the courts articulated and developed customary law. Beginning in 1254, the opinions of the *Parlement de Paris* were collected in the *Olim* reports. By the end of the fifteenth century, it was evident that the court officials should be the persons charged with drafting written customary laws.

The task of the courts in early French law was very different from that of courts today. Often the principal function of the trial in a customary law area was to discover and define the legal rules to be applied rather than to apply a preestablished rule to the particular facts of the case. This was so even after the customary laws were written down, although that accomplishment facilitated proof of the law considerably. The law continued to be customary in nature, even when written, so that old law could always be abrogated by disuse and new law could develop. As Olivier-Martin has noted, it was this idea that justified the periodic revision of the customary laws.[9]

The independence of the judiciary from the crown throughout the period of the monarchy, even when royal power appeared most absolute, has rightly been emphasized by Koschaker.[10] The resistance of the supreme courts, particularly the *Parlement de Paris,* to royal power is well known. Although the venal and hereditary nature of court positions made of the judiciary a self-interested, ritualist caste, this circumstance also had the great advantage of creating a cohesive judiciary, independent of administrative authorities and of the political branches of government. French law was thereby protected from the arbitrariness that prevailed in certain neighboring countries. Through litigation on concrete questions, the law was developed and applied by a professional body with a high moral idea of its own functions and of the law. Koschaker finds in these circumstances the basis for a close affinity of French and English law, as "judges' laws" (*Juristenrecht*), in contrast to German law, which was not the creation of an independent and coherent judiciary.

Although the *parlements* of prerevolutionary France, by their interference in administrative matters and their extreme conserva-

9. Olivier-Martin, *op. cit.,* no. 319, p. 423.
10. P. Koschaker, *Europa und das römische Recht* (1947), 177, 231 ff.

tism, prevented many reforms that might have saved the monarchy, they did not oppose reform when their privileges were not at stake. They were reasonable and wise in developing the law to meet changing needs. Equity was taken into consideration, and equitable solutions were incorporated into the law without difficulty. There was no need in France, as there was in England, to set up new courts in opposition to the existing ones, to develop outside the law a body of special rules based on equity. The royal prerogatives of grace and mercy did not lead to the creation of two concurrent sets of royal courts: royal grace and letters of rescission and redemption continued to be used for their intended purpose, administrative correction of overly rigorous legal solutions. They did not develop into a rival or complementary legal system.[11]

The work of scholarly writers was closely related to that of the courts. French scholarly writing was devoted to the study of both Roman law and customary law and, in comparison with the scholarship of other countries, manifested distinctive characteristics in both areas. In Romanist legal writing, the work of French scholars was in marked contrast to that of their German and Italian counterparts. While the Italians and Germans strove constantly to modernize Roman law, to adapt it to new social conditions, French Romanists of the Renaissance period, such as Cujas and Doneau, were more preoccupied with scholarly, and less with practical, concerns. This difference seems to reflect the different role assigned to Roman law in the French legal system, rather than a more theoretical and abstract approach on the part of the French. Since Roman law was treated as actual legislation in Germany and Italy, writers there naturally tried to develop and even distort it in order to justify the solutions desired in practice. In France, on the other hand, Roman law was not treated as legislation and customary law was free to depart from it. Roman law could thus be studied objectively without attempting to adapt it to current practical needs.

In their study of customary law, on the other hand, French writers were more practical and resisted the attraction of overly abstract theories. Their works consisted of procedural guides, expositions of customary law, commentaries on judicial decisions, and treatises, all based primarily on observation of court procedure and

11. See John P. Dawson, "Remedies of the French Chancery before 1789," in *Festschrift für Ernst Rabel* (1954), I, 99–140.

decisions. The writers' objective was to describe court practice and explain it systematically, and thus to facilitate legal research and use of the law. Under the influence of the seventeenth-century school of natural law, these eminently practical goals were supplemented by a desire to improve the law by making it more rational and uniform. National unification of the laws was the principal theme of a now-famous speech by the scholar Dumoulin in the sixteenth century and continued to be pressed by scholars throughout the seventeenth and eighteenth centuries. Finally, Pothier (1699–1772), after having written commentaries on the customary law of Orleans, began in 1760 to write treatises in which he set forth the basic principles of French law as abstracted from various customary laws and Roman law.

Even in these works, the "realism" of French scholarship is apparent, for they differ greatly from the doctrinaire works of other countries of continental Europe, which sought to distill universal principles of natural law. It is noteworthy that France contributed no masters of first rank to the school of natural law. For French jurists, the subject was too theoretical, too abstract. They never achieved the level of universality of Grotius, Pufendorf, or Christian Wolf. More modestly, they attempted to express the principles of natural law within the limited framework of the national legal system. This limitation of objectives paved the way for codification in France, thus assuring for French law a century of preeminence in Europe and the world.

Legislation, generally speaking, played a secondary role in France until the Revolution. The French kings were little concerned with legal reform, since law essentially meant private law and their main efforts were aimed at establishing a coherent system of administration. The prevailing idea was that the law existed apart from, prior to, and independent of the sovereign. The king of France, in his omnipotence, remained subject to natural and divine law, as well as to the "fundamental laws of the kingdom." Since his role did not include the creation or modification of law, he never thought of getting involved in this area. He believed himself authorized only to declare the law, by proclaiming existing customary law, in the interest of justice and sound administration.

Thus, until the seventeenth century, the monarchy limited itself to requiring and organizing the reduction of customary law to writing. Apart from that, it intervened only with partial, although sometimes quite important, measures in fields directly related to the administration of justice, namely evidence and procedure.[12]

During only two periods did legislation play a more important role. The first of these periods was that of the great ordinances drawn up on the initiative of Colbert during the reign of Louis XIV. These dealt with civil procedure (1667), criminal procedure (1670), commercial law (1673), and maritime law (1681). The first two of these ordinances unified French court procedure on the basis of quite detailed rules. The latter two "nationalized" French commercial law, which had until then been considered international because of its development and the nature of the courts that applied it.

The second period during which legislation played an important role was that of the ordinances of Chancellor Daguesseau during the reign of Louis XV. Unlike Colbert's ordinances, these dealt with pure private law. Three ordinances were promulgated at this time; they dealt with gifts (1731), wills (1735), and substitutions (i.e., perpetuities) (1747).

II   Codification

A historical view is essential to an understanding of the French codification and its import, since codification was a natural, indeed almost inevitable, product of existing conditions. It by no means constituted a complete break with tradition, and despite new methods and ideas that were introduced into the law, this tradition retained its practical interest and value. The chief reason for undertaking codification and carrying it through to completion was practical. The diversity of customary law and the overall lack of uniformity in French law could no longer be justified. The primary purpose of the codification was neither to satisfy doctri-

12. The *Ordonnance de Villars-Cotterets* (1539) substituted French for Latin as the language of the administration of justice. The *Ordonnance de Moulins* (1560) required written proof of obligations resulting from contracts above a certain amount.

naires nor to establish the reign of reason in France. Rather, it was
to unify the law nationally, thereby simplifying it and eliminating
obvious practical difficulties.

Nevertheless, the French Revolution, with its ideal of a rational
social order, was required to insure successful codification. Benefi-
cial as the codification was for the bulk of the population, it was
less so for legal practitioners, many of whom had made the most of
an unsatisfactory situation and were profiting handsomely from the
law's complexity. The livelihood of some depended on it. Relying
on natural law theories, promoters of codification proposed to create
a logical code whose provisions would embody rules of ideal justice, as perceived by human reason, relying as little as possible on
rules from the earlier law and a tradition considered obscurantist.
This was clearly the idea that gave the final impetus to codification
in France, and it was adopted by the codes' draftsmen as their goal.
The codes were to be the written reason (*ratio scripta*) of the universe. The conquests and prestige of Napoleon made this ideal
seem attainable.

If one looks beyond the revolutionary slogans and natural law
theories, however, one finds that the real accomplishment, in ret-
rospect, was quite different from the dreams and pretensions. As
our example, let us take the most famous of the codes, the Civil
Code, or Code Napoléon. Although the revolutionary Constitution
of 1791 provided that the French were to have a civil code, several early attempts had failed, and it was not until 1803 that the
commission was named which was to complete the Civil Code. By
then the lofty illusions of 1789 and 1793 had faded and there was
a total reaction against the revolutionary ideology. The code was
not completed until a few months before the declaration of the
Empire in 1804.

The draftsmen of the Civil Code were anything but radical.
They were lawyers and judges of the prerevolutionary era. Their
average age was close to sixty. How were these men to conceive
written reason? They could not be expected to forget their education, experience, and preconceptions. For them, written reason was
represented by traditional law. In the areas where French law was
already unified on the basis of Roman law, such as the law of obligations, it is hard to cite a single innovation. In other areas, the
draftsmen had to choose among the various customary laws (in-

cluding Roman law, which was the customary law of the Midi and of Alsace). But here too, what caution! In the area of matrimonial property, one can hardly maintain that a logical system was invented, for the code adopted as its general rule the centuries-old community property system as regulated in the customary law of Paris. Then, in order to accommodate the feelings and practices of the Midi, it provided for a dowry system that could be adopted by antenuptial contract.

It is true that the Civil Code's draftsmen made innovations in some areas. They greatly modified real property law in an attempt to simplify it, and eliminated many provisions of feudal origin. The law of succession was modified in the same way, and the new marriage law departed from canon law rules in many respects. Even in these areas, however, the Civil Code did not devise and sanction whole new theoretical systems; the break with prerevolutionary rules and ideas was less clear than was supposed.

The traditional nature and wisdom of the French codes are best attested by their durability. These supposedly revolutionary codes have withstood many changes of political system and are still in force today. Of the ten constitutions that France has had since the codification (1804, 1814, 1815, 1830, 1848, 1852, 1875, 1940, 1946, 1958), only the Charter of 1815 modified the Civil Code, abolishing divorce. The Civil Code has remained intact throughout all other changes of regime; amendments to it have been independent of new constitutions and constitutional legislation. The codification did not replace the historical and traditional French law with a logical and rational legal system.

Even the scope of the codification, which encompassed only a part of French law, reveals the persistence of tradition. Its domain was essentially the same as that of legislatively sanctioned written law before the Revolution. The Civil Code revised provisions previously found in Justinian's Digest (on contracts and delicts), in the written customary laws (on property, intestate succession, matrimonial property, and personal capacity), in royal ordinances (on gifts and wills), and in the *Corpus Juris Canonici* (on marriage). The Code of Civil Procedure was only a new edition of Colbert's 1667 civil procedure ordinance with few changes of either substance or style. The Commercial Code similarly reproduced Colbert's ordinances on commercial and maritime law. Only the Penal

Code and the Code of Criminal Procedure represented an effort to bring new fields into the domain of written law in France.

With the exception of criminal law, all public law remained uncodified, and it was not even considered necessary to state the exclusion expressly. French public law, which regulates the government's organization (constitutional law) and the relations between private individuals and governmental bodies (administrative law), is still outside the domain of codified law, just as it was at the time of the monarchy. In the area of constitutional law, French judges have not considered the preambles and bills of rights that have been added to constitutions to be supreme laws that prevail over all other legislation. This attitude constitutes retrogression rather than progress, for the prerevolutionary supreme courts tended to rely more heavily on the fundamental, though unwritten, laws of the kingdom than judges have since. These courts were unpopular, and judges have been hesitant to expose themselves again to the same criticism. Nor was codification the technique through which, in the nineteenth and twentieth centuries, new concepts were developed to regulate relations between governmental bodies and private individuals, assuring greater security in these relations and giving individuals better guarantees against arbitrary government action. The "administrative law" that has developed in the last century in France is not based on a code, but is rather a judge-made law like prerevolutionary French law and the common law of England. It matters little that the main body which has elaborated this law, the Council of State (*Conseil d'Etat*), does not belong to the hierarchy of regular courts and that structurally it is closely related to the executive branch of the government.

The codification, occurring during the Napoleonic era, did not depend originally on the idea of the omnipotence of the legislator. Such an idea was not accepted in prerevolutionary French law, and the promoters of the codification did not advocate it. Their point of departure was rather the idea that there existed a universal and unchanging natural law and that its principles should be articulated in order to promote justice and the public welfare.[13] The idea of national or popular sovereignty functioned only secondarily, to de-

13. Article 1 of the draft Civil Code said, "There is a universal, unchanging law that is the source of all positive law; this law is the natural reason that governs all peoples of the world."

termine the authority best qualified to discover and set forth the principles of natural law which were then to be the principles of the codes.

Although the promoters of the codification did not subscribe to the postulate that legislators are omnipotent, the question remains as to whether this idea was not in fact given additional impetus by their work, and whether the existence of the codes, whatever the views of their promoters, did not thus induce a profound transformation in the French concept of law. Clearly there was an evolution. The French codes were the product of the school of natural law, which proclaimed the existence of moral and legal principles, divinely decreed or intuitively discerned by human reason, anterior to all legislation and thus superior to the legislators. The codification's completion, however, saw a reversal in outlook. Success seems to have sapped the school of natural law of its strength and caused its decline. The codes desired by natural law theorists gave rise to a generation of positivists, who saw not only legislation but the law itself as a legislative creation.

In private law, the existence of a systematic body of legislative rules reflecting the contemporary conception of natural law seemed to preclude jurists from having recourse to other sources. Writers limited their efforts to the exegesis of code texts. Judges, required since the Revolution to rationalize their decisions, took refuge behind the provisions of the codes in order to avoid being accused of arbitrariness, even in cases where their decisions could properly have been justified by arguments from other sources. A positivist attitude in French jurists resulted from the codification and did not disappear until the end of the nineteenth century, when the solutions of the codes and the exigencies of justice no longer coincided. At that time, along with the development of new sociological concepts, natural law ideas experienced a renaissance.

Although public law was not codified, the private law codification did affect it significantly. Because public law, to the extent that it is law, attempts to implement principles of reason, justice, and fairness, public law jurists could not ignore a code which proclaimed the rules of justice and enjoyed the prestige of Napoleon's name. Consequently, following the codification, public law drew its principal inspiration from the rules and principles of the codes, as the written reason of the nineteenth century. Special justification was necessary in order for any departure from these rules not to be thought arbitrary. Public law gradually developed a certainty that had been unknown previously. The codification of private law exercised a powerful attraction on public law rules. Differences still exist in France between private and public law, but they are seldom arbitrary. Each is justified by considerations peculiar to public law: for example, the principle of the equality of citizens, the need to insure the permanent functioning of public services, and the need to insure governments a certain freedom of action. Civil servants and high government officials have ceased to be above the law.

In short, the codification has had important effects on French law and has contributed significantly to a transformation of the prevailing concept of law in France, but its effects have been independent of the will of its authors and were unforeseen by them. Conversely, the new characteristics that the authors expected of the codification proved largely illusory. The codification did not succeed in substituting a fully rational and logical law for France's historical and traditional law. It did not produce the break that had been expected between the solutions of the prerevolutionary system and those of the new system. Nor did it make the law accessible to the masses as had been intended.

PART TWO

Political, Administrative, and Judicial Organization of France

Since law provides support and reinforcement for a specific organization of society, its study must be based on an understanding of the essential elements of this social organization as it manifests itself in the political, or governmental, structure. In addition, law is dependent on the mechanisms that apply it. We shall describe the outlines of these mechanisms in studying France's administrative and judicial organization.

I   The Constitution

The Constitution of the French Republic, adopted October 4, 1958, is relatively new, and it is still difficult to predict the future development of a structure that was dominated until 1969 by the personality of General de Gaulle. We will limit ourselves here to a brief description of the political institutions set up by the Constitution of 1958. We shall mention in passing certain French traditions, attitudes, and feelings that are at least as important to a true understanding as the text of the Constitution itself.

Like every French constitution since 1791, the Constitution of the Fifth Republic is based on the principle of separation of powers.[1] French constitutional law scholars since the eighteenth-century philosophers have erected this principle into a dogma. Frenchmen grow up with the assumption that France's difficulties during the monarchy were the result of failure to respect the principle of separation of powers. A Frenchman can imagine only tyranny, arbitrariness, and corruption if this principle is ignored. Rationally and intuitively he is upset by real or imagined violations of it, in either the structure of his institutions or their activities.

The constitutional act of June 3, 1958, which instructed the executive to revise the prior constitution, provided that the new constitutional proposal should be based on five principles. These

1. The First Republic existed from 1792 to 1804; the Second from 1848 to 1852; the Third, established after the war of 1870, lasted until 1940; the Fourth from the liberation of France in 1944 until 1958; the Fifth was set up following the events of May–June, 1958.

included the following: "The executive and legislative branches must be effectively separated, so that each holds, independently and as its own responsibility, its full attributes; and . . . The judiciary must remain independent so as to be able to guarantee respect for the fundamental liberties set forth in the preamble of the Constitution of 1946 and the Declaration of the Rights of Man, to which it refers."

The Constitution was drafted in conformity with these directives. Nevertheless, the principle of separation of powers is subject to a variety of interpretations, as is evident from a glance at the constitutions of western democracies, all of which claim to implement it. The Constitution of 1958 clearly develops the principle in a way very different from that of previous French constitutions. It repudiates the traditional interpretation of the principle which had evolved under the Third and Fourth Republics. With these preliminary observations, let us now look at the position of the executive and legislative branches of government and of the judiciary under the Constitution of 1958 and in relation to French tradition. We shall then discuss the force of the constitutional rules themselves.

Section 1.　Executive Branch

A Frenchman raised and educated under the Third or Fourth Republic would be disturbed to begin his study of French political institutions by looking at the executive branch. He takes for granted the supremacy of the legislative branch, represented by Parliament. The Constitution of 1946 was particularly clear in this regard. Article 3 stated: "The people exercises [its national sovereignty] in constitutional matters by the vote of its delegates . . . . In all other respects, it exercises it through its representatives in the National Assembly." No reference was made to the executive branch, which was composed of a figurehead president of the republic and a council of ministers drawn almost entirely from members of Parliament and overturned by Parliament with notorious frequency. In French political tradition, parliamentary supremacy has been intimately associated with the very concept of democracy, since French experience had indicated that a strong executive was a threat to democracy and freedom.

The Constitution of 1958 repudiated this tradition. It put the executive branch on an equal footing with the legislative and even, at least temporarily, above it. The constitutional act of June 3, 1958, introduced this switch by declaring, as its first principle: "Universal suffrage is the sole source of power. Legislative and executive power derive exclusively from universal suffrage and the bodies elected by it." The Constitution of 1958, significantly, reversed the order of the foregoing, and speaks of the President of the Republic and the executive before dealing with Parliament. The dominant theme of the Constitution is the establishment of a new equilibrium between the executive and legislative branches by the imposition of strict limits on a Parliament that recently was omnipotent. In fact, the point of equilibrium has been passed; the Constitution institutes clear executive supremacy. Under the new Constitution, therefore, the executive branch deserves, both theoretically and practically, to be discussed before the legislative.

Executive power, according to the Constitution of 1958, is in the hands of the President of the Republic and his Government.[2] The President of the Republic is the "keystone of the Constitution." He is more than the chief executive. The Constitution makes him the virtual guardian of the Constitution, an arbiter above political parties charged with insuring the regular operation of public services (article 5), the guarantor of judicial independence (article 64), and a dictator of practically unlimited power in time of national emergency (article 16); it authorizes him to submit proposed laws to referendum (article 11) and to dissolve the National Assembly (article 12).

Despite these specific powers, with their broad reach in times of crisis, the President's main function continues to be as the chief

---

2. TRANSLATOR'S NOTE: The French term *gouvernement* has two distinct meanings, which can be confusing for an English-speaking reader. The first meaning is the same as our meaning of "the government," the totality of political organs that govern society, including the executive, legislative, and judicial branches. The second meaning has no precise equivalent in English and refers to a group of officials in the executive branch comprising the Council of Ministers and a significant number of other high appointed executive branch officials. It is contrasted with the lower-rank, civil service bureaucracy, or *administration*. For clarity the term *gouvernement* is translated "government" with a small "g" when used in its broadest, usual English sense, and "Government" with a capital "G" when it is used in its special French sense. *Administration* has been translated "administration" (see Section 2 of this part).

executive officer. This position is indicated by the various prerogatives and powers granted him by the Constitution: appointment of
the Prime Minister and, on the nomination of the latter, of the
other ministers (article 8), presidency of the Council of Ministers
(article 9), promulgation of statutes (article 10), signatory of ordinances and decrees adopted by the Council of Ministers (article
13), appointment of civil and military employees of the state (article 13), commander-in-chief of the armed forces (article 15), and
others. Since 1958 the position of the President of the Republic
has been further strengthened through constitutional amendment.
The Constitution originally provided for his election by an electoral college, but was amended in 1962 to provide for direct election by universal suffrage.

The Government is headed by the Prime Minister, who is appointed by the President. The other ministers are also appointed
and dismissed by the President, but his decision in their case must
be based on a proposal from the Prime Minister (article 8). The
Prime Minister can submit the Government's resignation to the
President (article 8) and he must do so where the National Assembly has adopted a motion of censure or has failed to approve the
platform or a general policy statement of the Government under
conditions stated in article 49. The constitutional act of June 3,
1958, posed as its third principle that "the Government must be
responsible to Parliament." The Constitution did incorporate this
principle; so from this point of view France is still a parliamentary
democracy, despite the increased power given to the executive.
Finally, the 1958 Constitution creates an incompatibility between
the function of member of the Government and the status of member of Parliament (article 23).

The Government determines and implements the nation's policies (article 20). On a more narrowly legal plane, it is important
to know how this power is to be exercised. There is a crucial division between subjects within the legislature's jurisdiction and those
of a "regulatory" nature. With respect to the former, the Government can only act if and to the extent that Parliament delegates
power to it; then it acts through ordinances (article 38). In the
"regulatory" sphere, however, the Government acts at its own discretion; the only limitation is that it must act through decrees proclaimed with the advice of the Council of State where its action

will amend legislatively passed statutes. The regulatory power granted to the Government constitutes a substantial part of what is theoretically the function of the legislative branch.[3] This redistribution of power toward the executive is particularly great because under the Constitution the regulatory area seems to be the rule and the statutory area the exception.

The new Constitution's description of the respective provinces of legislation and regulation is important for jurists. The concept of regulation, in particular, is completely revised and changed. One must take care not to confuse earlier regulations with regulations enacted pursuant to this constitution. The new concept of "ordinance," created by the Constitution (article 38), likewise deserves the attention of jurists. It does not correspond to the concept of ordinance under previous constitutions and is nearer in meaning to the old concept of legislative decrees, which the Government issued at various times under earlier constitutions on the basis of parliamentary delegations of power.

Reoriented as it is with respect to the legislative branch by the reestablishment of a balance that had previously been destroyed in the legislature's favor, the executive has retained its traditional independence from what used to be called the judicial branch and is now called the judicial authority. Here, French institutions can be explained historically. The supreme courts of prerevolutionary France, the *parlements*,[4] made themselves very unpopular by opposing all reforms to the traditional legal system. Assiduous in their defense of an antiquated system based on the inequality of social classes and on self-serving premises, they failed in their ambition of becoming the nation's representatives. Nor did they succeed in really controlling government action or in imposing procedural rules upon it. Of their many ill-advised interferences in politics and government, people remember their opposition to those organizational reforms that the monarchy did attempt from time to time. Abolition of the *parlements* was one of the first acts of the French Revolution, on November 3, 1789. The following year a law on judicial organization, which is still in force, proclaimed that "the judicial functions are distinct and will always remain separated

3. For this reason writers have suggested that it might be more accurate to speak of the governmental branch now than of the executive branch.
4. TRANSLATOR'S NOTE: See Part One, note 5, above.

from the executive functions" (law of August 16–24, 1790, title II, article 13). Judges are forbidden to concern themselves with executive action. Article 4 of the Civil Code clearly states that they cannot enact regulations. Nor can they give any order to a government agent: the common law's writ of mandamus disturbs Frenchmen greatly. The courts cannot even judge cases in which executive activities are at issue; such litigation might lead them to criticize or condemn such conduct, and indirectly to try to subordinate the executive to judicial control. A practical procedure, that of the "conflict," has been set up by statute; the executive can require the regular courts to renounce jurisdiction when the case in question is one over which, by virtue of the principle of separation of powers as thus understood, they lack jurisdiction. A special tribunal called the Court of Conflicts (*Tribunal des Conflits*), composed partly of judges and partly of administrators, has been created to handle jurisdictional disputes between the regular courts and the executive.

The lack of jurisdiction in the regular courts to hear cases involving the executive is a principle that dominates French law and has led some foreign jurists to question whether individual citizens are adequately protected against abuse of governmental power and whether France really subscribes to the rule of law. An affirmative answer to such questions is beyond doubt today. The Frenchman is at least as well protected as anyone against state power; often he is better protected. The only difference is that, in France, litigation involving the executive branch goes before tribunals that are independent of the regular courts. Although these tribunals, of which by far the most important is the Council of State, are "administrative courts" within the executive branch, the necessary precautions have been taken to insure their full independence from the "active administration." The independence and impartiality of these courts are unquestioned. In short, the French division between regular and administrative courts, like the separation in common law countries between courts of common law and those of equity, is explained by history. There, too, the existence of the equity courts was once contested; they seemed dangerous, subject to abuse, likely to encourage arbitrariness and destroy the "rule of law." Today these fears have faded and English equity is unquestionably "legal." It has come to be regarded as a progressive, rather than a regressive, force in the development of the law. Frenchmen view their administrative law in the same way. In the beginning, the exclusion of regular court jurisdiction over litigation involving the government was risky and on principle hard to defend. In practice, however, it has turned out well and has contributed to the development of French law. The administrative courts, totally independent of the executive in fact, have been able, because of their position at the very center of the executive branch, to establish a control over governmental action that would have been thought intolerable if attempted by regular judges.

Section 2.   Legislative Branch

Before 1958, the legislature had in fact gained almost unlimited power. It closely supervised executive action. Because the courts could not declare a statute passed by Parliament unconstitutional, constitutional limits on legislative power were purely formal.

The Constitution of 1958 reflects a strong reaction against this system. It severely restricted legislative prerogatives. The powers of the legislature today can be summarized into two principal points: (1) Parliament helps prepare and passes legislation; (2) it can force the Government to resign.

Although these are virtually the same powers that permitted past Parliaments to establish their omnipotence, various new rules in fact change everything. The National Assembly can still turn out the Government, but in doing so it now risks dissolution by the President of the Republic. The Government is no longer recruited from the National Assembly, or at least a member of Parliament who is appointed minister must give up his parliamentary seat until the next election. While these two rules do not restrict the rights of Parliament in theory, in reality a demand for the Government's resignation has ceased to be an attractive, risk-free operation for members of the National Assembly. In addition, the right to introduce a motion of censure that can force the Government's resignation has been restricted by the Constitution (article 49). Such a motion has been adopted only once since 1958, and in that case the Government resigned and Parliament was dissolved as the Constitution requires.

Parliament helps to prepare statutes. Here again nothing is

changed in theory. Parliament retains the legislative initiative and the right of amendment, and only Parliament can pass statutes. In reality, however, two new rules change everything. In the first place, bills and amendments formulated by a member of Parliament are inadmissible where their adoption would either reduce public resources or create or increase a public charge (article 40). A second and no less important limitation is that the legislative domain is restricted to specific subjects listed by the Constitution (article 34), beyond which one is in the regulatory area, reserved for executive action. Also, the duration of regular sessions of Parliament and the agenda for extraordinary sessions are strictly regulated by the Constitution (articles 28 and 29). And finally, we must mention the possibility of a referendum, by which the executive can bypass Parliament on specific questions.

Legislative power, as it is conceived and regulated by the Constitution of 1958, is far from the parliamentary omnipotence that the Third Republic developed and the Fourth Republic articulated in its Constitution. Before 1958, the Government was little more than a clerk to Parliament. Whatever executive power there was derived more from the existence of a generally excellent civil service than from the unstable Governments, which were preoccupied with daily parliamentary relations. The Constitution of 1958 reacted strongly against this slipping toward a principle of "unity of powers." The defects of the earlier system had exhausted public patience. Parliament was discredited. Having concentrated all power in itself, it had failed to deal effectively with the fundamental problems before it. The danger now is that the executive branch, rearmed by the Constitution, might become omnipotent in its turn and develop into a dictatorship, disregarding the principle that the Constitution was supposed to reestablish and that remains fundamental to any western-style democracy, the principle of separation of powers. The opposition has emphasized this danger, but it is hard to take seriously accusations of "personal concentration of power" and "dictatorship" from a press that is demonstrably free of governmental control; and General de Gaulle did step aside as soon as 52 percent of the voters rejected a constitutional reform he proposed, an action which his successor would no doubt repeat if the situation were to arise again. Nevertheless, there is no question but that Parliament at present is in eclipse, and this has become a

matter of concern even to many of the government's strongest supporters.

The legislative branch provided for by the Constitution of 1958
is composed of a Parliament of two assemblies, the National Assembly and the Senate. The National Assembly is elected for five
years by direct, universal suffrage. Senators are elected for nine
years by indirect suffrage. One-third of the Senate changes every
three years. In most respects, the two chambers have the same functions, but only the National Assembly can require the resignation
of the Government, and it can also override the Senate's opposition
to a bill.

Another assembly provided for by the Constitution (articles 69–
71) is the Economic and Social Council, which has a purely advisory role. It must be consulted on all programs or bills of an economic or social character (article 70) and may be consulted on any
proposals or bills for statutes, ordinances, or decrees (article 69).

Section 3. Judiciary

Traditional doctrine recognizes the existence of a third branch, or
power (*pouvoir*), of government, in addition to the legislative and
executive. This third power is the judiciary. Frenchmen have always had some difficulty, however, thinking of the courts as exercising a "power" comparable to those exercised by Parliament and
the executive. The judiciary does not have the prestige in France
that it has in England. Nor does it have or aspire to the functions
and responsibility of judges in the United States. Few political
questions of concern to the nation's executive come before the
judiciary, since French courts are not allowed to review the constitutionality of legislation or to control the activity to the executive. Jurisdiction in this latter area is entrusted to a body within
the executive branch, the Council of State. Even in the private and
criminal law areas, the courts' powers are restricted by the codification, which at least theoretically seems to solve all problems. In
these circumstances, a Frenchman must exert himself if he is to
think of the courts as constituting a true branch, or power, given
what this somewhat poorly chosen term, *pouvoir,* connotes for him.
The Constitution of 1958 reconciled theory with facts by speaking
of the judiciary simply as the "judicial authority" (articles 64–
66), instead of the judicial power, or branch.

Actually, all that this term is supposed to imply is that the courts shall be independent of both the executive and legislative branches. This is self-evident to the French jurist. The creation by the Constitution of 1946 of the Superior Council of the Magistrature was intended to reinforce this independence by eliminating some obvious dangers. Although the Superior Council of the Magistrature was retained by the Constitution of 1958, its powers were reduced and its structure altered (article 65). This weakening is deplored by many.

A foreigner may be confused by the existence in the French legal system of administrative courts that perform judicial functions without belonging to the "judicial branch" of government. This confusing situation has a historical explanation and does not disturb people in France in the way that the recent development of administrative tribunals in England and the United States has drawn criticism in those countries.

French courts, while independent in their judicial activities, readily accept legislative and executive jurisdiction over the organization of the administration of justice. They do not regard the Ministry of Justice as threatening their prerogatives in any way. Nor do the courts claim any exclusive power to establish their own procedure or to organize and regulate the judiciary, lawyers, and other auxiliaries of the judicial system. Civil and criminal procedure are regulated in France by legislatively enacted codes. Similarly, statutes and decrees fix the organization and regulation not only of judges, but of others who hold legal jobs as well.

Section 4. Authority and Strength of Constitutional Rules

French constitutions have traditionally been rigid documents. Constitutional rules are adopted and are subject to amendment only by special procedures. The Constitution of 1958 has followed tradition in this regard. The Constitution itself was approved by a referendum, and amendments to it require approval either in a referendum or by a special majority of Parliament. In 1962 the electorate approved, by a substantial majority, an amendment providing for the direct election of the President by universal suffrage. In 1969, on the other hand, it rejected a proposal to establish "regions" in France with considerable autonomy and, in connection therewith, to change the Senate fundamentally. The rejection of this proposal led to the resignation of the President of the Republic, who had placed his prestige behind it. Nevertheless French tradition has never accepted a real supervision over the constitutionality of legislation. There has been a refusal to conceive of the people as a separate, fourth factor.

During the period when Parliament established its supremacy, the distinction between the legislative branch and the people was regarded simply as a device to limit the sovereignty of Parliament, and in reality to give supremacy to one of the other branches of government, the executive or the judicial. To distinguish between the legislative branch and the people appeared to Frenchmen in principle illegitimate and in practice a threat to individual liberties, which could be guaranteed effectively only by the elected Parliament. Frenchmen had become used to fearing an executive dictatorship, but not a legislative one. Nor were they prepared to accept what one of them called, with a kind of Jacobin emotion and sense of protest, a "government by judges."

The Constitution of 1958 has taken a step forward in this area. It clearly has not given the right to examine the constitutionality of legislation to the judiciary as a whole, or even to a constitutional court especially created for that purpose. Nevertheless the principles proclaimed by the Constitution are better protected than in the past against possible legislative infringement, while earlier institutions have been retained and continue to provide protection against possible infringements of these principles by the executive.

What happens if there are violations of the Constitution by the legislative branch? The Constitution of 1958 has created an organ to prevent such violations: the Constitutional Council (title VII, articles 56–63). In addition to various other functions, the Constitutional Council determines the constitutionality of statutes *prior to their taking effect* whenever the law is an "organic statute" by virtue of its object,[5] and whenever the council is requested to do so by the President of the Republic, the Prime Minister, the Presi-

5. This term denotes statutes of particular constitutional importance for which the Constitution has provided or which are necessary to implement the Constitution's provisions. The Constitution of 1958 called for eighteen organic statutes; these were promulgated between November 7 and December 29, 1958.

dent of the Senate, or the President of the National Assembly. Its decisions are final, unappealable, and binding on all branches of government and all administrative and judicial officials (article 62). The Constitutional Council has had to determine on several occasions whether a particular bill transgresses the regulatory power which the Constitution grants to the executive branch. In July, 1971, it rendered a decision which has been the subject of much comment, on a matter referred to it by the President of the Senate (who belongs to an opposition party). The council declared unconstitutional several provisions of a law on associations, on the ground that they violated the principle of freedom of association, which is referred to by the preamble of the Constitution.

What happens if the executive violates the Constitution? Here the pre-1958 rules remain in force. The Constitution is treated just as any other statute. The Constitutional Council has no jurisdiction other than that just described. Only the Council of State has jurisdiction to determine whether acts of the executive are illegal or unconstitutional. In this area, the new Constitution seems inadequate, and one wonders whether it gives sufficient attention to the matter of regulations. Their use is no longer restricted to the creation of subsidiary legislation and implementation in areas already covered by statute. Regulations now have their own sphere of operation, parallel to that of legislative action. In such a situation it is shocking to have an administrative court, at least theoretically part of the executive branch, as the only body able to review the constitutionality of regulations. Although the independence of the Council of State within the executive branch is universally recognized, the Constitution can be criticized on this point for having ignored the principle of separation of powers and sanctioned a degree of executive supremacy that may be dangerous.

Respect for the Constitution, and especially for the principle of independence of the executive from judicial control, is imposed on the judiciary by binding jurisdictional rules, which are enforced by the Court of Conflicts and by various Civil and Penal Code rules such as that forbidding judges to give general or regulatory decisions on issues submitted to them (Civil Code, article 5).

II   Administrative Organization

The administration plays a considerable role in all modern countries by reason of the importance of the services people expect from it and the development in modern states of the notion of public services and the "public sector" of the economy.

In consequence, there has been a steady evolution since the Revolution, with a progressive increase in the tasks assumed by the administration. This evolution has been accelerated recently during two periods of extensive nationalization, first in 1936 when the "Popular Front" took control of the government and then in 1945 with the liberation and the establishment of the Fourth Republic. In the first period, the railroads and the Bank of France were nationalized and a national social security administration was created. Immediately after the liberation, there were important nationalizations in banking, insurance, energy (coal, gas, and electricity), radio, maritime and air transport, and other specific industries (the Renault industrial complex, defense industries, and the like).

These ever-increasing administrative functions have been carried out until recently through a variety of public law entities, the most important of which was the state itself. As the tendency toward governmental direction and guidance of activities in the private sector has become more prominent, the situation has grown much more complex. Along with the traditional public law entities, the state has created other bodies to assist in the performance of its new functions. Often these bodies seem superficially to be ordinary private organizations. For a variety of reasons the government has found it advantageous to "disguise itself" in directing a "public service," and has thus organized a corporation of which it is the sole shareholder. In numerous other cases it has joined with private individuals to form a "mixed corporation," in which it may or may not have a controlling voice.[6]

The administrative agencies and public services run by the state are grouped into ministerial departments under the authority of various ministers, although the precise number of departments and

6. P. Weil, Le droit administratif, no. 52 in series Que Sais-je? (3rd ed.; 1968).

the allocation of services between them changes from time to time.[7] In addition to the minister's staff, composed of a few persons linked directly to the minister, a ministerial department is normally made up of (1) a central administration with various subdivisions and (2) external branches. Sometimes there are also advisory councils and committees. The central administration is situated in Paris and deals with matters arising throughout the country. The external services, on the other hand, are composed of ministerial agents stationed in specific localities with authority to settle minor problems themselves. Their existence corresponds to the need for some deconcentration of administrative power and personnel.

The most important central administrative officials outside the capital are the prefects, who are stationed in each of France's ninety-five departments.[8] The office of prefect was created by Napoleon on the pattern of the intendant of prerevolutionary France and has many special functions. But the prefect is above all, in addition to his special functions, the Government's chief official in his department, and as such, supervises all of the various ministries' external offices in his department. In addition, he has a power of administrative tutelage, and thus some control, over the manner in which departments and communes manage the affairs designated by law as within their sphere of primary responsibility. Deconcentration through external offices of the ministries is contrasted in French legal terminology with decentralization,[9] which delegates certain powers in the jurisdiction of particular administrative agencies either to territorial subdivisions or to autonomous institutions with specific functions.

Administratively, metropolitan France is divided into ninety-five departments.[10] These are subdivided into arrondissements, the ar-

7. The first Cabinet of the Fifth Republic, formed in January, 1959, included the prime minister, one deputy prime minister, four ministers of state, fourteen ministers, and six secretaries of state. The variety of titles reflects a desire to establish a hierarchy within the Government.

8. The department of Paris, recently substituted for the department of the Seine, has a special organization, including two prefects, the prefect of Paris and the prefect of police. These two prefects divide the functions of prefects of other departments and also perform some functions that belong to the mayors of the communes in other departments.

9. See C. Eisenmann, *Centralisation et décentralisation* (1948) and J. Bou-Louis, "Décentralisation" and "Déconcentration" in *Répertoire Dalloz* (1957).

10. Including Corsica and the "territory" of Belfort.

rondissements into cantons, and the cantons into communes. Arrondissements and cantons are utilized solely for deconcentration, but departments and communes are used to accomplish both deconcentration and decentralization. It was within these various divisions that Napoleon in his time organized all French government services, from courts to hospitals, from mortgage registries to prisons. "Regions," made up of several departments, have also been created for the provision of some public services; for instance, there are now sixteen education regions, nine military regions, and thirty-four regions for the inspection of bridges and highways.[11]

The jurisdiction of departments is relatively limited. Departments are managed by general councils, made up of general councilors (*conseillers généraux*), who are elected by universal suffrage within the cantonal structure. The general council normally holds only two sessions a year and the duration of the sessions is limited by statute. The official who carries out the decisions of the general council is the prefect, who in this connection has a double role. His second role is supervision of the general council on behalf of the central government. He attends its deliberations and can initiate proceedings to invalidate its decisions.

The commune replaced the prerevolutionary parish, which still exists in the ecclesiastical organization of France; it is the most important division in the French administrative organization. France is made up of 38,000 communes in all, whose populations vary greatly. Paris, Lyon, and Marseille are each single communes, while communes of less than one hundred inhabitants are also frequent. Communal affairs are run by a municipal council elected by universal suffrage; this council elects from its membership an executive committee, made up of a mayor and one or more assistant mayors to act on its behalf.[12] The French mayor is an elected official, rather than a career civil servant, contrary to the situation in many other countries.

The commune, represented by its municipal council, generally

11. These figures are for 1960. The number of educational regions has been increased substantially since then. A vast reorganization of the regional system was proposed by the government in 1969 and was rejected in a referendum.

12. Paris has a special organization, in which the municipal council chooses a president; the mayors of the twenty arrondissements of Paris are officials appointed by the central government and are little more than custodians of the records of civil status.

deals with its affairs as it judges best. Its powers are defined by statute, however, in two respects. First, there are some services that the municipal council is required by statute to provide. And second, it is forbidden to provide certain services or to act in certain areas. The definition of municipal council jurisdiction is in some cases statutory, but often it is found in the decisions of the Council of State.[13]

In addition to the departments and communes, the decentralization of government activities in France has been accomplished by the creation of various public corporations (*éstablissements publics*). "Communes and departments provide a great variety of services, whose common characteristic is that they are local. Public corporations, on the other hand, provide services that are functionally specialized, in areas such as culture, commerce, or the improvement of real estate." [14] Chambers of commerce, universities, and savings banks are examples of public corporations. There are many types of public corporations, and their legal regulation varies correspondingly, with special statutes regulating either individual corporations or categories of them. For example, a special law regulates public corporations of an industrial or commercial character, which have become particularly numerous and important since World War II.

The public corporation is an official, integrated part of the governmental structure and must be distinguished from another category of organization, the corporations of public interest (*établissements d'utilité publique*). Most corporations of public interest are privately created associations or foundations, whose goals have allowed them to be "recognized as of public service." This recognition entails special benefits for them concerning their legal capacity and tax status. One of the few characteristics common to all public corporations is that they are legal persons and thus have financial autonomy. Another of their characteristics is that of specialization; no public institution can undertake activities outside its area of specialization.

The French civil service is aware of the importance of its tasks

13. Invalidation of the decisions of the municipal council must be requested first from the prefect; the prefect's decision to invalidate or uphold the position of the municipal council can then be taken to the administrative courts and on appeal to the Council of State.

14. M. Waline, *Droit administratif* (8th ed.; 1959), 352.

and of its role in the nation's life; it has developed traditions and attained a cohesiveness that one seldom finds in the civil service of other countries. This professionalism has its disadvantages. Traditions can develop into bureaucratic routine, and an *esprit de corps* often engenders an expectation of special privileges. At times the French civil service seems to exist for its own benefit rather than for that of the nation as a whole. There are, however, clear advantages that may outweigh these disadvantages. The civil service's solid traditions give civil servants a definite sense of the public welfare that is generally honest and sound. The frequent changes of government have been bearable in France only because the country has had a reliable civil service with well-established traditions.

The word *service* itself has almost no meaning in France outside of the civil service. A Frenchman would never think of using that concept to characterize the activity of a manufacturer of automobiles or household utensils, or that of an insurance company or a movie-house. For the person outside the civil service, the profit motive outweighs any consideration of the service to be rendered the community. To the French this seems legitimate, and they would be suspicious should he cover himself with a veil of virtue by proclaiming his devotion to society. For the man who wants to serve society, there exists, in the eyes of Frenchmen, a clear route. He should enter the civil service and devote his whole career to it. For this reason, the French civil service attracts some top-flight people, as well as some who are less noble and view a civil service career as a peaceful and secure way of life. The great entrance examinations that used to exist (for the Council of State, the Comptroller General's office, and the diplomatic corps, for example) and today's National School of Administration have attracted many top French university graduates.

The French civil service, always conscious of its responsibilities and particularly so since it achieved complete independence from the judiciary in 1790, has understood that it must fight the dangers that threaten the powerful, such as arbitrariness and corruption. As its recruitment and esprit have become democratic, the civil service has placed limits on its own power and has developed an institution designed to regularize its operation and minimize abuses. This institution is the Council of State, the true control mechanism of the French civil service.

Divided into sections, the Council of State is often asked—and sometimes it must be asked—for its advice on government legislative and regulatory proposals. But it has another function, equally essential, that makes it unique. The Council of State is best known to jurists as the supreme court of administrative law, with jurisdiction to control administrative action in almost all areas. On the petition of private individuals, the Council of State can either invalidate administrative actions or award damages or other remedies to individuals wrongly injured by such action. Every French executive official, from the President of the Republic to village mayor, with ministers and prefects between the two, is subject in his official actions to the Council of State's criticism and censure. And the council also has control over the activity of independent administrative agencies and their officials, and over the activity of certain elected bodies, such as the departmental general councils and the municipal councils. It has created the French "administrative law" over the last one hundred years. The result is that a legal structure has, perhaps more completely in France than in any other country, replaced an earlier structure that allowed much arbitrary action and many situations in which the government could not be held liable for improper action on its part. French public law can be understood only through a knowledge of the Council of State and particularly its unique esprit. This esprit has grown out of its participation, aside from its judicial functions, in the work of the active civil service, its members' devotion to public service, their comprehension of administrative necessities, and also its determination to curb abuses and misuses of power, to guarantee the equality of citizens, and to insure a healthy civil service.[15]

The overall structure of the Council of State is easy to describe. In addition to four actively "administrative" sections, it includes a litigation section to settle disputes brought before it. This latter section employs many more people than the four administrative sections combined and is subdivided into eleven three-man subsections. Disputes are normally disposed of by a particular subsection,

15. An excellent book on the Council of State is C. J. Hamson's *Pouvoir discrétionnaire et contrôle juridictionnel de l'administration* (1958). This book appeared in English in 1954 under the title *Executive Discretion and Judicial Control*. Also see M. Letourneur and J. Méric, *Conseil d'Etat et juridictions administratives* (1955).

or by two subsections sitting together, depending on the nature of the dispute. Difficult questions are decided by the litigation section as such, which for this purpose is composed of its president, assistant president, the presidents of the various subsections, and three other judges. Exceptional cases are decided by the full litigation assembly (*assemblée plénière du contentieux*). This body has a total of nineteen members and is very similar to the litigation section just described, except that it also includes the vice president of the council and four councilors elected each year by the council from its administrative sections.[16]

The Council of State has found it useful to have within its structure, as do the regular courts, a government representative.[17] The master of petitions (*maître des requêtes*) fills this role, with the title commissioner of the Government (*commissaire du gouvernement*). The title is rather poorly chosen, since it implies a subordination to the executive, whereas the commissioner frequently argues for the invalidation of administrative measures or for an award in damages against the state. In addition, the council has a number of clerks, called *auditeurs*, assigned to it; they prepare advisory memoranda for the council.

Several characteristics of the Council of State should be emphasized. First, there is great cohesion within the council. Most of its members enter at the age of twenty-five and spend their whole careers there, only absenting themselves for brief outside missions. Second, one should note the collaboration within the Council of State between persons of widely differing age and experience; this makes the council less susceptible to bureaucratic routine than the supreme courts of most other countries. And finally, the council has close ties with the active administration. Some members of the Council of State participate in active administration, while others settle litigated disputes. All belong to the same small, homogeneous body and work in the same buildings. Some members of the Council of State are recruited, not through competitive examinations,

16. The Council of State disposed of 4,949 cases in 1957–58. Of these, 243 were decided by the litigation section and 62 by the full litigation assembly. The rest were decided either by two subsections sitting together (3,127) or by a single subsection (1,517).

17. TRANSLATOR'S NOTE: See translator's note and text beginning on p. 59, below, for a discussion of the institution of the *ministère public,* or Public Ministry.

but on the basis of their experience in the active administration. In addition, the heads of the various administrative agencies are called upon to cooperate in the council's nonlitigious work. The effect of these various rules is to give the Government confidence in the Council of State, which for this reason can reach decisions that a different body would be unable to impose. The independence of the Council of State is illustrated by numerous decisions where it has readily affirmed the rule it thought most just under the law, even at the risk of provoking a serious governmental crisis and embarrassment, whether political or financial.

The Council of State was at one time the court of first instance in all administrative law disputes, but in 1953 it was relieved of this function and new lower administrative courts were created to lessen congestion in the Council of State. There are twenty-four lower administrative courts in metropolitan France,[18] each with three members to give judgment and often a fourth to act as commissioner of the Government. The Council of State is now generally only a court of retrial or appeal, since cases are decided in the first instance by the lower administrative courts or by some other administrative court with specialized jurisdiction.[19] This principle, however, is subject to important exceptions, and there are many categories of disputes where the law still provides for initial hearing by the Council of State. This is particularly true where the constitutional or legal status of an administrative act is challenged. The Council of State retains great influence in other cases, since ordinarily any judgment rendered by a lower administrative court can be taken to it on appeal, or even for trial *de novo*, without regard to the amount in controversy.[20]

18. Before the reform of 1953 these courts were called interdepartmental councils of the prefecture (*Conseils [inter-départementaux] de préfecture*).

19. There are in fact forty different types of administrative courts. See Waline, *op. cit.*, no. 234 ff., pp. 144 ff.

20. Decisions of special administrative courts, on the other hand, ordinarily can only be appealed to the Council of State on questions of law.

III   Judicial Organization

There is neither a single comprehensive statute governing the whole French judiciary nor a single treatise covering the whole subject. The reasons for this lack derive from the historical development of the judiciary and the structure of French legal education. Separation of powers, as that concept is ordinarily understood in France, dictates that administrative courts be regarded as an administrative service and be studied with administrative law, rather than as part of the judicial structure. To the French jurist, therefore, the words *judicial organization* refer only to those courts which decide cases in the private and criminal law areas. Treatises on "civil procedure" cover only those principles and rules that are common to private and penal law courts and those that are peculiar to civil law litigation. To discover the procedural rules governing criminal, commercial, and labor courts, one must supplement these works with specialized treatises on criminal procedure and labor and commercial law.

We have followed tradition in examining the regulation of French administrative procedure and litigation in the chapter on administrative organization. We will, therefore, limit ourselves here to a description of the courts in the private and criminal law areas. We will then discuss the Court of Cassation, which supervises the lower courts in these two areas.

French private law courts were substantially reorganized in 1958. Before this reform the court of general jurisdiction, except where statutes provided expressly to the contrary, was in the first instance the civil court (*tribunal civil*), of which there was usually one in each arrondissement. Above them were twenty-seven courts of appeals (*Cours d'appel*), with appellate jurisdiction where the dispute was sufficiently important. Alongside these courts, there were others, generally known as courts of exceptional jurisdiction. These courts could hear only those cases over which a statute expressly gave them jurisdiction. The oldest courts of exceptional jurisdiction were the justices of the peace (*justices de paix*), with jurisdiction over minor cases, and the commercial courts (*tribunaux de commerce*), with jurisdiction over some commercial disputes.

Each canton had its justice of the peace, and appeals from this court went, where the dispute was sufficiently important, to the civil court, which then gave judgment as the court of last resort (except for the possibility of petition on questions of law to the Court of Cassation). The commercial court was generally located in the arrondissement, and litigants could, where the case was sufficiently important, appeal from its decisions to the court of appeals. Other, more recently created courts of exceptional jurisdiction were the labor boards (*conseils de prud'hommes*), which ousted the jurisdiction of the justices of the peace in disputes between workers or employees and employers; the joint rural lease commissions (*tribunaux paritaires de baux ruraux*), with jurisdiction over disputes between lessors and lessees of rural land; the landlord-tenant judges (*juges des loyers*), with jurisdiction over disputes between lessors and lessees of residential property;[21] and the social security commissions of first instance (*commissions de première instance de sécurité sociale*). It is appropriate also to note here the special jurisdiction of the president of the civil court, apart from that of the civil court itself, and the summary jurisdiction in civil and commercial matters that belonged to the president of the civil and commercial courts in some emergency situations.

The reform of December, 1958, has profoundly changed both the structure and terminology in this area. The civil court has taken the name court of major jurisdiction (*tribunal de grande instance*). Apart from this change in terminology, two modifications concerning it are of note. First, many of these courts have been abolished; 172 courts of major jurisdiction have replaced 353 civil courts. Second, the courts of major jurisdiction have lost much of the appellate jurisdiction that belonged to the civil courts. Henceforth appeals from decisions of the justices of the peace (whose name has been changed to courts of minor jurisdiction), labor boards, joint rural lease commissions, and social security commissions of first instance go to the courts of appeals.[22] This principle, however, can be set aside by decree, so as to give the courts of major jurisdiction appellate jurisdiction in certain areas.

21. The landlord-tenant judge, however, was merely the justice of the peace or the president of the civil court, depending on the amount in controversy.

22. Before the reform of 1958 there were special courts of appeals for these last two categories of courts; they have been abolished.

Another basic aspect of the reform was the abolition of the justices of the peace. In truth, this abolition was more a promotion. The new court of minor jurisdiction was substituted for the justice of the peace and given a position between that of the old justice of the peace and that of the old civil court. First, the court of minor jurisdiction will generally be a court which sits in the capital of the arrondissement instead of the capital of the canton; 455 courts of minor jurisdiction were set up for all of France. On the other hand, the rules governing recruitment of the judiciary have been standardized so that judges of the courts of minor jurisdiction will no longer seem to belong to an inferior part of the judiciary. And finally, the jurisdiction of these courts has been considerably enlarged in comparison with that of the old justices of the peace, and appeals from their decisions, like appeals from the courts of major jurisdiction, generally go to the courts of appeals.[23]

The position of the courts of appeals was not changed by the 1958 reform except for the enlargement of their jurisdiction. Similarly, the reform left in existence most of the courts of exceptional jurisdiction. There thus exist in France at present 236 commercial courts and 359 labor boards (or sections thereof).

Courts are divided into chambers where their workload justifies it. Thus, the Paris court of appeals has twenty-five chambers[24] and the Paris court of major jurisdiction has twenty-seven, themselves subdivided into sections.

For criminal cases, different courts have jurisdiction depending on whether the offense alleged, judged by the penalty involved, is classified as a major offense (crime), an intermediate offense punishable by brief imprisonment or fine (délit), or a minor offense (contravention). Major offenses are judged, in first and last instance, by the court of assize (Cour d'assies), a court composed of three magistrates and nine jurors, who are selected by lot for each session of the court of assize from a previously established list. Intermediate offenses are judged, in first instance, by the correctional court (tribunal correctionnel), the criminal law equivalent of the court of major jurisdiction. Appeals, if any, go to the correctional

23. The court of minor jurisdiction has jurisdiction when the amount in controversy is less than 5,000 francs (c.US $1,000). Its decision is subject to appeal where the amount in controversy exceeds 2,500 francs (c.US $500).
24. Each of these chambers is subdivided into two sections.

appeals chamber (*Chambre des appels correctionnels*) of the court
of appeals. Minor offenses are handled by the police court (*tribunal
de police*),[25] which corresponds to the court of minor jurisdiction.
Appeals, if any, go to the court of appeals.

There have been times when special criminal courts existed to
judge specific political or economic offenses. The only special
courts existing today are the High Court of Justice (*Haute Cour
de Justice*), established by the Constitution of 1958 to judge cases
of high treason, and the military courts, to judge certain special offenses committed by military personnel. There also are maritime
courts, which judge specific offenses involving the merchant
marine.

Finally, children up to eighteen years of age who commit intermediate or minor offenses are tried by special children's courts,
made up of one professional judge and two nonprofessional assistants. A major offense committed by a sixteen- or seventeen-year-old
minor is judged by the court of assize for children (*Cour d'assises
des enfants*), made up of one court of appeals judge, two special
children's judges, and nine jurors.

Above all these civil and criminal courts sits the French supreme
court, called the Court of Cassation (*Cour de cassation*). It is
composed at the present time of one criminal and one civil chamber; with the latter itself subdivided into three civil sections, a
commercial section, and a social section.[26] Cases taken to the Court
of Cassation are generally heard by a single section. Particularly
delicate cases and those likely to create conflicts with earlier decisions can be referred to "mixed chambers" (formerly the civil
assembly [*Assemblée plénière civile*]), a special grouping of the
president and one representative of each civil section of the civil
chamber, and in some cases, the president and a councilor from
the criminal chamber. Finally, there are circumstances, which we

25. Called before 1958 the *tribunal de simple police*.
26. Before 1947 the Court of Cassation was differently organized. In addition
to the criminal chamber, there were three chambers on the civil side, a "request"
chamber, a civil chamber, and a social chamber. Most civil cases came first to the
request chamber, which decided if the appeal had a chance of success. If its decision was affirmative, it sent the case on to the civil chamber. If it was negative,
it dismissed the appeal by a reasoned decision. The social chamber, created in
1938, had immediate jurisdiction over and decided appeals in certain kinds of
cases.

will discuss presently, where a case can be heard by the full court (*Assemblée plénière,* formerly called the *Chambres réunies*) of the Court of Cassation.[27]

Within the judicial hierarchy, the Court of Cassation is unique. As a rule, it considers only questions of law and leaves all factual questions for determination by other courts. It is impossible to reach the Court of Cassation by complaining that the lower courts have made a mistake of fact, such as having incorrectly evaluated the amount of damage suffered by the plaintiff or having found X guilty of theft when he was innocent. The Court of Cassation hears only questions of law, or so at least goes the general rule. There are exceptional cases where the principle is set aside, but the primary problem is the practical, applied meaning of this abstraction, since the line between questions of fact and law is always difficult to draw and sometimes is conceived by the Court of Cassation in a way that may be theoretically difficult to justify. The Court of Cassation's role is not, as scholars sometimes seem to think, to guard the purity of this distinction. Rather, it is to insure the consistency of French judicial decisions, so as to avoid there being a better chance of winning a lawsuit in a Marseille court, say, than in a Le Havre court. The Court of Cassation intervenes wherever intervention seems required to fulfill the court's function, without too much concern as to whether the question to be considered ought, strictly speaking, to be called a question of law.[28] Only two primary factors limit the overextension of its jurisdiction. The court may fear a loss of effectiveness through overexposure. And its own procedures prevent the court, for example, from taking evidence freely.

Since it generally considers only questions of law, the Court of Cassation seldom considers the whole of a lawsuit. Thus, exceptional cases aside, it cannot dispose of disputes definitively. Either of two things happens. If the court decides that the law has been correctly interpreted in the case, it will reject the petition. If it

27. This terminology dates from 1967. Prior to these reforms, the present mixed chambers were known as the *Assemblée plénière,* and the role of the present *Assemblée plénière* devolved on the plenum of the court (*Chambres réunies*).

28. See G. Marty, *La distinction du fait et du droit* (1929), 365–66. "The Court of Cassation should intervene whenever, because of the character of the decision appealed, its judgment can have a general effect and help avoid future difficulties."

decides that the lower court judges have made an error of law, it will quash their decision and send the dispute back to a new court of the same level as the one whose decision is quashed. This new court—the court of rehearing—has jurisdiction over the whole dispute. On the point of law that was submitted to the Court of Cassation, it may adopt the court's point of view, in which case the litigation is terminated and the new court's decision is final. If the court of rehearing, however, refuses to follow the Court of Cassation, as it has the right to do, a new petition to that court can be taken. In such a case, the dispute comes before the full court of the Court of Cassation. Where the full court quashes the decision against which the second petition is brought, it again sends the case back to a court of the same level. On the point of law which the Court of Cassation has decided, this new court must yield to the opinion of the full court.

Any decision of any court whatsoever can be brought before the Court of Cassation, without regard to the amount in controversy, provided only that the decision involved is not appealable to another court. Decisions of the justices of the peace and of the police courts are in fact often submitted to the Court of Cassation. This is possible even where the amount in controversy in the case is too small to allow an appeal to the court of appeals. A case that seems to be a trifling matter can raise basic issues of law, on which the Court of Cassation can usefully speak so that the people throughout France will be subject to the same law and judged in the same way.

Among the French courts of general jurisdiction, only the court of minor jurisdiction and the police court in the criminal area are composed of a single judge. And among the courts of exceptional jurisdiction, the landlord-tenant courts, the referees' courts (*juridiction des référés*), and the court of the president of the court of major jurisdiction (*juridiction du president du tribunal de grande instance*) are single-judge tribunals. In all other cases, the principle of judicial collegiality prevails. In most courts, three judges collaborate in a decision, and in the Court of Cassation the minimum number is seven. The courts of assize are composed of three professional magistrates and nine jurors.[29] Similarly in other courts

29. Since 1941 the judges and jurors have joined together to decide both on the question of guilt and on the penalty.

(labor boards, joint rural lease commissions), laymen are associated with judges in the settlement of disputes. Various attempts have been made in France to establish more single-judge courts, most notably in 1945. But these attempts have failed; the statutes in question have been repealed, in large part because of the resistance of the judiciary itself to the idea of giving judgment singly in criminal cases.

Although criminal and civil courts have different names, the same judges in fact sit in the courts of major jurisdiction and the correctional courts, on the one hand, and in the courts of minor jurisdiction and the police courts, on the other. Except in courts where the volume of litigation justifies several specialized chambers, the same judges hear civil cases one day and criminal cases the next. Similarly, the courts of appeals hear on appeal both civil and criminal cases.

All criminal courts, courts of major jurisdiction, courts of appeals, and the Court of Cassation have attached to them representatives of the Ministry of Justice, whose functions we shall explain in detail in Part Three, below. There is no representative of this ministry, on the other hand, attached to the civil courts of exceptional jurisdiction.

All decisions rendered by French courts must contain written reasons, except those of the courts of assize. This obligation to rationalize decisions did not appear in France until a fairly late date. It was related to the creation of the Court of Cassation in 1789, and was intended to facilitate that court's supervisory activities. The writing of opinions in France is a highly technical matter.[30] It seems that judges adopted the techniques used before the Revolution by French lawyers in their written summations. It is an accepted principle in France that good judicial opinions are short. The higher a court is in the hierarchy, the shorter its opinions.

The brevity of French opinions ordinarily does not detract from their clarity. In fact, French jurists consider conciseness a prerequisite to clarity, since it requires the court to eliminate all that is superfluous and to weigh each word of its opinion. One should

30. Whether this tradition will endure is at present open to doubt. The Paris Court of Appeals has moved away from the century-old tradition in a conspicuous —but so far unique—decision rendered in 1967.

also note that for many years only a part of every judicial opinion was published in the case reports. In addition to published reasons (*motifs*) and a disposition (*dispositif*), a part that was not published, called the conditions (*qualités*), was drafted by the parties' lawyers relating the whole procedural context. A decree of December 22, 1958, abolished conditions and a ministerial circular of February 17, 1959, required, because of this abolition, that courts be sure that their opinions constitute "a whole, whose reading alone indicates the requests and positions of both sides, in fact and in law, the reasons for the decision, and finally the decision itself." It remains to be seen how much these admonitions will be heeded, and whether and how much the form of French judicial opinions will in fact change. The failure to publish the conditions makes the reading of pre-1958 French opinions a difficult task, for which some initiation is required.

If they so desire, Frenchmen can take their disputes to private arbitration for settlement instead of going into the state's court system. This possibility is excluded, however, in cases where the law requires communication of the dispute to the Ministry of Justice. This exception excludes all criminal cases and those civil cases in which either the state or a person lacking capacity (minor, insane person, spendthrift for whom a supervisor has been appointed) is involved, as well as a fairly large number of cases involving questions of public policy. The parties generally authorize their arbitrators to act as amicable compounders (*amiables compositeurs*). The import of this authorization is ambiguous. It is said that it allows the arbitrators to decide "equitably." Its purpose, however, is often more limited, i.e., to permit the arbitrators to ignore minor rules (as opposed to the basic principles) of procedure, and in particular to exclude an appeal based on an error of law committed by the arbitrators. The organization of arbitration in France is far from satisfactory. The execution of arbitration awards often depends largely on the good will of the parties. Nevertheless, arbitration is frequently utilized in France, particularly in commercial disputes, and above all in the area of international commerce. The amicable compounder clause then prevents appeal from the arbitration award by an assertion that the arbitrators have not applied the law required by a system of conflicts of laws, a system which itself is often ambiguous.

PART THREE

French Lawyers

The way law is created, developed, and applied depends in large measure on the men who work with it. It is doubtful whether true law can exist in the absence of a class or caste of specialized lawyers. The recruitment and education of lawyers—whether it be through inheritance, as was the case in earlier times, or through university training—can have a decisive effect on their concept of the law and on how this law will really develop. For this reason, we will in Part Three examine. French legal education and the legal professions.

I   Legal Education

As in other countries of the Romano-Germanic legal tradition, legal education in France today is primarily an academic, university education, divorced from legal practice. A university degree is ordinarily required in order to qualify for top legal jobs, such as advocate (*avocat*), judge, and law professor. The lawyer's strictly professional training comes only after he has spent several years in a university and earned the degree of license in law (*licence en droit*).

The rule is certainly not absolute. Theoretically, one can become a notary (*notaire*) or a bailiff (*huissier*) simply by going through professional apprenticeships and passing examinations organized by the profession itself. To qualify for most legal jobs, however, in addition to such apprenticeships and examinations, one must hold an academic degree. The degree required is a license in law for judges and advocates and capacity (*capacité*) in law for reporters (*greffiers*), *avoués*, and *agréés*. Even notaries and bailiffs will do their best to obtain one, without which they will feel socially inferior to other members of the legal profession. It is assumed in France that true lawyers have degrees.

The rule that requires French judges and advocates to possess academic degrees is ancient. We know that as early as 1268 a majority of judges in the *Parlement de Paris* were trained lawyers, and by 1319 all judges on the various supreme courts appear to have received university training. Even in the lower courts, there were educated lawyers as early as the reign of Saint-Louis. It was not until the end of the fifteenth century (1499), however, that lower court judges were expressly forbidden to decide cases if they had no university degree. Thereafter, one of the principal lower courts, the court of *bailliage,* had to have a presiding officer with a law degree.[1] As for advocates, it seems that as early as the fifteenth, and perhaps even the fourteenth, century they had to have a license in law degree.[2] Nevertheless the importance of this requirement can be overstated. Until a reorganization of the University of Paris in 1679, the license in law could be attained in a single year, and there were even cases where it was purchased for money. Only in 1679 was a true program of disciplined studies, lasting three years, introduced. And even this did not prevent a serious deterioration in the quality of legal education during the eighteenth century. The present organization of law faculties is based on an 1804 statute, which reestablished the faculties after the Revolution had abolished them in 1793.

Today French jurists must hold a university degree in order to practice their profession, and apart from any legal obligation, they expect to seek and possess such a degree. This has important consequences for the character and attitudes of French jurists.

The education given by the universities is not a practical training and in some ways even conflicts with the kind of training required by practitioners. Like other European universities, French universities used to teach primarily Roman and canon law. It was only in 1679 that a chair of French law was created at the University of Paris. Today French law faculties certainly put primary emphasis on French law, but the instruction given their students, future lawyers, still goes far beyond this. Other subjects are also taught, sometimes to broaden the lawyer's general background and help him understand legal problems and sometimes simply because in France it has been within the law faculties that instruction in

1. This requirement was first formulated in the *Ordonnance Cabochienne* (1413), which was passed by King Charles VI under threat of mob violence and annulled several months later.

2. R. Delachenal, *Histoire des avocats au Parlement de Paris, 1306–1600* (1885), 6 ff.

various relatively new social sciences has been organized.[3] The breadth of his curriculum encourages the French law student to see legal problems from above and to consider them in all their general aspects, historical, economic, and social. He does not see them, and is not encouraged to see them, from the practitioner's point of view.

The technical aspect of legal problems receives little emphasis in law faculties, where we tend to live in the realm of ideas and pride ourselves in not worrying about the more mundane, and sometimes sordid, problems of legal practice. There will be time after graduation for the student to learn "the craft," and the devices and tricks that it involves. In his university years, he must live in the realm of ideas and breathe the pure air of principle. He must not be concerned with material considerations, which will become and remain his master during the rest of his life. This attitude seems particularly important to the French law faculties because they are composed, in large part, of students between eighteen and twenty-two or twenty-three years old, many of whom have not yet finally decided to become professional lawyers.

University legal education is sought not only by those looking toward legal careers. A great many persons who will not eventually become professional lawyers go through the law faculties. The explanations for this are, first, that this path is at present the normal one for persons who want to make a career in the civil service,[4] and second, that the French have a traditional bias in favor of legal education. It is an axiom in France that legal studies open all doors. A knowledge of the law, at least elementary, is highly valued. The Frenchman considers such familiarity with law an almost essential element of a person's general education; the French public does not regard the law as something esoteric and mysterious, as the English regard their common law. These attitudes lead Frenchmen, as has already been noted, to see legal

3. A French university even now comprises only five "faculties": Law and Economics, Humanities (*Lettres*), Science, Medicine, and Pharmacy. There are in addition two faculties of Divinity (Roman Catholic and Protestant) within the University of Strasbourg.

4. Economics has been dissociated from law only since 1955. Basic principles of economics are still taught, however, within the curriculum of the law schools, and legal principles are taught within the curriculum of the economics degree.

problems where a foreigner would see political or economic problems. One would have an incomplete and untrue picture of the French legal system if one disregarded this tendency and were not aware of its explanation in the wide diffusion of legal culture among the most diverse elements in French society.

The student educated in a French law faculty is accustomed to think of the law in terms of principles, rather than of practice and procedure. If he becomes a professional lawyer, life and experience will no doubt correct this attitude. Nevertheless, he may well retain something of the idea that, above practice and routine, there is a realm of principle and legal theory in which a few privileged persons are allowed to live. He continues to respect and admire the person who has not had to "lower himself" to practice. The law professor, as pure jurisconsult, enjoys in France—and here we continue an extremely old tradition[5]—particular prestige.

The superiority which a French jurist, because of his education, naturally accords to principle over procedure has its practical disadvantages. Too often the legally educated Frenchman neglects the practical aspects of a problem, even when they are of crucial importance. He is satisfied to pose a principle, to make a solemn declaration, without asking how this principle will be applied or even whether it can be applied.

The theoretical Declarations of Rights proclaimed by French constitution-makers are rightly contrasted to the American Bill of Rights, which is enforced in practical terms by judicial control over questions of constitutionality. One contrasts still more forcefully these same French Declarations of Rights to the habeas corpus procedure that has been organized by English lawyers. These observations in fact have a validity well beyond the confines of constitutional law; they can be made in every area of the law. Problems of evidence and procedure are hardly touched by legal writers in France. The subject of execution of judgments, similarly neglected by the writers, seems to be of little more interest to the legislator. He seems to think his job is finished when he has stated what the law is and does not concern himself with effectively guaranteeing that it will be respected. The same observations are valid for criminal law and administrative law. There also, the Frenchman too

5. See F. Schulz, *Principles of Roman Law* (1936).

often thinks it is enough to state principles. Too rarely does he give his attention to implementing and insuring respect for the principles stated.[6]

Certainly one cannot place the whole blame for this weakness on French legal education and the French law faculties. It seems clear, however, that they aggravate these problems and tend to give French law an academic and theoretical character which is sometimes excessive.

II   The Legal Professions

France has no statute dealing generally with all legal activities or the whole of the legal profession. There are, however, some positions within the legal system that are regulated by statute and restricted to persons belonging to particular professional organizations. Provided that these specific monopolies are respected, any Frenchman can call himself a lawyer and provide legal services. We need not, therefore, enumerate all the positions that are considered related to the French legal system. We will confine ourselves to a few remarks concerning the principal legal careers that are regulated by statute.

Section 1.   Magistrates

The term *magistrate* is applied to three groups of persons in France: judges, agents of the Public Ministry, and officials working in the central administration of justice.

§1.   Judges
In the French judicial structure, there are many different kinds of courts, and judges in some of them have special names and ranks. Our description here will be limited to the most general case, that of the career judge who sits in a court within the regular, rather than the administrative, court hierarchy.

6. See Alexander H. Pekelis, *Law and Social Action* (1950), 42 ff.

Ordinarily, litigation in France is handled by a career judiciary. This is true in civil cases in the courts of minor jurisdiction (*tribunaux d'instance*) and the courts of major jurisdiction (*tribunaux de grande instance*) and in criminal cases in the police courts (*tribunaux de police*) and the correctional courts (*tribunaux correctionnels*). It is also true in the courts of appeals and the Court of Cassation.

The manner of becoming a career magistrate was revised by ordinance of December 22, 1958. The law student who has obtained the degree of license in law (*licence en droit*) is qualified to take a competitive admission examination for the National Magistracy School (*Ecole nationale de la magistrature,* formerly the *Centre nationale d'études judiciaires*).[7] Upon admission, he attains the status of a law clerk (*auditeur de justice*)[8] and from then on is a part of the magistrature. At the end of three years of studies, composed of both scholarly work and apprenticeship training, he will take another examination and then become a full-fledged magistrate, as either a deputy judge or a deputy prosecutor. The National Magistracy School, modeled after the National School of Administration (*Ecole nationale d'administration*), is open to both men and women. Many women have entered the judiciary since it was opened to them in 1946. A maximum of 10 percent of the magistrature can be recruited, on the recommendation of the Superior Council of the Magistrature (*Conseil supérieur de la magistrature*), without going through this institution. The magistrate ordinarily enters the judiciary in this way before he is twenty-seven years old and then progresses up through the hierarchy, with the hope of ending his career on the Court of Cassation.

The way judges are recruited in France, the way their careers are structured, and the way they are promoted cannot help but have important consequences for the personality of judges and

7. Various categories of persons can be admitted to the National Magistracy School without taking the competitive examinations. For such persons, the program of studies at the school lasts only two years.

8. One must not confuse these *auditeurs de justice* with the *attachés de justice,* a position created by a decree of January 7, 1959. The *attachés de justice* are officials that can be assigned to the Court of Cassation, a court of appeals, or a court of major jurisdiction to perform certain administrative functions. They are not magistrates.

for the application of the law. The magistrate's career in France is often chosen because of a family tradition, and sometimes because of a strong inclination in that direction. In addition, however, it attracts some relatively unambitious men, who prefer the security of a modest but sure salary to the hazards of battle, the risks of business life, or the uncertainties of competition. A person who chooses the career of magistrate can look forward to a tranquil life, at least the first few years of which will usually be spent in a provincial city.

Nor will his life be troubled by excessive responsibility. Judges sit alone in French courts only for minor civil cases and to hear violations of police regulations. A case of any importance will go to a court composed of several judges. In addition, it is a principle of French law that court opinions must be anonymous. The writing of minority opinions is not only unknown; it is strictly forbidden. The secrecy of judicial deliberations is imposed on judges by their very oath of office, and one never knows whether a particular judgment or opinion was rendered by a unanimous court, whether there was a minority in opposition, or who constituted the minority if there was one. For this reason, a judge has little occasion to assert his personality outside of court deliberations. He will not be rendered famous by his opinions, even when he reaches the apex of the hierarchy.

These observations are important and increase the authority and reliability of judicial opinions. The French judge naturally follows precedent although he is under no legal obligation to do so. He is not tempted to assert his own personal opinion against established case law. Therefore, the rule of *stare decisis* is less necessary in France than in other countries, and it may be that this is why it has never been imposed.

Another consequence of the same observations is that the French judge naturally avoids any position that would put him particularly in public view or give him excessive responsibility. France has no judicial control over the constitutionality of statutes. No French constitution has ever formally forbidden this control, but the French courts have never wanted it. They themselves abandoned the tradition of the prerevolutionary *parlements* (supreme courts), which, in the absence of a parliament in the modern sense, tried to represent the national will. France now has a modern Parliament, and the judiciary has readily subordinated itself to its decisions.

A final consequence of these same factors is that the French judge does not like to put himself in the limelight by creating rules of law. In practice, certainly, he must do so. The judicial function is not, and cannot be, one of mechanically applying known, pre-existing rules to particular cases. But the French judge tries to give the impression that this is his job. In his opinions, he always pretends to apply a statute. Almost never will he rely upon general, unwritten principles or formulas of equity that, to a third person, might seem to invite or allow judicial initiative and arbitrariness. One must know this mental disposition of the French judge in order to understand the "principles of interpretation" that are applied to the statutes and codes of French law.

To be sure, judges are respected in France, but because of what we have said, they do not have the importance and prestige in France that they have in some other countries. The French Court of Cassation, having willingly restricted itself to as technical a legal role as possible, provokes neither the wild praise nor the vehement criticism that are, in changing times and climates of opinion, the lot of the Supreme Court of the United States. French judges are glad of their anonymity and, having been judges from their youth, do not derive the same reward from their status that English judges do, nor do they have as close relations with the bar as do English and American judges.

This brings us to another observation that is essential to an understanding of French law. In France one rarely finds a judge who was an advocate before coming to the bench. Thus, he does not share the advocate's approach to problems and his relations with the bar do not have the same basis as in common law countries. The French judge enters the judiciary directly from his university. His basic education is theoretical and academic. He has learned to see the law in terms of principles. He has a slight distrust for advocates, who try to pull him down to the level of concrete, factual circumstances and thus to draw him away from the security of his principles. The French judge will let the advocate speak. He will listen to him without ever interrupting, although this often leads to interminable presentations of argument and to abuses. But the judge will continue to wait; he will not announce his decision in the case immediately after the advocates retire. He takes his time to weigh the arguments so eloquently presented by the two sides. He must deliberate upon the case. Judgment will not be given until a week or more after the hearing ends. This period of deliberation seems as necessary to French judges as it may appear shocking to English and American lawyers. No doubt the principal reason for the contrast to common law procedure is the traditional collaboration in common law countries between the judge and a jury, which must be released as soon as possible. Further reasons, however, are the different relationships between judges and advocates in various countries, the varying conceptions of the advocate's role, the different forms in which arguments are presented, and the greater preoccupation which the French judge has, compared with his English and American counterpart, with rendering a decision that is in full accord with principle and thus not limited to the facts of the particular dispute before him.

The French judge has gone through a law faculty and is conscious of having received from that institution his basic education. Regardless of his feeling toward his teachers, he is marked for life by his stay in the faculty. He continues to consider the law essentially as a body of principles. His point of view is very different from the practitioner's procedural approach. No doubt, as a judge he associates with advocates and comes to see legal problems from a practical angle. But his views do not depend, as those of the advocate are thought to depend, on the unique position of the parties. The French judge, within the family of lawyers, feels closer to the law professor, who was his teacher, than to the advocate, whose collaboration is not entirely disinterested. The advocate knows this and sometimes, in difficult cases, seeks the advice of a law professor to strengthen his position. Compared to his American or English counterpart, the French judge is something of a theoretician, who is particularly interested in the coherence of legal principles and the harmony of the system. These attitudes unquestionably have influenced the development of French law.

The French judge cannot be dismissed and so is fully independent of the executive branch of the government. Also, appointed for

life, he is not dependent on any electoral body. But can a desire for
advancement not compromise his independence? This question can
be answered unequivocally in the negative.[9]

The promotion of judges, in fact, does not depend at all on their
political attitude. No doubt it can be advantageous for a magistrate
to have personal connections with individuals who will recommend
to the ministry that he be promoted. Such recommendations have
often been criticized and it was partly in reaction against them that
the Superior Council of the Magistracy was created. In any case,
however, such recommendations are usually based on personal relationships, independent of the possible political attitude of the magistrate in question, and are completely unrelated to any services that
the magistrate has rendered, or might render, to a politically influential individual or to the executive.

The independence of the French judiciary should be obvious if
we note certain characteristics of French justice. Let us recall the
collegiality of judges that exists in all important cases and the anonymity of judicial opinions. Also, there is the fact that the courts do
not control the constitutionality of French legislation and that
politically important cases thus usually escape them. Another
factor is the existence of administrative courts in France, which
deprive the ordinary courts of jurisdiction over most cases where
the state or an administrative agency is concerned. And finally,
there was until recently the weakness of the executive branch and
the frequent Government changes. All of these factors have helped
reinforce the complete independence, in relation to the political
branches of government, that French judges derive from their con-
science and their tradition. The system of promotion of judges
applied in France has other inconveniences, but it does not compromise the independence of the judiciary. French judges can demonstrate their independence of the Government without any risk to
their careers. Unfortunately it is much more difficult for them to remain independent of the pressures of public opinion, guided and
sometimes misled by a press eager for sensation and scandal. If preventive detention is used too often, it may well be to satisfy a public

9. Since the French Constitution of 1946, the promotion of judges has depended partly on recommendation by the Superior Council of the Magistrature
Unfortunately, the role of the council was restricted by the Constitution of 1958
and the executive branch was given greater control over its composition.

opinion that has been developed by a press that will another day de-
cry abuse of the same preventive detention.

§2. *The Public Ministry*

A second category of French magistrates is composed of agents of
the Public Ministry (*ministère public*): procurators, procurators
general, advocates general, and their assistants.[10] In each court of
major jurisdictions, correctional court, court of assize, court of appeals, and in the Court of Cassation, there are, in addition to the
judges, one or more agents of the Public Ministry.

The role of the Public Ministry is not to defend the interests of
the state or to give legal opinions and advice to the executive. Although the Public Ministry is attached to the Ministry of Justice, it
represents and defends not the interests of the state or the executive,
but those of society and of the law. It has an important role in the
criminal area, where it is charged with prosecution, under judicial
supervision, of delinquents. In civil cases, its role is less central, but
equally important. Litigation between private individuals in France
is not thought to involve only those individuals. The Public Ministry insures that the interests of persons requiring special protection
(such as minors and insane persons) are properly protected, and that
the principles of law, the bases of public order, are not ignored. To
this end, the ministry often submits a brief to the court when it is
considering a case.

Because the state also holds itself out as the defender of law,
order, and social morality, one can easily leap to the erroneous conclusion that the Public Ministry and its agents are representatives of
the state. If this were so, it would indeed be shocking to see the
Public Ministry endowed with its various privileges and one would
be led to suspect that it exists to spy on and influence judges, thus
threatening their independence. For a proper evaluation of the institution of the Public Ministry, one must put aside all preconceptions and examine its characteristics and functions as they operate,

10. TRANSLATOR'S NOTE: The somewhat awkward term "Public Ministry" has
been used here to translate the French term *ministère public* in order to emphasize
that the French institution has no English or American counterpart. It is described sufficiently in the text to obviate further definition here. Occasionally I
have substituted the terms "Ministry of Justice" or "prosecutor" in other chapters when this did not seem to create confusion and could facilitate comprehension
of the main point asserted in the text.

without being misled by appearances which can produce a distorted
picture of its role and activities. The Public Ministry, like most
French legal institutions, has a basis in tradition. In some cases, the
functions it served earlier in its historical development are reflected
in the rules governing its organization and operation, although it has
long since ceased in fact to be used, or even usable, for such ends.

There is no doubt that, historically, the Public Ministry was the
sovereign's representative in court. The term procurator for the Republic (*procureur de la Republique*), which succeeded that of procurator for the king (*procureur du roi*), leaves little question in that
regard. In France the Public Ministry originally had functions comparable to those exercised in England and the United States today
by the solicitor general and the attorney general. The major difference was that, because English justice was centralized in the royal
courts in London, only a single attorney general was required,
whereas France was less centralized and so had to have one procurator for the king in every important court.

The earlier situation, in which the Public Ministry was the state's
representative in court, is still reflected in some rules. The agents of
the Public Ministry are appointed and discharged freely by the
executive. They are organized hierarchically and can be instructed
by and are responsible to the Minister of Justice. Their situation,
however, began to change as early as the fourteenth century. The
primary reason why the rules just mentioned remain is that the
agents of the Public Ministry have various other administrative
duties in addition to their functions in court. For example, they supervise the registers of civil status and the records on convicted criminals and collect statistics on the administration of justice.

While participating in the administration of justice, the agents of
the Public Ministry now have almost complete autonomy, which
has converted them into representatives of society more than representatives of the state.[11] In their court activities, they are now true
magistrates rather than agents of the executive and are formally recognized as such. They are magistrates by virtue of their recruitment,
their relations with the judiciary, and their independence. An adage

---

11. In cases before the civil and administrative courts, the state retains ordinary
advocates and *avoués* to represent it, and it hires their services as would any other
client.

says, "While the pen is servile, the tongue is free." The magistrate in the Public Ministry who, because of instructions he has received, must present a written brief for a particular position can assert his own point of view in his oral presentation and develop arguments in opposition to his written position.[12]

Agents of the Public Ministry are selected by the same examination as judges. After graduation from the National Magistracy School, one must choose between a career as a magistrate on the bench (judge) and one as a pleading and prosecuting magistrate (agent of the Public Ministry). The two careers are quite distinct and attract different personality types. The magistrature of the bench ensures greater independence and more time for study and reflection, while the pleading and prosecuting magistrature is more suitable to active, responsibility-seeking men and usually leads to more rapid advancement. Even so, the choice made after this examination is not final. Although judges rarely enter the Public Ministry, movement in the opposite direction is common, particularly at the senior level, since there are more appellate court judges and thus more vacancies to be filled than there are positions of advocate general and chief prosecutor.

Prosecuting magistrates and judges have constant contact and consider themselves part of a single corps, but at the same time each group has its own responsibilities, and often their points of view differ. It would never occur to a judge that the magistrates attached to the Public Ministry are there to spy on him or influence his judgments other than by honest legal arguments. Nor would it ever occur to the agent of the Public Ministry that he could be asked to do such things. It is clear that the independence of the judiciary is not affected; judgments which reject the position of the Public Ministry are frequent.

§3. *The Central Administration of Justice*
Finally, other magistrates work together in Paris at the Ministry of Justice and form what is called the Chancellery. The Ministry of

12. In most cases, the Public Ministry operates independently of government policies, except where the latter, pursuant to the principle of discretionary prosecution, requests the Public Ministry not to prosecute with vigor the enforcement of particular laws.

Justice is divided into four large departments: personnel, civil litigation, criminal litigation, and penitentiary administration and the seal.

The following are some of the principal functions performed by these departments: preparation of the budget for the administration of justice, which must be approved annually by Parliament; drafting of new statutes involving civil and criminal justice; updating of files on each magistrate and preparation for meetings of the Council of the Magistrature; preparation of statistics on the administration of justice; publication of official reports of judicial decisions; record-keeping on convicted criminals; supervision of prisons and reform schools; administration and care of a service of foreign legislation and international law, which includes a very large library; and annual examinations for admission to the magistrature.

Section 2.   *Advocates*

Advocates (*avocats*), with magistrates and law professors, form the aristocracy of the French legal profession. It is an aristocracy based on two factors. First, admission is dependent upon holding a university degree. And second, its function is to serve society in the interest of justice and not simply to provide a living for its members.

The two factors are traditional and derive from a class structure that disappeared long ago on the political level in France, but exists still, however weakly, on the social level. The idea that a profession is less noble because it helps one earn his livelihood is no longer widely held in France. Nevertheless, the feeling has not completely disappeared, and advocates are very proud that theirs is an activity which, aside from any pecuniary interest, constitutes a kind of public service. It was only recently (by a law of December 31, 1957), and then with some exceptions, that advocates were given the right to sue for their fees. As in Roman times, an advocate's services were theoretically free for his client, who then recognized the service performed by giving the advocate a remuneration that he could afford and regarded as appropriate. For the same reason, the French bar is hostile to contingent fee agreements; an advocate cannot be remunerated by a share of his client's recovery. Such an arrangement, which many people consider ideal, is indignantly rejected by the bar, for it seems to conflict with the public service character of the advocate's function and associates him with material considerations that are inconsistent with his dignity and character as a disinterested servant of the law. In addition, for many years advocates were prohibited from forming professional partnerships, which were regarded as inconsistent with the notion of a public trust. This rule was relaxed in 1954, and now local bar associations can authorize partnerships among advocates.[13]

The rule that the advocate's career is open only to persons holding a degree of license in law is also derived from the conception of law that France inherited from Rome. The aristocracy of the profession cannot possibly have an education limited to practical matters. The advocate's activity and thought must be inspired by a liberal background. Legal practice unenriched by such an education and by legal theory is without nobility or merit; it is a trade, not a profession. The requirement that an advocate hold the degree, together with the traditions that regulate his activities, have to this day reserved the career to sons of the middle class, although other legal careers are more accessible to candidates of more modest background. We have here another reason, less readily admitted than that discussed above, why French advocates as a group consider themselves superior to other jurists. The economic decline of the middle class and the easier entrance to the faculties of law for those of modest means threaten these aspects of the advocate's career only in the long run. Young men from working-class families, once in the university, seldom choose to enter the law faculty; they are much more likely to choose the faculties of science or letters. In addition, of the various legal careers available, they will rarely choose that of the advocate.

The above discussion should illustrate the differences between the French advocate and the American lawyer. One should not be deceived by the similarity of the words "bar" and *barreau*. There is a gulf between them that cannot be filled by creating international bar associations. The French advocate differs also from the German

13. A person interested in the French conception of the advocate's role should be sure to read R. Savatier's description of the attitudes of the liberal professions in *Les Métamorphoses économiques et sociales du droit privé d'aujourd'hui* (1959), II, 186–233.

Rechtsanwalt in that the advocate's function is limited to representing his client in court. In France, procedural documents are not prepared by the advocate, but by another jurist, the *avoué*.

Advocates must belong to bar associations (*barreaux*), which supervise and can discipline their members, subject to the possibility of court appeal. Every city with a *tribunal* or a court of appeals and at least six advocates has its own bar. There is, however, no overall organization grouping all these local associations. An advocate who is a member of a bar association can litigate anywhere in France, except before the Court of Cassation, which has a special bar. Admission to a bar association is granted by the association itself, under the supervision of the courts. But an association can admit a candidate only if he holds the license in law. Since 1942, candidates have also been required to have a certificate of aptitude to the profession of advocate (C.A.P.A.), which is awarded on the basis of a special examination organized collectively by the faculties of law, the magistrates, the advocates, and other legal organizations. The candidate is admitted first as an apprentice advocate and becomes a full advocate after three years, losing the tax advantages as well as the restrictions of apprenticeship.

Although the assistance of an advocate is never obligatory in France, it is rare for a litigant, civil or criminal, not to use his services. To do so in the regular courts (except at the lowest level) would imply that the litigant was placing himself at the court's mercy or intended to present his arguments himself, since advocates have an effective monopoly there. No one but an advocate can appear on behalf of another. In the commercial and administrative courts and the lowest regular courts the advocates' monopoly is less exclusive, but litigants still frequently ask them to defend their interests.

French advocacy tends to keep French law in the realm of principles, divorced from procedural questions. One must admit that the advocate argues primarily from the facts, when he tries to present the case to the judge in the light most favorable to his client. He is not always an incisive jurist and will readily admit this fact. Here too there is a tradition: the French advocate is heir to the Roman orator, not to the jurisconsult. But the advocate is not tied to procedure. He does not draft the instruments or give the notices that procedural rules require; other lawyers do this. The advocate argues in a way that raises the debate above the procedural level, introduces general considerations, invokes legal principles, and gives the hearing a very different appearance from that of hearings in England or America. The law's application is necessarily affected.

Section 3. Other Legal Careers

There are in France a number of other legal careers, in addition to those discussed above. Precise delineation of function and detailed regulation are provided for specified officers of the court who depend on governmental appointment, which carries with it a limitation on the number of persons authorized to fulfill the assigned function. The primary categories thus delineated and regulated are the *avoués* before the courts of major jurisdiction and the courts of appeals, the advocates who practice before the Council of State and the Court of Cassation, notaries (*notaires*), court reporters (*greffiers*), and bailiffs (*huissiers*).

An *avoué* must participate in all proceedings before the courts of major jurisdiction and the courts of appeals. He drafts the parties' statements of claim and briefs. Litigants cannot bypass him. The advocate before the Council of State and the Court of Cassation fills the functions normally performed by both the *avoué* and the advocate in the lower courts.

The notary, who is a very different official from the English notary public, and even more different from the American notary public, plays an extremely important role. He does all conveyancing, drafts wills and marriage contracts, drafts acts of incorporation, and authenticates instruments of all kinds. Frequently referred to as the "family counselor," he is well regarded and the very symbol of respectability.

Court reporters and bailiffs return us to the area of litigation. Court reporters prepare the transcripts of court hearings and actually write out and distribute judgments for the courts. Bailiffs are responsible for serving summonses and for the execution of judgments.

In addition to the professional groups that are recognized and regulated by statute, others have been organized by the courts themselves to discharge specific functions under court supervision. Thus, there are organizations of trustees in bankruptcy, liquidators of corporations, administrators of unclaimed estates, attorneys in particular commercial courts, and so on. At first sight, some of these tasks may not seem exclusively, or even primarily, legal. Nevertheless, they are entrusted to lawyers, and for this reason are considered legal careers.

Aside from these named categories, finally, one must remember that other legal jobs can be performed by anyone. A law degree, usually the license in law, is a prerequisite only for those few careers that are specifically regulated. In fact, the very term *lawyer* refers more to a person who has received a legal education than to one who has a legal job. Anyone can open and freely operate a legal office in France, and legal work is done under a variety of names: claims collector, advocate-counselor, business agent, real estate manager, and so on. The law and the courts do not interfere as long as the monopoly granted to specific categories of lawyers is respected and there is no violation of the penal laws that set standards of behavior.[14]

Many lawyers work at these various kinds of jobs. Some are independent and others come together in associations that set group standards and thus provide some guarantee of their respectability. Others work for large organizations, such as banks, insurance companies, and businesses of all sorts. Many such organizations prefer to have their own legal departments to handle their legal problems; they feel this arrangement is more economical and provides greater expertise through specialization.

Various government departments also have legal sections made up of lawyers to advise them on their relations with other government offices and with private individuals and to help draft proposed laws, decrees, and departmental instructions within their area of responsibility. In addition, top government administrators and directors of banks and businesses of all sorts are often lawyers, since a legal education is one of the most highly prized personal assets in France (and until a few years ago the study of economics was coupled with the study of law).

Nevertheless in France, unlike Germany and some other countries, government administrators are not required to have law degrees. To be eligible for admission to the civil service, it is ordinarily required that one hold a degree, but not necessarily a law degree, or

14. The Ministry of Justice has prepared a bill that would regulate these professions and set standards of competence and ethics.

even a university degree in the strict sense. Specifically, degrees from the Institutes of Political Science are recognized as qualifying one for admission to the National School of Administration. Every graduating class from this school includes persons whose education has been in literature, history, and science and who are certainly not lawyers.

Note to Part Three

In a very recent development, an important statute (law number 71–1130 of December 31, 1971) reorganized parts of the legal profession. The new law creates and defines a "new profession of advocate." This new profession is the result of a fusion of advocates, *avoués*, and *agréés* in their practice before the lower civil and commercial courts. Thus the law has partially abolished the separation of functions of the *avoué* and the advocate. The advocate henceforth will fulfill all of the functions of a lawyer in the lower courts. In addition, the possibility of advocates practicing together as a multimember law firm is expanded under the new law. Title II of the new statute regulates the out-of-court practice of law by persons who have not previously been subject to any special professional regulation. The purpose of this part of the statute is to insure the honesty and competence of persons who call themselves legal counselors (*conseillers juridiques*) or something similar. Title III of the statute excludes from all practice of law any person who has been convicted of a crime or has gone bankrupt and not rehabilitated himself. The statute takes effect September 16, 1972.

PART FOUR

The French Concept
of Law

In a survey of the French concept of law, several questions should be considered. What force do Frenchmen attribute to the law as a factor of social organization and how do they expect it to relate to other social forces? To the extent that law is composed of a body of rules, what are the meaning and characteristics of the notion of "legal rules"? This part treats the role of law in society, the concept of legal rules, and the categorization of such rules as imperative or suppletive, a distinction of primary importance to French law.

I   Role of Law in Society

According to a well-known Latin saying, "wherever society is, law is" (*ubi societas, ibi jus*). In linking the ideas of law and society, this adage implies that law plays a fundamental role in all societies, or at least in all political societies.

Comparative law does not bear out this postulate. There are societies in which the concept of law seems not to exist. The customs that our education predisposes us to regard as legal are in no way distinguished, either objectively or in the eyes of those who follow them, from other social behavior and usages that we would not call legal. This is true of all primitive societies ruled by "custom" alone.

In other societies, law does not appear as an autonomous discipline, and one can again wonder whether "law" exists as such. To people living in these societies, the rules that we traditionally consider legal are imposed by religion. Neither their origin nor their characteristics distinguish them from other religious rules. Their primary object does not seem to be the organization of society or the resolution of social conflicts. Rather, they inform men of their duties and tell them how they ought to behave in order to please God, with all the consequences that violation can have in this world and the next. This view prevails in Islamic, and, with certain reservations, Hindu communities. It has frequently been noted that the word *fiqh* in the former and *dharma* in the latter do not entirely correspond to our word *law*. Rather, they refer to a science of the duties of man that is tied to religion and is much more comprehensive than our idea of law.

In other societies, although our concept of law exists, law plays but a secondary role and is accorded no prestige. The law is considered something to which one may have to turn as a last resort, but which normally should not have to be used. *Law* connotes only penal law and exists for the punishment of scoundrels and criminals. The honest citizen is not concerned with it; his existence will be guided by higher principles. Law is made for barbarians and does not dominate the organization of civilized nations. This is the traditional Chinese conception of law and has spread throughout the Far East. It is also the distant goal of Communist societies, in which Marx and Engels prophesied law would fall into disuse.

Even if one considers only Europe, the concept of law is less uniform than is generally thought. It is no doubt true that in Soviet Russia, as in Germany, England, and France, law is recognized as an autonomous institution and is thought to play an important role in social life. Despite these generalities, however, very important differences exist in the conceptions of law in each.

Soviet jurists profess as their ideal a Communist society in which law would be superfluous. It should disappear along with that other mechanism of constraint, the state. At the present stage of development of the Union of Soviet Socialist Republics, the socialist stage, the need for the state and law, remains. Nevertheless, law as such is unworthy of veneration. It is not the verbal expression of a pre-existing natural justice. It is a mere tool of those who govern and is used by them to accomplish the ends they set themselves. Because of the ends it serves, we are told, Soviet law is fundamentally different from "bourgeois" law.

According to Soviet doctrine, law is essentially political and thus does not control those who govern, since it is they who make the political choices. The USSR is not a state based on law (*Rechtsstaat*). It does not know the rule of law in the English sense, and its principle of socialist legality has neither the same basis nor the same scope as the apparently corresponding western principle. This all follows from Marxist-Leninist doctrine, which proclaims that in the last analysis what matters is the organization of production—the society's "economic infrastructure." Law is only a scaffolding for purposes of construction; thus it is either naive or hypocritical to make a fetish of it.

If we look to the more limited Europe of the western-style democracies, can we find the unity that has thus far eluded us concerning the concept and role of law? This too is doubtful, since the English conception differs greatly in certain respects from the continental.

The English conceive of law essentially as a means of solving disputes, of reestablishing a threatened or disturbed peace. England's common law has been built by the courts in disputes submitted to them, and has been profoundly influenced by this method of formation. The observation has often been made that English law was born of procedure, a fact which has implications not only for the technical form of the law but for legal philosophy as well. English law excels in the consideration of concrete problems and in the discovery and application of practical formulae. It shows a distrust for broad principles and overly abstract generalizations. It does not try to formulate rules of conduct, but aims only to act effectively when the social order is disturbed. Thus, the object of criminal law is not so much to discover the truth and punish the guilty as to avoid the conviction of innocent persons, while maintaining sufficient security for society as a whole.[1] English law is not an educating or moralizing law, but an esoteric, technicians' law. Its methods and language are little known to those to whom it applies. Whatever is unrelated to litigation, such as the organization of government and the operating rules of administrative organs, is in the realm of political science and does not concern jurists.

The continental conception of law, which prevails in France, is very different. Although law is certainly the concern of jurists, it is not their concern alone. It involves the whole population, because it establishes the very principles of social order and thus tells citizens how they should behave, in accordance with the community's ideas of what is moral and just. Law should not be, and is not, an esoteric science; rather, it must be accessible to the greatest possible number of persons. Because it has an educational role, it is linked to the whole prevailing existential philosophy. It takes the place of social morality and, for some, aspires to replace religion itself.

1. This idea is borrowed from Professor C. J. Hamson, who developed it in lectures given in January–March, 1959, at the University of Paris Faculty of Law, entitled *Les grands contrastes du droit français et du droit anglais*.

This continental conception of law is tied to the way in which law has been dealt with as a scholarly activity in the universities. There is a tendency to disregard the distinction between law in the narrow sense, in its litigious and jurisdictional aspects, and the other social sciences, particularly political science and economics. Jurists concentrate on the problems of establishing a just social order and naturally turn their attention to law reform. On the other hand, they are not captivated by, and may even avoid, problems of procedure and the practical application of legal rules. The legal rule itself, conceived as a rule of conduct, has a generality and a form different from that in English law. It aspires to rationality and is often phrased in universal terms. It may well become moralizing. Codification, written constitutions, bills of rights, and laws containing only general principles are important, since they permit the exposition not only of the principles of social order, but also of its tendencies and hopes for improvement.

This is the conception that prevails generally in continental Europe. Within this regional unity, it is more difficult to isolate a strictly French conception that can be contrasted with a German, Danish, or Spanish conception. There are of course obvious differences among the various European legal systems, but these relate more to particular substantive rules, techniques, and legal institutions than to their general conception of law. The reason is that throughout Europe the general conception of law has been formed in the same way—by the gradual interaction of scholarship and practice. To discover contrasts between Norwegian, German, Italian, Greek, Portuguese, and French law, it is easier to speak of particular areas of the law, such as constitutional, administrative, or criminal law or procedure than of law in general. It is more difficult to draw general contrasts between the legal systems of these various countries. Nevertheless, let us try to do just that.

Generally speaking, French jurists are less dogmatic, less concerned with pure logic, and less exacting in their search for consistency in the law than are Germans, Italians, and Spaniards. Frenchmen regard legal concepts as somewhat relative, and the idea of a world unification of law seems to them visionary. Having a century-old code and having seen it reinterpreted to serve changing needs and values, they recognize the life of the law and the impotence of legislation.[2] One of the present characteristics of French law is the emphasis given in law teaching and writing to judicial decisions. Another characteristic, which is considered a shortcoming, is the lack of development in France of studies devoted to legal philosophy and general legal theory.

Among the peoples of Europe the French probably hold law in the greatest esteem. This is natural for a people that is particularly conservative. Despotism and arbitrary government were replaced by the rule of law in France earlier and more completely than in other countries. None of the spectacular political crises that have marked the last 150 years of French history have been crises of law. Koschaker has emphasized, in contrasting French and German tendencies, how readily Frenchmen regard as legal those problems the political aspect of which appears predominant elsewhere.[3] Churchill similarly commented on how surprised the English were at the preoccupation of French army and navy officers with legal matters.[4] There were long and bitter debates in France over whether the Vichy government was legally formed, whether it exercised its powers according to the law, and whether the powers granted to the new European organizations were compatible with the French legal concept of sovereignty. The French love legal discussions just as they love problems of language and grammar, and it is not always the jurists who are the most exacting and punctilious in these discussions.

This last observation leads us to the following conclusion. Two conceptions of law exist in France side by side, intermingling, with one or the other predominating according to personalities and circumstances. The first conception of law is clearly related to political science and is, therefore, that of the majority of the citizens, especially of the nonlawyers. Law, according to this conception, merges to a large extent with the idea of justice. Its goal is the realization of a particular political and economic order, and its essence is in the general ideas that inspire it, not in the technical rules by which it

2. These expressions form the titles of two well-known books in France: J. Cruet, *La vie du droit et l'impuissance des lois* (1908), and G. Morin, *La révolte des faits contre le code civil* (1920).

3. P. Koschaker, *Europa und das römische Recht* (1947), 169–70.

4. W. Churchill, *The Hinge of Fate,* Vol. IV of *The Second World War* (1951), 574–75.

is expressed. Law aspires to universality and to the perfection of a just society.

Another conception coexists with the foregoing and is more particularly characteristic of lawyers, who are involved in the administration of justice. Lawyers are more inclined to view law in terms of the legal rules used in practice and applied by the courts. They place more emphasis on procedure and sanctions and less on statements of general principle and rules of ideal conduct. They may question whether constitutional law in the absence of judicial review, or international law in the absence of an international court, is really law at all. All things considered, a French lawyer's view of the law is quite similar to the English conception, while the more popular French conception resembles that espoused in the Soviet Union.

We have represented one of these conceptions as being that of the nonlawyers and the other that of the lawyers. Although this generalization is correct, it often happens that lawyers escape the lawyers' approach. They become involved in political science or become philosophers and then see no contradiction in placing themselves on the ground that we have defined as being that of the nonlawyers. This has happened with some of the best French lawyers.

In the universities and in legal scholarship how influential are the philosophers? The practitioners? In this respect, the countries of Western Europe occupy an intermediate position between England and the USSR. Among the countries of Western Europe, France is no doubt closer than its neighbors to England for reasons related to a distinct tradition, to passing practical circumstances, and to particular mental attitudes. Even so, it is not certain that different conceptions of law are held by the legal practitioners of France, Germany, and Italy.

II   Legal Rules

Just as legal systems and lawyers differ in their conceptions of law as a whole and of its role in society, the legal rule—the vehicle for expressing legal commands—is not conceived in the same way everywhere or by everyone. We shall limit ourselves here to a discussion of the difference between the French concept of *règle juridique* and the corresponding English concept of the legal rule. Let us note, however, that the same contrast exists, with slight variations, between the Anglo-American common law system as a whole and the continental system, to which the USSR and the Communist countries of Eastern Europe continue, for this purpose, to belong.

The French concept of *règle juridique* is not the exact equivalent of what the English understand by a legal rule: the concept of *règle juridique* has a greater generality than that of the legal rule.[5] This difference is very understandable for anyone who reflects on the different ways in which French and English law have been formed and keeps in mind the general conceptions of law and of its role that prevail on the two sides of the Channel.

In the common law, the legal rule is ordinarily formulated by the judge. He faces a very precise, concrete question and responds to that question by applying a particular legal rule. He naturally has in mind the particular question posed as he formulates the rule and does not elaborate a rule that goes beyond the terms of this question. This is so true that if a slightly different question comes before another judge later, he will consider himself justified in distinguishing this question from the preceding. The overall appearance of English law resembles an impressionist painting; the legal rules, considered individually, are but points. One must step back in order to detect the general patterns of the composition.

The situation in France is completely different. The law is not essentially judges' law, but rather a law of jurists and the universities. French law has an aversion to case studies and seeks clarity

5. The difference between the attitudes of French and English lawyers in this respect appears clearly if one considers the related notions of French "public order" (*ordre public*) and English "public policy" and the way in which they are conceived and applied by French and English courts. French writers and judges readily grant the relativity of the concept of public order and the fact that it changes over time with circumstances. They think it would be both useless and dangerous to try to define its limits. English writers and judges, on the other hand, have constantly tried to specify the cases where one can have recourse to the idea of public policy; they ask whether the courts can apply the concept to new situations or if all its possible uses have not been exhausted by the various precedents that have already used the notion. On this subject, see Philippe Malaurie, *L'ordre public et le contrat: Etude de droit civil comparé* (*France, Angleterre, URSS*) (1952).

by looking beyond the decisions in particular cases to the principles proclaimed by the legislator and legal writers. What the English call a legal rule the French regard as the disposition of a dispute. Rules only exist at a higher level of abstraction. The very concept of rule implies generality—abstraction. The rule is not a point, but rather a directional line. This ought to be as true of the legal rule (*le règle juridique*) as of the instrument that bears the same name, *le règle* (the ruler).

For a Frenchman, the English jurist's legal rule is nothing but an isolated judicial decision; it is not a *règle juridique*. For an Englishman, the French jurist's *règle juridique* is not a legal rule. It does not have the precision that is the essence of such a rule. Rather, it is a legal principle. Contrary to what one might suppose, this difference has more than theoretical interest. Its practical importance is considerable.

Because of this difference in the conception of the legal rule, legislative techniques in France and England are dissimilar. Legislatures in both countries try to formulate legal rules, but the realization of this intention is very different precisely because the French *règle juridique* is not equivalent to the English legal rule. An English statute will necessarily deal explicitly with particular problems. A French statute will go into less detail, will give the judge more discretion, will not try to foresee all problems, and may include general formulae that to a common lawyer seem to negate its effects as law and make it more a general principle than a command.

In England, there is a saying that a statute is meaningless until interpreted by the courts. The explanation given for the saying is that the legislator, no matter how hard he tries, cannot attain the degree of precision characteristic of true legal rules. It is attainable only by a judge in a concrete case. This seems even more true to a common lawyer, if he considers French statutes. Principles such as those of articles 2,[6] 1134,[7] and 1382[8] of the Civil Code have for an

6. *Code Civil*, art. 2: "Statutes apply only for the future; they have no retroactive effect."

7. *Ibid.*, art. 1134: "Legally formed agreements take the place of statutes for those who have made them. They can only be set aside upon mutual consent or for causes established by law. They must be performed in good faith."

8. *Ibid.*, art. 1382: "Any act whatsoever by a man that causes damage to another obligates the person at fault to repair the damage."

English jurist *a fortiori* no meaning as legal rules. The English jurist will always seek to know how the rule has been interpreted by French judges in particular cases. This is of course a legitimate interest and one that will be shared by his French counterpart. The difference between the two only appears at the termination of such research. If the common lawyer finds a decision on a particular point that interests him, he feels that he has finally found the legal rule for which he was searching and assumes that a Frenchman would think the same. And on the other hand, if he finds no judicial decision dealing with this particular point, he is inclined to disregard the French code article, not conceiving that this article itself could be regarded as establishing a legal rule. For the Frenchman, the statutory text has a very different value, for in such texts the legal rule to be followed is always found.

In the examples given, we have intentionally taken extreme cases, articles which embody legal rules so general that even Frenchmen are apt to speak of them as "principles." The observation made above, however, is of general validity. It is true as well with respect to articles that French jurists see without hesitation as the expression of legal rules in the strict sense. The English jurist still will not see a legal rule.

As an example, let us take articles 146 and 180 of the Civil Code, by virtue of which the French judge will pronounce the nullity of marriage for error as to the qualities of the person.[9] Frenchmen are not shocked by the generality of these articles and find that they contain perfectly ordinary legal rules. The legislator is not expected to go into greater detail and would be criticized if he did. The English jurist, on the other hand, will find a legal rule only in judgments deciding that errors concerning the nationality, health, chastity, or criminal record of one of the spouses is, or is not, a grounds for the nullity of the marriage. For a Frenchman, the legal rule exists at a higher level, as expressed in the texts of articles 146 and 180. The judicial decisions are nothing but "applications of the rule."

9. *Ibid.*, art. 146: "There is no marriage when there is no consent." *Ibid.*, art. 180: "A marriage contracted without the free consent of both spouses, or of one of them, can only be attacked by such parties themselves, or by the one whose consent was not free."

In contracts, let us take article 1150 of the Civil Code.[10] French-men know very well that this article raises various questions. Not everything is resolved by saying that when there is a failure to perform a contract, compensation is due only for such damage as was foreseeable when the contract was made. The courts must decide whether only the nature of the loss has to be foreseeable (loss of a suitcase entrusted to a carrier) or whether the amount of the loss must also have been foreseeable (valuable contents of the suitcase). Nevertheless, this does not prevent us from regarding article 1150 as a true legal rule, since the French distinguish between the legal rule and the application which it requires. For the common lawyer, the only true legal rule is in what the French consider the particular applications of the rule, its interpretation by writers and judges. Legislative techniques differ in the two systems for this reason. One might even say that the very possibility of codification depends on the French conception of legal rules.

Another difference between the two systems that results from the contrast between the French and English conceptions of the legal rule relates to the role of scholarly writing and judicial opinions. Both have greater latitude in the French system than in the common law precisely because only the former distinguishes between the legal rule on the one hand and its application and interpretation on the other. In common law countries, a sudden change in case law is a serious thing. If a previously accepted rule can be repudiated, what will become of the security of legal relations? Why should other rules not be repudiated as well? In France, even the question is not the same. Since a dissenting writer or a change in the courts' position on a question affects only the interpretation of a legal rule in its previous application, it is not so dangerous. A certain flexibility in the courts' position is acceptable, since the danger thereby created to the security of legal relations is limited. There is no danger of its undermining the law as a whole. The legal rules, conceived of as entities superior to judicial decisions, form a solid framework that limits the effect of changes in the courts' position or that of dissenting writers. A different attitude toward scholarly writing and judicial decisions is the consequence of the different

10. *Ibid.*, art. 1150: "The debtor is liable only for those damages that were foreseen or could have been foreseen at the time of contracting, unless the non-performance is the result of his fraud."

conceptions in France and England concerning the very notions of *règle juridique* and legal rule.

An English lawyer looking at French law should not expect to find legal rules that are the full equivalent of legal rules in the common law. He should remember that French law is more doctrinal and academic than English law and that the legal rule is more abstract, more like a legal principle than a legal rule as those terms are used with reference to English law. He should remember that judicial decisions do not pose legal rules, but only apply preexisting rules which have significance beyond a particular case. If he understands these things, he can understand the technique of codification, as well as the lesser authority that judicial decisions have in French law as compared to the common law.

French judicial decisions always cite statutory provisions in their support. This is only possible because of the generality of the code and statute articles. These are often principles rather than commands. It is important to know how they have been applied, because judges will give considerable weight to this factor and will usually interpret a statute in the future as they have in the past. But one must keep in mind that in France the legal rule is found in the legislative provisions themselves, no matter how general they may be, and not in their application by the courts. It is because of this that French law is a "written law." It is essential to bear this in mind in order to understand not only how changes in courts' positions are possible in France, but also the limits of these changes.

Seemingly corresponding French and English terms are in fact not equivalent. The English "legal rule" is not the same as the *règle juridique;* for the Frenchman, the former is an isolated decision, a mere application of the rule. The French *règle juridique* corresponds more closely to the legal principle that in common law countries is induced by writers rather than proclaimed by the legislator. By *principe juridique,* the French designate a legal rule whose importance they wish to emphasize or, as in common law countries, a basic idea that explains several legal rules.[11]

Our intention in making these observations is simply to describe an important and confusing divergence between two legal systems.

11. See Jean Boulanger, "Principes généraux du droit et droit positif," *Le droit privé français au milieu du XXᵉ siècle* (*Etudes offertes à Georges Ripert*) (1950), I, 51 ff.

The terminology of the subject, however, is far from precise, and the manner in which the legislator expresses himself varies considerably. One can easily find French statutes and code provisions that are sufficiently precise to satisfy the English lawyer's notion of a legal rule. This is particularly so in areas such as criminal law and tax law where the principle of strict interpretation prevails.

Like all legislators, French legislators are sometimes tempted to try to foresee everything and make of the courts quasi-mechanical instruments of their will. French writers have criticized this poor legislative technique and decried the resulting defective legislation. The draftsmen of the Napoleonic codes, products of a sound tradition, were able to resist this temptation and did not surrender to the illusion that they could foresee everything. This is the source of these codes', and particularly the Civil Code's, exceptional value, long life, and influence on other countries. The drafters of the French codes were able to find a happy medium in the articles they drafted, between the detailed formulation that was adopted in the 1794 Prussian *Allgemeines Landrecht* and the overly general expressions that are often found in constitutions and declarations of rights. They thereby gave French law a framework which experience has shown to be sufficiently firm and flexible. For these qualities, we are indebted to their conception of the legal rule, to their understanding that in its legislative expression the law should have a greater generality than the decision required of a judge in a particular case.

The reason that the French concept of *règle juridique* is broader than the English lawyer's concept of legal rule is that the former is formulated by legislators rather than by the judge. Perhaps the same reason can explain another difference between French law and the common law. Many questions that are considered questions of law in common law countries are regarded as simple questions of fact in France.

The distinction between questions of fact and questions of law is always difficult to apply. In all countries, the importance and effect of the distinction have been greatly influenced by practical considerations. Thus the distinction has different meanings according to the particular consequences attached to it: for example, definition of the jurisdiction of the French Court of Cassation, definition of the respective spheres of competence of the judge and jury in England, necessity for the parties to prove facts only. Because the functions of the distinction are different in France and in England, the distinction is of course not made in the same way.

There is, however, one general observation which we want to make on this subject. There is a natural tendency in common law countries to consider the questions that come before a judge, and which he has resolved or must resolve, as questions of law. In France, on the contrary, since the elaboration of the law is regarded as essentially the function of the legislator, there is the opposite natural tendency, the tendency to see the judge as the person whose basic job it is to decide factual issues and to apply in the particular circumstances of the case preestablished legal principles.

The way a legal rule should be interpreted is of course a question of law in France, but the particular application of the rule is not as important as the very existence of that rule. French jurists can, therefore, more readily than common lawyers disregard the doubtful cases, where it is not clear whether the judges have decided a question of law, having general validity, or a simple question of fact, whose significance is restricted to the case. English digests and practitioners' treatises, on the contrary, are often full of judicial decisions of purely factual interest. The authors of these works dare not take the responsibility of deciding whether a decision poses a legal rule or simply contains an evaluation of the factual circumstances of the case. Writers have noted, and deplored, the excessive bulk of the common law as a result of this obliteration of the distinction between law and fact.[12]

III   Imperative and Suppletive Rules

The distinction between imperative and suppletive rules is an essential part of a French lawyer's view of the law. Nevertheless, because of the common law lawyer's different conception of legal rules, the distinction between suppletive and imperative rules is unknown in England and often completely incomprehensi-

12. See Sir Maurice S. Amos, "Have We Too Much Law?" in *Journal of the Society of Public Teachers of Law* (1931), 1 ff.

ble to the common law lawyer.[13] For him, all statutes and rules of law are imperative by definition. They state a command and dictate the solution to be given in a particular case.

French jurists, however, distinguish according to the circumstances in which the rule of law is to be applied. In some cases, rules are to be applied without regard to the intention of the individuals concerned, whereas in other cases the intention of these individuals is important. The statutory rule applies only if those affected by it have not excluded its application. In the first case, a French jurist speaks of an imperative rule, in the second of a suppletive rule.

The distinction between imperative and suppletive rules is explained better by examples than by abstract formulae. Article 144 of the Civil Code, which provides that men under eighteen years of age and women under fifteen cannot marry, is an imperative rule. Its application cannot be avoided by an agreement between the parties that they will be married even though they are not of age. Similarly, article 1674 of the Civil Code, according to which the sale of an immovable can be invalidated if the seller can show that he was paid less than 7/12 of its full value, is an imperative rule. And the rule that a mortgage must be expressed in a notarial act in order to be valid (article 2127, Civil Code) is imperative.

On the other hand, examples of suppletive rules are those providing that a debt is to be paid at the domicile of the debtor (article 1247, Civil Code), that a seller warrants the thing sold against latent defects (article 1641, Civil Code), and that gifts must be counted as part of the donee's share of the donor's succession (article 843, Civil Code). These provisions govern only if the interested parties have not regulated their affairs otherwise. Contracting parties are perfectly free to provide that a debt is payable at the creditor's domicile or anywhere else. They can provide that a sale is without warranty. They can stipulate that a donation is not subject to return and is not to be counted as part of the donee's share in the donor's succession.

The basis of the distinction is clear. It comes down to the following simple question: can private individuals, if they so desire, set aside the rules established by the legislator and regulate their rela-

---

13. The notion of dispositive rules of law, likewise, is unique to countries that regard the law as a rule of social organization rather than simply as a technique for settling disputes.

tions by other rules that they adopt? How could this distinction, which seems so elementary to a French, Spanish, Italian, or German lawyer, have remained unknown in the common law world, where the best lawyers sometimes have difficulty understanding it? Civil law jurists find this lack in common law all the more surprising because of the practical utility of the distinction. Its practical importance is so great that we can hardly imagine a legal system without it. For any legal text, it is important to know whether a person can argue to the judge, "Yes, this rule is contrary to my position, but it should not be applied in this case, since my opponent and I agreed to exclude it."

The question comes up in many contexts. The legislator must be constantly aware of it as he legislates. He must know what sort of law he is passing and often will specify whether it is imperative or suppletive. In the first case, he will say "notwithstanding any agreement to the contrary"; in the second, "unless otherwise agreed." Why should the common law world not know this elementary distinction?

Although we have described the distinction between imperative and suppletive rules as a general one, it is in fact used in France only by private law lawyers. It is not used in public law. Public law lawyers simply assume that all rules of public law are imperative. This assumption is so commonly accepted that one frequently finds French authors confusing the concepts of imperative legal rules and rules of public law. Writers condemn "the invasion of private law by public law" when they see that freedom of contract is more restricted now than it once was. If "imperative legal rules" were synonymous with "public law rules" and "suppletive legal rules" were synonymous with "private law rules," one could understand why the distinction is not current in common law countries, since the distinction between public law and private law is rarely used.

Ancient as the confusion between imperative rules and public law rules may be—it is even found in certain texts of Justinian's Digest—this confusion is almost universally condemned by legal scholars. It is based on a false notion of public law. We will see that the proposition that all public law rules are imperative is far from self-evident. But even more important, no one has ever doubted that within the realm of private law one finds both suppletive and imperative rules. Thus, the distinction between suppletive and imperative rules is not equivalent, either logically or historically, to the distinction between private and public law.

Still, it is a fact that our distinction between imperative and suppletive laws is used only by private law jurists and seems foreign to writers on public law. This observation suggests the following question: is the distinction not tied to the phenomenon of codification, since only private law has been codified in France? To answer this question, let us look first at Anglo-American law and see how, without using the concept of suppletive law, it solves problems that we would think dependent on this concept.

If we look first at statutes enacted by the United States Congress or the British Parliament, we are astounded to discover many provisions that we would automatically consider suppletive. "Unless otherwise agreed, the said provision will apply as between the parties," proclaims the legislature. Thus, English and American statutes are familiar with the phenomenon that we characterize by the term, unknown to them, of suppletive law. Still, statutes and acts of Parliament, while technically different, are related to our codes and form a law that is regarded to a certain extent as exceptional, in derogation of the common law. How would such questions be dealt with in the pure common law?

Where we would utilize the idea of suppletive law, the English lawyer places himself at a different vantage point, that of the contract. He starts from the principle that the law's function is simply to enforce obligations voluntarily undertaken by private individuals, not to "make a contract" for them. Starting from this premise, the problem seems to be simply one of interpretation. But upon reflection it becomes apparent that the problem is more complex, since the parties' language may be imprecise, or they may have expressed their intentions incompletely. Contracting parties rarely take the trouble to express their intentions precisely or in sufficient detail. For this reason, it is clear that in reality the law must either "make a contract" for private individuals, or it must decide that the parties have not reached an understanding and that there is no contract between them. To adopt this latter position is usually an unsatisfactory solution. Thus G. C. Grismore states:

> In view of these facts, it becomes apparent that the problem involved in determining the rights and duties created by a contract is twofold. It is only in part a

problem of determining the manifested intentions of the parties, a process which is rightly called interpretation. To a large extent it also involves the problem of making provision for contingencies that have arisen in the course of performance, which were not thought of, and consequently were not provided for at all, and, also, of making provision for more or less trivial details of performance that were left unspecified, either consciously or unconsciously. This latter process is not a matter of interpretation but rather of "making a contract" for the parties.[14]

At first, the common law refused to recognize that two distinct problems were involved. In both cases one spoke of interpretation, as if it were always a matter of determining the parties' intentions and the meaning of their words. Today things have changed. After his chapter entitled "Determination of the Rights and Duties of the Parties: The Interpretation of Contracts," Grismore entitles his next chapter "Determination of the Rights and Duties of the Parties: On Making a Contract for the Parties." In this chapter, he studies in detail "constructive conditions," which in Anglo-American law the courts read into a contract unless the parties have expressly excluded them. This is the realm of suppletive law.

One can understand the different approach of American jurists to this problem. Because they traditionally view what we call suppletive legal rules as clauses or stipulations implicit in a contract, they do not call them legal rules and can hardly avoid speaking of contractual interpretation. Recently, however, they have begun to recognize that they are actually making legal rules. The concept of "suppletive law" seems about to appear, to accompany the new understanding of the proper sphere for "interpretation of contracts."

In a different but analogous area French legal scholarship has finally discovered that when we speak of "interpretation of the law" we are in fact dealing with two completely distinct phenomena. Sometimes we are actually trying to determine the true meaning of a provision by studying its terms and considering the reason for and the background of its enactment. In such a case, it is proper to speak of interpretation of the law. In other cases, however, we try to solve a particular problem by using legal provisions which are clear but

14. G. C. Grismore, *Principles of the Law of Contract* (1947), sec. 91.

do not directly apply to the problem in question. In this case, as Aubry and Rau noted, the problem is very different. It is no longer a question of interpreting a law, but rather, aside from any problem of interpretation, of searching for a new legal rule.[15] All of Geny's work and his plea for "free scientific research" in the area of legal science are based on this distinction.

In the common law, instead of starting from a legal provision and asking whether it is imperative or suppletive and thus whether or not the parties can validly exclude it, one starts from the contract and asks whether, considering the parties' agreement and commercial usage, a contract exists which is sufficiently precise, bearing in mind that the contract must be the work of the parties and not of the courts.

If you were to codify the commercial usage to which the parties are presumed to refer you would have the French notion of suppletive law. The disadvantage that Americans and Englishmen see in such codification is that it would give a purely legal appearance to something that is, as is any custom or usage, a "mixture of law and fact." In addition, legislative action here might impinge upon the most fundamental principle in the contractual area: the right of the parties to regulate their relations as they see fit. The English prefer to indulge a legal fiction that commercial usages are implicitly accepted as contractual conditions by the parties. While this approach does depend on a fiction, it respects the fundamental principle of freedom of contract. The discussions that have taken place in France about the binding or nonbinding force of usages and customs do not encourage common law lawyers to accept the French approach in this area. They fear that by making suppletive legal rules come from a legislative decision they would provide a wedge by which state intervention would quickly come to dominate the law of contracts. They feel safer if, instead of a legislative rule, they can invoke a fictional intention of the parties based on commercial usage, which in some cases will be local or confined to particular trade groups, leaving the state and, so it sometimes seems, the law itself out of consideration.

15. Aubry and Rau, *Cours de droit civil français* (6th ed., by E. Bartin; 1936), I, no. 40. Compare the distinction made by German writers between *Gesetzesanalogie* and *Rechtsanalogie: Motive zu dem Entwurfe eines BGB für das deutsche Reich* (1888), 14–17.

The absence of the concept of suppletive law in common law countries goes far to explain the apparent and much discussed difference between the approach of French and Anglo-American courts to contract interpretation. In France the legislator himself, through suppletive legal rules, provides the means to interpret the contract as would "a reasonable man," for whom the legislator has substituted himself. Thus, where the results of "objective interpretation" on the basis of suppletive legal rules appear unjust or incorrect, the judge will be impelled to a subjective interpretation of the contract, i.e., a search for the "true intention" of the parties. In common law countries, since the category of suppletive law has not been recognized, a judge interpreting a contract begins by doing what the legislator has done in France. It is easy to see why in these countries "objective interpretation" of contracts is most evident, even if in actual fact the relations between objective and subjective interpretation are in the end the same, or virtually the same, as in French law.

Both French jurists and English and American jurists can learn something from the analysis of this problem in the case of the neighboring system. French jurists should notice how common law lawyers deal with this problem. Rather than considering the distinction between imperative and suppletive laws as one of the general principles of French law, as they usually do, they should ask if it would not be better to deal with it, as do the English and Americans, in connection with the law of contracts. The issue in a particular case would be clearer if, instead of starting from an abstraction and asking whether a particular law is imperative or suppletive, they would start from the other side and ask whether the parties' attempt to exclude by agreement the application of the legal rule is valid or not: does this agreement violate public policy? The distinction between imperative and suppletive laws is but one aspect of the notion of public order (*ordre public*), and its discussion belongs in the context of article 6 of the Civil Code, which provides that "private individuals may not by agreement derogate from laws based on public order or considerations of morality." M. Julliot de la Morandière, in a course which he once taught at the University of Paris Faculty of Law on the concept of public order, asserted that the use and meaning of this principle would be much clearer if, instead of studying it from the point of view of general public order, which is hard to define, one would look at it from the standpoint of specific, individual contracts, of which one would ask whether or not they contravene public order. That is the approach taken by the common law lawyer and it is certainly preferable to the civilian approach.

For example, consider the problem of clauses excluding liability. The validity of such clauses becomes a difficult problem if one escalates the debate unnecessarily and asks whether article 1148 ff. or article 1382 ff., in their respective spheres, is imperative or suppletive. The question is much easier to deal with if, instead of trying to determine the nature or character of the legislative rule, one looks at the particular agreement that has been concluded and asks whether or not the agreement is contrary to public policy.

In addition, the common law example can help clarify the situation in French law with respect to public law. What is the significance of the oft-repeated affirmation that all laws in the public law area are imperative? The state, through its administrative organs, concludes contracts with private individuals. Although these contracts are less flexible than private law contracts and are subject to preestablished general terms and conditions, it would be extraordinary if everything in the contractual relations thus established were covered either by statutory provision or by contract clauses. Lawyers in the public law field have not recognized this problem because administrative law is neither written nor codified law. Therefore, they start from the same point of view as common law lawyers. Case law in the administrative law area is full of judgments interpreting contracts. Many of these judgments actually interpret neither the will of the parties nor a legal or contractual provision. Often they really establish suppletive law, although judges are seldom aware of this and do not use the term. Thus one can see how even in France the distinction between suppletive and imperative law has remained unrecognized in the eyes of certain jurists and how it could be replaced, as in the common law countries, by the use of other techniques, particularly in the area where the law is uncodified and judge-made. Here the courts quite naturally decide cases on the basis of the facts, or the supposed facts, of the particular case without stating a rule of law.

For common law lawyers there is no question but that the distinction between suppletive and imperative laws can be of use. It helps them to see, as they are seeing more and more clearly, that the problems once dealt with under the heading of "contract interpretation" are complex. Sometimes the question posed is one of pure fact: what did the parties intend? what did they decide? These are questions of interpretation of contracts in the true sense. But in other cases, the court must complete the parties' contract. It must make the contract for them. How should this be done, by adopting what rules? This is a question of law—suppletive law.

To a Frenchman it seems that the writings of common law lawyers would be clearer if they used the distinction between imperative and suppletive laws. Judges do "make contracts for the parties" when they insert provisions in the contract that the parties would have been able either to include or exclude from it. On the other hand, it is not "making a contract for the parties," and even less "interpreting the contract," to subject it to rules that the parties could not have excluded by agreement. A Frenchman would never think of considering as suppletive article 1147 of the Civil Code, which provides that the debtor is discharged if performance becomes impossible as a result of *force majeure*.

It would seem equally unreasonable to view the Anglo-American common law theories of frustration of adventure or failure of consideration as questions of contractual interpretation or as manifestations of the courts' power to "make a contract" for the parties. The French Council of State has never connected the theory of *imprévision,* in the cases where they have accepted it, with the interpretation of contracts. Thus, it seems that the French distinction between suppletive and imperative laws would help common law jurists to distinguish, in the law of contracts, between three kinds of rules: those the parties have agreed upon (actual interpretation of the contract), those which the law imposes (imperative legal rules), and those which, without being imposed by the law, are ordinarily included in the contract by the courts, unless the parties have expressly excluded them, by applying accepted standards of good faith and commercial usage. These last rules are, in the eyes of a French lawyer, the exclusive sphere of suppletive law.

Is the agreement by which the parties attempt to exclude a particular law valid? The answer to this question will determine for the French lawyer whether the law is imperative or suppletive. Nevertheless, the terms *imperative law* and *law of public order (ordre public)* are sometimes used in other contexts unconnected with any agreement by which parties attempt to avoid a rule. For example, one uses this terminology to indicate that the judge can invoke a particular law on his own motion. It is also used to indicate that a rule can be invoked by the parties for the first time at the appeal stage of litigation, and to indicate that a law applies immediately to contracts concluded prior to its enactment. The concept of imperative law, in these various senses, has no relation to the concept of suppletive law. The words *imperative law* are used in a completely different sense than that we have discussed above. There is no doubt but that in this regard our terminology is confused. All we can do here is to note this fact and deplore it.

PART FIVE

The Organization
of French Law

In many countries a fundamental task of legal science, often its most important one, is to divide the law into branches and to analyze and classify legal rules according to these divisions. In today's complex societies, it is only possible to know the law where legal categories and distinctions give order to the variegated mass of rules that bind us. Although legal classification is often the work of scholars, its use is not limited to the academic and pedagogic. It is important in the area of conflict of laws, where characterization is essential. But most important, in domestic law an established structure is a necessary prerequisite for any legal research.

When a jurist has a legal problem, whether practical or theoretical, his first step is to determine the branch of law to which the problem belongs. Does the question call into play rules and principles of civil law, administrative law, or procedure? And further, is it a problem of personal capacity, succession, or marriage arrangements concerning property? Consciously or unconsciously, the jurist must put the problem in context. He will not understand the problem, much less know where to begin research to solve it, until he has situated it within the divisions and categories that form his legal system.

But contrary to what one might suppose, this categorization is not just a simple preliminary operation which then allows the jurist to do his research and discover the legal rules applicable to the question at hand. No doubt this is its most important function; it imparts an organization to the law and facilitates research. Nevertheless, as we shall see, the problem is more subtle than this. Legal classification, aside from this technical aspect, has its own value.

Although French law is unquestionably a single whole, its various branches often claim a certain independence of each other. Each asserts its own particularity. What do their claims mean?

In each branch of the law, special importance is given to fundamental policies related to the function of the rules in question. For example, in commercial law one stresses the practical needs of commerce, in administrative law one emphasizes the necessity for public services to function regularly, and in labor law special importance is (or at least was) given to stability of employment. These are considerations particular to a specific area of the law and must receive primary attention when one is dealing with rules in that area, but they have little importance in other places. The preoccupation of all lawyers to achieve just results is implemented in different ways by civil, penal, and tax law specialists. They do not see problems from the same vantage point. For this reason, the difference between various branches of the law is not simply one of subject matter. Sometimes the rules are conceived, interpreted, and applied in a special way.

This is the basis for the concept of particularity (*particularisme*) of the various branches of law. By seeing problems from a special point of view, the commercial lawyer and the criminal lawyer will sometimes feel that a perfectly proper civil law rule must be critically examined before being accepted in commercial law or criminal law. It must be asked whether the rule in question conflicts with the primary functions to be served by these branches. In other words, each branch of the law accepts the rules elaborated by other branches only after an independent evaluation of their worth. They reserve the right to exclude a particular rule if it is unacceptable, or even inappropriate, to their goals.

The particularity of various branches of the law is desirable insofar as it introduces distinctions and nuances that are justified by different points of view and do not constitute real internal contradictions in the legal system. For example, there is no reason why the concept of "trader" should be defined in the same way by commercial law in order to decide the jurisdictional limits of commercial courts and the applicability of bankruptcy rules, and in tax law in order to determine which persons are liable to pay a license fee and which activities are subject to a tax on commercial profits. Nor is there any reason why special rules should not apply to government contracts by virtue of the government's special position as representative of the public welfare.

Nevertheless, to minimize confusion within the legal system one must avoid unduly accentuating the particularity of the various branches of the law and of too readily accepting distinctions which lack a rational basis and therefore can lead to unacceptable contradictions. In addition, attention to questions of terminology and great care in the statement of rules are required. The authority of the law will be compromised if we are led to interpret rules in ways which contradict their apparent meaning and scope.

When the lawyer determines that his problem requires the application of rules from a particular branch of the law, and then from a particular subcategory of that branch, he is not just trying to situate the question in order to find the particular legal rule that will finally permit him to answer it. His whole attitude toward the problem and his method of investigation will be influenced by the categorization upon which he settles.

This observation may be verified simply by noting the specialization that exists among lawyers. The most eminent contracts authority will refuse to give an opinion on a question of criminal law. The reason for this is not simply that the complexity of the law requires specialization. To a certain extent, that very specialization in one area of the law makes a person less able to deal with questions in another area. The ways of stating, discussing, and disposing of questions depend partly on the nature of the question and the category of rules which must be applied to it. Tax and divorce specialists may well see a problem differently from the criminal law specialist. Their attitudes toward interpreting legal rules are not necessarily the same, and their instincts will not affect them in the same way. One has to be retuned before moving from one area of the law to another. As a result of legal classification, lawyers within a single legal system often feel like strangers when dealing with each other. When they abandon their area of specialization, they will at least experience the same uncertainty and reservation that any lawyer experiences when he gives a client advice on a question of foreign law.

The preceding observations explain why we have chosen to include Part Five in this book. Our first objective is to familiarize the reader with the organization of French law and the objective content of its various divisions. When a question arises, one must know to what extent it is a problem of civil, commercial, administrative, or criminal law in order to know what materials to use in studying the problem. Secondly, and this is much more difficult, we shall try to explain the differences in method and approach that dominate the various branches, categories, and subcategories of French law.

I   Public Law and Private Law

For a Frenchman, the most basic distinction is that between public law and private law. The line between public and private law may sometimes be unclear. The very principle of the distinction, from the point of view of logic or rationality, may be disputed. But the distinction, based on a tradition as ancient as the Roman Empire, remains the basic division in French law. French lawyers are either private law specialists or public law specialists. It matters little that both sometimes claim the same contested area and sometimes deal with the same questions. Looking at the administration of justice, one finds separate supreme courts for private law matters (Court of Cassation) and public law matters (Council of State). Again, it is unimportant that some public law questions are within the jurisdiction of the private law courts and thus come before the Court of Cassation. The basic principle is not compromised by its exceptions. Public law and private law are the two great categories of French law.

What is the basis of this distinction? The oldest criterion proposed is the famous description by Ulpian in the *Digest* (D.1.2.1.1.): *Publicum jus est, quod ad statum rei Romanae spectat; privatum, quod ad singulorum utilitatem* ("Public law is that which concerns the state of the commonwealth; private law that which is for the use of private individuals"). This statement is open to various interpretations, but no distinction between public and private law has or can have the precision of a mathematical formula. Like Ulpian, we shall eschew the search for such precision and propose a basis for the distinction in very broad terms. Some legal rules involve the state: these are rules of public law. Others regulate the relations between private individuals: these are rules of private law.

This criterion has been the object of very active scholarly criticism. It is argued that all legal rules involve the state, since they are all intended to insure some order in society and the state's fundamental role is precisely to guarantee order and public peace. Relations between individuals involve, at the same time as the individuals themselves, society as a whole. Individuals are not always free to act as they see fit. It is fallacious to contrast rules which involve the state with rules governing the relations between individuals.

These criticisms are invalid. They result from a frequent confusion between two distinctions, the one under consideration here, between public and private law, and one examined earlier, the distinction between imperative and suppletive rules.[1] It is true that private individuals are free to organize their relations only within certain defined limits. The interest of the state, or rather of society, must be considered and prohibits total individual freedom of action. But it does not follow that we are never concerned with the relations between individuals. When B marries G, or X sells or gives something to Y, the relations thus created are relations between B and G, or X and Y, even though those relations are necessarily subject to certain imperative legal rules. Private law does not mean, as is so often asserted, that individuals can do as they wish without restriction.

In other relationships, however, it is apparent that the state is a *party*. A is hired by the state as a teacher in a public school. B is required by the state to pay taxes. C undertakes to supply equipment to the navy. D is injured in an explosion at a state armory. In all of these cases, there is a new element. We are no longer dealing with relations between two private individuals of equal status under the authority of the state. We are now concerned with a problem in which one party is a private individual—the teacher, taxpayer, supplier, accident victim—and the other party is the state, represented by one of its various agencies or departments. This relationship is a public law relationship. The same is true in the case of a dispute over the election of a parliamentarian or of the President of the Republic. Here we are in the domain of public law because we are dealing with a matter concerning the state's constitution and organization (*status rei publicae*).

One does not have to be a legal positivist to see a considerable difference between the two situations. Even if one argues that the distinction is theoretically unjustified, because the principles of natural law impose the same standard of moral conduct on the state

1. In agreement, see Charles Eisenmann, "Droit public, droit privé," *Revue de droit public et de la science politique* (1952), 903; H. Mazeaud, *Leçons de droit civil* (2nd ed.; 1959), I, 46–47.

as on private individuals, one cannot ignore the practical fact that it is the state which administers justice in our societies. The state will be more easily persuaded to apply legal principles in relations between individuals subject to its control than in those where, one might say, it has a conflict of interests. Thus, practically, the distinction between public and private law always has a certain validity. It is reinforced theoretically if one accepts the doctrines of legal positivism and thus regards the law basically as the command of the state. If it is the state that creates legal norms, or if one admits that the state can modify them when it so desires, the application of legal rules to relations to which the state is a party will always be somewhat optional. The contrast between public and private law is even clearer if one takes this position.

As the distinction between public and private law is understood in France, it is the simple observation of a fact: The state is directly involved in some legal relations (in and out of litigation), while other relations exist simply between private individuals. Although this factual observation is indisputable, we must still examine to what extent it justifies different regulation of the two categories of relations, and to what extent this regulation is in fact different. These are two further questions, which do not affect the basic validity of the distinction. Still, the answers to these questions will largely determine the theoretical and practical importance of the distinction. It should be obvious that the public versus private law distinction arises only because it has definite practical and theoretical importance, but a failure to recognize this fact seems to be the source of confusion surrounding the matter. The confusion is compounded by the fact that some writers see the matter from the ideal point of view (first question) and some from the point of view of positive law (second question) without always clearly stating which. The criticisms they exchange are usually a result of this confusion or of the critic's failure really to understand the position and the different perspective of the person criticized.

Let us look first, in order to establish a solid foundation, at the second question: What is and what has been the practical import of the distinction between public law and private law? The practical importance of the distinction has always been considerable. One can even say that for centuries private law alone existed, in that public law was so rudimentary as hardly to merit the name of law.

F. Schulz has shown that this was the case in Roman law.[2] The work of the jurisconsults during the classical period, and the Digest too, deals only with the private law of Rome. Nothing was written in Roman times on public law, either as a whole or in its various branches. The jurists recognized its existence, but did not consider it a proper subject for their study. Both prudence and principle dictated that they not write on it. It was more a matter of government, of public administration than of law. It was enough to note the seeds for future growth, as Ulpian did when he suggested that the law might one day develop in a new area and in his relatively insignificant definition contrasted public law to the law of the present, private law. Definitions of this period in the area of natural law were written in the same spirit. Here too it was hoped that someday it would become positive law.

The situation was the same in prerevolutionary France. Even the expression *public law* was lost for centuries. It did not appear again until the fourteenth century, and when it came into use, it referred more to what we would call today political science than to actual legal rules. The confusion continued until the French Revolution. Until then, the law, whether of Roman origin or French customary law, was private law. Canon law might provide an exception, but the legal prescriptions here were rules relating to the organization and structure of the church, more principles of administration and government than true rules of law. A rudimentary public law did begin to develop in the areas of public international law and church-state relations, which are concerned with the relations between equals, but not in constitutional or administrative law, headings that still appeared neither in books nor in university curricula. It is true that litigants sometimes invoked the "fundamental law of the kingdom" and principles of natural law. And there were efforts to regularize governmental operations. The *legists* appeared and tried to create a public law in the image of private law. But both internally and internationally, the legal character of the rules that the government followed (or was supposed to follow) was contested. The courts encountered strong opposition when they tried to consider and render legal judgments on the action of government administrators. The executive branch considered that this was unac-

2. F. Schulz, *Principles of Roman Law* (1936).

ceptable interference with the business of government, which is and ought to remain distinct from law and the courts. The rule of law was far from established. The existence of a true public law remained disputed throughout the prerevolutionary period.

The Revolution did not try to change the basic principle that had been accepted throughout the prerevolutionary period concerning the separation of powers between the executive and the judiciary. On the contrary, a statute of the revolutionary period, the law of August 16–24, 1790, proclaimed this principle in clear legislative terms for the first time: it prohibited the courts from interfering with the executive or hearing litigation to which the government was a party. This law is the basic text that still dominates the structure of French law, although it has never been elevated to the status of constitutional principle. Henceforth, the situation was clear. Public law could develop. The executive, purified by the Revolution and reorganized under the Empire, would be subject to legal principles, its arbitrariness would be curbed, and its actions would be subject to supervision. But all this had to happen outside the private law courts. This was the principle proclaimed by the law of 1790. Secondly, the principles applied to direct and control the action of government officials would be principles suited to the government's needs. They would not be purely and simply, as might be feared if the control were to lie with the ordinary courts, principles of private law, badly adapted at best to these needs. This second principle was not clearly formulated by any statute, but it seems to be a kind of logical corollary of the first principle.[3] The independence of the executive from the private law courts would make no sense if the government were still purely and simply subject to private law rules. The Civil Code does not so state, but it has always been assumed that it proclaims French law governing the relations between private individuals and is not applicable to relations in which the government is a party.

In the years following the basic law of 1790 that proclaimed the

3. Nevertheless, the principle of administrative law's full independence from civil law was not accepted automatically. It was not until 1873 that a resounding opinion of the Court of Conflicts in the *Blanco* case (February 8, 1873, S.1873. 3.153) affirmed clearly that, even in the absence of particular legislation, the government's liability "cannot be governed by the principles set forth in the Civil Code." See A. de Laubadère, *Traité élémentaire de droit administratif* (1953), no. 32, p. 31.

permanent separation of executive from judicial power in France, the French executive branch was reorganized. Napoleon, completing the work of the Revolution, organized it rationally and in the strict hierarchical manner that still characterizes it today. In the newly established conditions of order and integrity, mechanisms were created to combat arbitrariness and to prevent abuse of authority. It was not enough to impose a new legal order on private individuals. The government itself had to be the first to respect the law and provide a virtuous example. Law had to govern its activities. Public law had to develop along with private law.

The Council of State, established in 1800, was to be the principal institutional architect of this development. Two important dates in its history illustrate the development of public law as a new branch of French law. The first important date in the history of the Council of State and the development of French public law is 1872. In this year, it was established that the Council of State was completely independent in the exercise of its judicial functions. Its jurisdiction was "delegated," not "retained."[4] The second important date is 1889, the year of the *Cadot* decision.[5] In this decision, the Council of State decided, and successfully imposed, the idea that it had a general jurisdiction in the administrative law area. It has jurisdiction without special statutory authority being required in any category of cases. From the moment the executive acts, the Council of State can be asked to determine the propriety of the action. The Council of State can decide that the government has certain discretionary powers, and in such a case no judicial review is possible. But it is the Council of State itself and not the government which has the power to decide whether or not a particular act is within this discretionary area, whether or not it is an "act of government." And the Council of State has progressively restricted this area.

Today these two principles are beyond discussion. It is perfectly clear that executive action in France is governed by proper legal

4. *Law of May 24, 1872.* "Delegated" jurisdiction means that the Council of State gives judgments that are self-executory. In a system of retained jurisdiction, the Council of State would only draft proposed decisions, which would not acquire executory force until approved by the chief executive. See M. Waline, *Droit administratif* (8th ed.; 1959), no. 38, p. 29.

5. Council of State, December 13, 1889 (D.P.1891.3.41, S.1892.3.17, note by Hauriou).

rules that cannot be evaded. Public law has almost made up the head start that private law had over it. It has attained a degree of development comparable to the latter.

The characteristics and development of the Council of State's case law show that this high tribunal applies true law in the sense that we ordinarily understand that term. It matters little to petitioners that they must go before an administrative court rather than a private law court. The government itself, with respect to many of its activities, no longer sees any substantial reason to avoid the supervision of the private law courts. In such areas, it no longer claims any special privilege and it accepts the application of private law rules.[6] For this reason, the respective jurisdictions of the administrative and regular courts are no longer exclusively based on the distinction between public and private law, and the distinction itself in turn has become less clear. The state and the government are frequently also subject to private law rules, and this too results in some confusion. Nevertheless the basis for the distinction between public and private law is clear. One should not be confused by the identity between public and private law rules in certain areas,[7] but that seems to be exactly what has happened in France. Nor does the distinction lose its validity simply because special courts no longer deal exclusively with questions of public law.[8]

French executive action has come to be subject to judicial supervision, ordinarily by administrative courts and in exceptional cases by the regular courts, both of which apply true legal rules when exercising this supervision.

This evolution of legal restrictions on the executive branch of the government has been faster and more complete than the evolution of constitutional law and control of Parliament. The Constitution of 1958 is the first French constitution to have organized a Constitutional Council with an effective check on the constitutionality

6. Nationalized enterprises have usually been made expressly subject to the rules of private law. Concerning the difficulties created by this approach, deriving from the fact that these are, nevertheless, public law relationships, see R. Houin, "La gestion des entreprises publiques et les méthodes du droit commercial," in *La distinction du droit privé et du droit public et l'entreprise publique*, Archives de philosophie du droit (new ser.; 1952), 79–107.

7. French and Belgian law are also identical on many points.

8. See, in the work cited above at note 6, the article by J. Rivero, "Le régime des entreprises nationalisées et l'évolution du droit administratif," 147–71.

of statutes. Unlike administrative law, French constitutional law has remained of more interest to political scientists than to lawyers. Since it consists primarily of a description of the organization, functions, and workings of the various organs of government, it involves few problems subject to litigation. It has thus remained very different from private law and other branches of the law which are primarily concerned with litigable problems.

The second question that we shall examine is the following: Is it *proper* for practical consequences to flow from the distinction between private and public law? In other words, is it desirable and reasonable that the relations to which the state is a party should be regulated by rules different from those which govern the relations between private individuals?

Frenchmen answer this question unhesitatingly in the affirmative. Public law situations are often very similar to private law situations, so that in many cases identical rules can be applied. Some of today's differences between public and private law rules are purely accidental. They can be explained only as the legacy of tradition, evidence of the growing pains of public law, a result of the continued existence of administrative courts that are completely independent of the private law courts.

In some areas, however, Frenchmen feel that the same rules are not appropriate for both public law and private law. The public interest and private interests cannot receive the same consideration. Sometimes private interests must be subordinated to the general welfare. This subordination is required both by social morality and by common sense. It has been required in all continental systems, from that of the individualistic Roman lawyers to that of the German National Socialists. The latter's declaration that *Gemeinnutz geht vor Eigennutz* ("The common good comes before self-interest") is a replica of Paul's statement in the Digest: *Publicum interesse privatorum commodis praefertur* ("Public welfare takes precedence over private convenience"). The most that one can ask is that the cases in which this principle applies be specified and that the rules to be applied in public law cases be made clear. But there will always be some cases in which its application appears justified.

Individuals who enter into private law relations may have previously been legally unrelated, with no reciprocal rights or obligations. The state, on the other hand, has a permanent legal relationship with its citizens, and public law must reflect this difference. For instance, although it is a guiding principle of modern French public law that citizens have equal rights to government services and that any unjust disturbance of this equality must be corrected, it is hard to see what relevance this principle could have for private law. Although a great resemblance between public and private law is natural, certain factors preclude a complete identity between the two bodies of rules. Public law lawyers pay particular attention to characteristics that are peculiar to public law relations, to the problems that are unique to it, and to the ideas that ought to lead to the modification, relaxation, or rejection in public law of some private law rules and the creation of doctrines unique to public law.

Public law is of more recent formation than private law. Because it lacks a traditional foundation and is more easily influenced and modified by a kind of political sensitivity, public law remains less certain and more changeable, at least in some respects, than private law. French "publicists" (lawyers in the public law field) see things differently from "privatists." Thus, the codification approach, to which privatists are so attached, does not interest publicists. Publicists are not considered, and do not want to be considered, pure lawyers. Public law was free to develop only because its architects considered factors and ideas that were foreign to private law. Publicists have, and legitimately try to maintain, the outlook of the government official and the politician to supplement their legal training. They pride themselves on being less restricted by routine than ordinary jurists. They try constantly to improve the law and are not satisfied simply to discover and apply it. Frenchmen find it essential for the well-being of the law that they maintain this attitude and insure that public law has some originality as compared to private law.

The distinction between public and private law, even if one accepts the criterion which we have used, is in fact less stable and less clear than one might suppose. The boundary between public and private law can, and in practice does, vary with the changing conception of the state and its role. For many years criminal law was regarded as regulating the private law relations between the person who caused damage and the person injured (or his family). More recently, however, it has become a matter of public law, as the idea has become current that crime is primarily a matter of concern to society and that it is the responsibility of the state, and not of the injured person or his family, to prevent it. Similarly, the process of nationalization of industries has brought under public law regulation a whole sector of the economy that previously was completely regulated by private law. Even civil procedure these days is difficult to classify as public law or private law. The fact that a judge intervenes to settle disputes between private individuals is insufficient to take this dispute out of the realm of private law, but one can wonder if the response should be the same when the powers of the government are increased and particularly when the right to initiate action to settle the dispute is given to a public official, the representative of the Public Ministry (*ministère public*). In other words, the fact that a legal problem is regulated by imperative rules does not seem to us sufficient to remove it from the realm of private law. But the contrary seems to be the case when the problem brings into direct contact the state and private individuals, rather than just several private persons under the control and tutelage of the state. The line between these two categories of cases will often be hard to draw, and this is why people often confuse public law and imperative legal rules on the one hand and private law and freedom of contract on the other.

One other consideration also softens the contrast between public and private law. Increasingly, the social significance of relationships between private individuals is legally important. In more and more cases, private individuals are treated as participants in a public service as a result of their individual initiative and activity. The closing of a private transport company, a strike in the bread-baking industry, and the suspension of business by a large bank are thought to be as intolerable as the closing of a service run by the government. When ideas of this sort are accepted, public law principles come into play and modify the traditional rules of private law. As the idea of public service becomes a part of private law, private law becomes more like public law. For these reasons, the distinction in modern France between private law and public law has become less distinct than it once was, and in many cases the rules of private law are becoming similar in substance to those of public law.

II   Civil Law

A description of the various branches of French law must begin with that branch whose age and technical perfection have made it preeminent: civil law.

What is the civil law? The expression civil law (*jus civile*) originally designated the law that was applicable between citizens (*civis*), as opposed to the different set of legal rules called the *jus gentium*, which applied between noncitizens and between a citizen and a noncitizen. There are still some traces of this distinction in present French legal terminology.[9] In general, however, the old notion of laws which are the privilege of citizens alone has disappeared, and the concept of civil law in French law today has nothing in common with the old Roman notion of *jus civile*, as distinguished from *jus gentium*. The term *civil law* has also ceased to be used in France, as it was before the French Revolution of 1789[10] and as it still is in England, to distinguish Roman law or national law from canon law. The words *civil law* have taken a different meaning today, becoming nearly the equivalent of private law. Civil law today is the law that is applicable between individuals, whether or not they are citizens; it is contrasted only with the legal rules that affect the state. Civil law is thus distinguished from public law and criminal law; it constitutes all of private law, except for a very few areas which tradition or the circumstances of modern life have kept somewhat independent of it. The distinction between civil law and canon law fell into disuse with the secularization in 1792 of the law of civil status and of marriage, when civil law absorbed those matters dealing with affairs between individuals that had formerly been in the exclusive jurisdiction of canon law. There still is, to be sure, a canon law regulating these matters, and many Frenchmen continue to attach great weight to it. But there is now, in addition to the rules of canon law, an increasingly divergent set of civil law rules in the same areas, so that French national law

9. Article 11 of the Civil Code contrasts "civil rights," the enjoyment of which is restricted to Frenchmen, with other rights, for which the nationality of a person is not relevant.

10. Domat's famous book *Les lois civiles* thus referred to Roman law.

never makes reference to canon law. Individuals are invited and obliged by the church to observe two sets of rules concurrently. As Frenchmen they obey civil law rules; as Christians, canon law rules.

Nevertheless, commercial law, which was traditionally distinguished from civil law, must still be treated as a separate category for some purposes. Parallel to the Civil Code, France has a commercial code; the rules of French private law are still different in certain respects depending on whether one envisages relations between businessmen or those between nonbusinessmen, and "commercial acts" and acts which are not termed "commercial acts."[11] For the last fifty years, there has also been a tendency for labor law to become as distinct as commercial law.[12] Rural law, too, tends to take on a certain particularity within civil law.[13] And civil procedure is not included in the French concept of civil law.

The best way to understand the meaning and scope of the French concept of civil law is to study the recent commercial editions of the Civil Code or the treatises and elementary manuals on French civil law. According to these manuals, the broad divisions of civil law seem to be the following:

1. Law of persons: physical and moral persons, attributes of personality (name, domicile, acts of civil status), capacity of minors and the insane and the protection of their interests.

2. Family law: marriage, divorce, separation, filiation, obligations of maintenance.

3. Property law: movables and immovables, contents and transmission of real rights.

4. Law of obligations: contract in general and particular contracts, delicts, unjust enrichment.

5. Law of matrimonial property relations: the statutory community, conventional systems established by marriage contract.

6. Law of succession: intestate and testamentary.

These divisions are made by writers for teaching purposes on the basis of the Civil Code. They are not, however, fully satisfactory and do not exhaust the contents of the Civil Code.

11. On commercial law, see below, pp. 112 ff.
12. See below, pp. 137 ff.
13. See R. Savatier, *Les métamorphoses économiques et sociales du droit privé d'aujourd'hui* (1959), III, 211–30.

The attention of the foreign lawyer ought to be called to the following points. For various reasons, certain questions are not studied at the point where it would logically seem they ought to be. Suretyship is studied at the end of contracts, although its source need not be a contract. Donations are studied with succession rather than as a special type of contract. Various questions which do not, properly speaking, belong to civil law, on the other hand, are studied in books on civil law because for one reason or another they have been regulated in the Civil Code. Examples are questions concerning promulgation, publication, and nonretroactivity of laws, and regulations concerning the registers of civil status, as well as many questions of evidence, the distinction between authentic acts and acts under private signature, organization of the notaries, *res judicata,* and procedure (the procedure in actions for divorce and concerning status and purge of mortgages). All of private international law, including the law relating to nationality, on the other hand, is treated in special works, even though the general principles governing this area were originally and still partly are, dealt with in the Civil Code.

In addition to the subjects dealt with in the Civil Code, civil law includes various other matters, such as copyright law. These questions, however, are ordinarily omitted from, or dealt with in a fairly summary way in, general civil law treatises, so that it is better to consult special treatises concerned with them. The general civil law treatises will also be insufficient for the study of certain questions that have developed recently.

Civil law is the center, the very heart, of French law. What we have said above concerning the distinction between public law and private law explains this. Public law is more recently formed than private law, and it is less pure than civil law, since it includes questions of administrative practice and general policy goals. Also, civil law, based on the Roman tradition and developed through the ages, has attained greater technical perfection and stability than has public law, which is subject to the vicissitudes of political crises. Lawyers rejoice in this stability. French privatists are proud of their Civil Code, which has celebrated its 150th anniversary[14] and becomes ever more firmly established, as contrasted with the many

14. See *Travaux de la Semaine internationale de droit, Paris, 1950: L'influence du code civil dans le monde* (1954).

constitutions that France has had during the same period. To them the Civil Code seems to be the most lasting and the only true constitution of France.

French law faculties of the early nineteenth century, reorganized by Napoleon in 1805, taught only civil law, Roman law, and criminal law. Even today civil law is for Frenchmen the law *par excellence*. Its principles and methods are what law students must learn. The study of other branches of the law begins from these principles and methods; their study consists of explaining deviations from the general principles and methods of civil law.

This predominance is threatened today. Some educators are asking whether, in view of the considerable development of public law, the traditional approach to education should be retained. Do not the present importance and special characteristics and nature of public law require that it be studied separately? Does not the traditional private law education inhibit education in public law by emphasizing considerations, such as security of legal relations and equality of the parties, that are of secondary importance in public law? In general, this question is now answered in the negative. Public law might not profit in being separated from private law. Such a separation would seem to contradict the last fifty years' development, which has tended more and more strictly to subject administrative action to legal principles. Many consider it a fine thing that administrators and political scientists, in as great numbers as possible, should receive a legal education and in particular study the civil law. It seems the best guaranty of an administration dominated by concern for legality. Public law specialists generally are very willing to remain in the law faculties; all they ask is that a larger place be given to subjects related to public law and that the study of these subjects be expanded, either in the law faculties or in associated institutes of political science. Such institutes exist today in some universities, and in particular the *Institut d'études politiques* of the University of Paris, successor to the former *Ecole libre des sciences politiques,* enjoys a good reputation.

The French Civil Code, originally adopted in 1804, was the object of an attempted general revision following World War II. The Commission for the Reform of the Civil Code was set up in 1945 and worked for twenty years. It prepared reform proposals for an introductory title, title I (persons and the family), and title II (gifts, successions, and wills), but was dissolved in 1965 after a reversal of policy at the Ministry of Justice. The idea of creating a completely new civil code has been abandoned, but the proposals prepared by the commission have been very substantially utilized in new legislation amending the Civil Code in various ways.

III   Commercial Law

Commercial law has a history that makes it distinct from civil law. It was developed originally by international tribunals that existed at markets and fairs and in port cities. It grew from the custom of merchants and maritime customs, i.e., from international customs. In prerevolutionary France, these unique sources made commercial law very different from civil law, which traced its origins to either Roman law or regional customs. Even before the Revolution, however, the special character of regular commercial law was compromised by the decline of the international fairs, just as that of maritime commercial law was by the decline of great commercial organizations and the rise of state mercantile policy. The international tribunals disappeared, and the special national tribunals (consular and maritime courts) created in their place and which sought to follow their course only partially replaced them. In addition, the French monarchy attempted to "nationalize" both regular and maritime commercial law through Colbert's *Ordonnances* of the late seventeenth century. Since then, commercial law has increasingly become a branch of the national civil law, and its autonomy as a special branch has become increasingly difficult to understand and defend.[15] The organization of commercial activity in guilds, however, allowed commercial law to retain some autonomy until the Revolution. Another reason for this continued autonomy was that prerevolutionary legal scholars neglected commercial law completely. To them commercial law seemed like little more than the daily practices of men of little social importance, merchants. Such practices were obviously of little interest or worth compared to

15. In the same way, mercantile law was absorbed in England by the general law of the land during the eighteenth century.

the glorious principles of Roman law and the customary law of land and succession, the very bases of stable fortunes and family position.

Because the Revolution aspired to rid France of all class distinctions, it abolished the commercial guilds and thus took away the strongest support for a separate commercial law. Still, commercial law was not merged with the rest of the civil law. Probably the principal reason was that few lawyers were competent in both kinds of law; there were civil and commercial lawyers. Thus the separation between civil and commercial law continued and, along with the Civil Code, the Commercial Code was drafted. This code went into effect in 1807, but has never had the prestige of the Civil Code. It was not supported by a tradition of the same value, and in addition, had the misfortune of being drafted between two crucial periods. It came after the guilds, but before the industrial revolution, the machine age, and the development of transport, all of which were to revolutionize both regular and maritime commerce.

Nevertheless, maritime commercial law still has some cohesiveness. Its particularity was always greater than that of regular commercial law. Maritime commerce is by nature international and has remained in the hands of a class of businessmen united by the particular risks they bear. On the other hand, Frenchmen discuss whether there remains today any reason to consider internal commercial law as an autonomous branch of civil law. The guilds having been abolished and the principle of freedom of commerce and industry established, internal commercial law no longer regulates a particular social class. For many it seems like nothing more than a heterogeneous grouping of rules concerning various contracts and activities which may be carried on by anyone who so desires. Now one is governed by commercial law as soon as he does something that falls in the new legal category of "acts of commerce," but not because he is in a particular profession. Still, this principle is difficult to maintain against an opposite tradition, and the code itself has distorted it in various ways. Sometimes an act is an act of commerce just because it is performed by a person in the interest of, or in connection with, his profession (commercial undertakings, theory of the accessory act). In addition, certain special institutions are established for those who perform acts of commerce regularly or as their profession (bankruptcy, commercial registers).

Thus, since the enactment of the Commercial Code, the basic rationale for commercial law has been unclear, and the whole organization of the subject reflects this weakness. After the code even more than before, the area has lacked general principles; it is a mixture of rules that cannot be dealt with as a logical whole. And its basic principles have to be found in the Civil Code.

The industrial revolution of the nineteenth and twentieth centuries has only accentuated the problem. Increasingly, commercial law has become the legislative regulation of business and business institutions. It is less and less the product of an international, or even national, custom of merchants. Merchants have lost even their name and are now called businessmen. The new name is a sign of the change.

What does modern commercial law contain? For the most part, it is made up of legal rules governing institutions that are particularly important to business: for example, all kinds of business organizations, checks, bills of exchange, industrial and commercial property, banking, stock exchange transactions, and bankruptcy.[16]

With the tendency toward a planned economy and regulated professions, commercial law increasingly resembles administrative law. This appearance is strengthened by the tendencies of recent commercial law treatises, which have been adapted to new curricula and include a discussion of business taxes. Nevertheless, the jurist who studies French private law must bear in mind that some parts of private law are split in two: civil law and commercial law. Ordinarily, civil law furnishes the principles; exceptions to these principles, some more justified than others, will be found when the relationship in question is one of business. This split exists with respect to numerous contracts: for example, transport, insurance, sale, lease, pledge, and compromise. The formation of such contracts, their proof, and their effects may differ according to whether or not they are subject to commercial law rules. Similarly, problems of capacity are seen differently by civil law and commercial law. There are other problems of maritime commercial law and of recent formation in internal commercial law that are regulated principally by commercial law, with civil law seldom having any role at all: banking and stock exchange transactions, business organizations, and negotiable instruments. Finally, one should note that France has special

16. In France bankruptcy is available only to businessmen.

commercial courts, the judges of which are elected by the business-men of the district and need not be lawyers.

Should commercial law continue to be considered an independent branch of the law or should it be merged with civil law? This question is being asked in France today as in other countries, but the majority of commercial law specialists are opposed to a merger and insist upon the particularity of commercial law.[17]

That part of modern commercial law that resembles administrative law would certainly be sufficient to preserve it as an object of special study in France. But what about the pure private law relationships? Is there still a rationale for the distinction between civil and commercial contracts of sale? The tools that were once unique to businessmen are now used regularly by nonbusinessmen. Private fortunes are increasingly composed of shares and bonds of business organizations. Payments are increasingly, and sometimes obligatorily, made by check. All share companies and limited partnerships are regulated by the commercial law, no matter what their purposes. Thus commercial law seems to be business law, in a general sense, rather than special rules applicable only to those who engage in commerce.[18]

But let us pause and examine, in conclusion, the extent to which this business law still has the characteristics that commercial law originally had: Is it still a custom of merchants? Is it still international? These two characteristics, as we recognized above, are clearly still important in maritime commercial law.[19] It must inevitably be international, and those interested have been able to insure this through international maritime conventions, whose terms are then incorporated into national legislation and form contracts. There is no question that maritime law has a very great independence within French law. Its language, so different from the language of other branches of French law, illustrates this clearly. In addition, the prin-

17. See particularly the preface to Hamel and Legarde, *Traité de droit commercial* (1954), I; Julliot de la Morandière, Rodière, and Houin, *Droit commercial et droit fiscal des affaires* (1959), I, no. 2. For the contrary position see Ripert, *Traité élémentaire de droit commercial* (4th ed., P. Durand and R. Roblot; 1959), no. 12, p. 8.

18. Concerning this development and the concept of business law as contrasted with commercial law, see R. Savatier, *op. cit. supra*, III, 196–210.

19. In Italy there still is, in addition to the Civil Code, a Code of Navigation, which encompasses both the public (administrative) law and private (commercial) law aspects of maritime and air law.

ciples of maritime law often diverge from those of civil law. This same observation could be made about air law, and to a lesser extent, about river law.

With respect to regular commercial law, the continuation of these ancient characteristics is less obvious. But still, some particularity is evident here if one considers the international aspects of this law. Some institutions are governed by international conventions (international transport, patents, trademarks, negotiable instruments). In other cases, a unique commercial law has developed on the fringes of legal regulation, by various means, old and new, that were familiar to the custom of merchants, such as the use of form contracts and arbitration. As a result of such practices, even this part of commercial law has kept a certain originality within the legal system. The problem is that the lawyer, today as before, feels uncomfortable with these extralegal mechanisms, and the commentaries he writes on commercial law, as it is formulated and described in legislation, do scant justice to this originality. Nevertheless, the originality remains and is real. It is for this reason that any attempt to unify the commercial law in a single code may be illusory.

A commission was set up after World War II for the purpose of revising the Commercial Code and corporation law. This commission, however, suffered the same fate as the Commission for the Reform of the Civil Code. It also has been dissolved and its work has been used by the Ministry of Justice as the basis for legislative proposals. In this way very extensive reforms have been made in corporation law, bankruptcy, commercial registers, and admiralty law.

IV   Criminal Law

Criminal law, also called penal law, occupies a special position in the French legal system. It is now incontestably a branch of public law. Theft, murder, assault, and battery are not just private matters between perpetrator and victim or his representatives. There is a violation of public order with which penal law is concerned. Independently of any civil compensation that civil law may require him to pay, the criminal must also account to society for his actions, even though it is not the direct interest of the state which he has injured as would have been the case if there were counterfeiting or trespassing on public property.

Although criminal law is part of public law, it is nevertheless traditionally considered in France the concern of privatists. Public law jurists deal with it only in one exceptional case, that of crimes committed by the President of the Republic or members of the Government in the exercise of their official functions. These crimes are within the jurisdiction of a special court, the High Court of Justice (*Haute Cour de Justice*), which was established by the Constitution of 1958 (articles 67 and 68).

Aside from this exceptional case, criminal law is left to the privatists. The main reason for this apparent anomaly is that the courts with jurisdiction to administer criminal law and pronounce convictions and sentences are always the regular private law courts and never, except for certain very minor offenses, the administrative courts. This is the case even where the accused is a government employee accused of an offense committed in the exercise of his duties. Here, the desire to insure individuals the guaranties offered by the regular courts and their procedures has prevailed over the fear of court interference in the activity of government administrators that might hamper their actions.[20]

The regular courts' power to judge the action of government administrators from a penal point of view does not seem to have been abused in any way and the jurisdiction of these courts is solidly established. In France it would be regarded as a dangerous privilege for the government, and as a rule full of danger for officials, to exclude the jurisdiction of the regular courts in this area. At the present time, there is, however, considerable concern over the power given to the executive under a variety of circumstances to apply clearly repressive sanctions, outside of the classical type of penalty. Examples of such sanctions are closure of a business establishment, prohibition from exercising a profession, and denial of a passport. The Council of State of course does have a power of review of such sanctions, but

20. Contrary to the principle that prevailed in prerevolutionary France that "every judge is a prosecutor," criminal court judges, with few exceptions, can no longer take jurisdiction on their own initiative. Still, the government is not completely protected, since the right to initiate criminal proceedings belongs not only to the government, through the Public Ministry; the person injured by a criminal offense generally also has that right.

many persons deplore the refusal to grant jurisdiction over them to the regular courts. The practice of administrative internment, in particular, has clearly been abused. The conditions that encouraged this at the end of World War II and during the Algerian battle for independence have, however, disappeared, and the situation, while still not completely satisfactory, has improved considerably.

Criminal law is based on a much weaker tradition than civil law. The Roman tradition in the area is of little relevance. The Roman jurisconsults never achieved the perfection in criminal law that characterizes their private law work. And in any case, the solutions given in ancient Rome have little connection with the ideas that prevail today.

Failing a Roman tradition, criminal law developed in prerevolutionary France on the basis of customary notions, which evolved in important ways under the influence of canon law.[21] As soon as criminal law became a matter of public concern and ceased to be simply a squaring of accounts between the criminal and the victim under the supervision of the state, the repression of criminal activity came to be thought of in France as posing a problem for the public rather than legal problems. Of course it was up to the courts to fix penalties, but they did not consider it to be the highest of their functions. Lawyers so ignored criminal law that no important criminal law treatise existed in France until the eighteenth century.[22] It was only when, at this time, the natural rights of man became a matter of concern, that the importance, and even the possible existence, of criminal law was noticed. Only then did the idea develop that one might limit, in this area as well as others, the possible abuses of police power by creating a penal code and a code of criminal procedure. After some preliminary work during the revolutionary period, these two codes were produced in the First Empire. This work has not preserved the same degree of prestige today as has the Civil Code. Nevertheless, it is quite possible that it is in this area that codification constituted the greatest advance.

Because there was no solid Roman criminal law tradition, the

21. The basic work in this area is still A. Esmein, *Histoire de la procédure criminelle en France* (1892).
22. The first important works were Jousse, *Traité de la justice criminelle* (4 vols.; 1761); Muyart de Vouglans, *Institutes de droit criminel* (1767); and Rousseau de Lacombe, *Traité des matières criminelles* (7th ed.; 1788).

study of criminal law has been relatively neglected in France. There have been few "criminalists," and the important works on criminal law have been written by judges, who are the practitioners in the area, rather than by legal scholars. A professor of law who devoted himself to something so unexalted would ordinarily leave aside the purely legal side of the question and become, rather than a criminalist, a criminologist, concerned with the sociological aspects of criminal behavior and its suppression rather than with the formal rules of criminal law and procedure. He would ordinarily write in the area of "general" penal law.[23] Special penal law never has been a required subject for French law students; it is regarded as a subject for practitioners.

The fact that, on the one hand, criminal law is a part of public law and, on the other, is administered by the regular courts, provides a key to understanding certain attitudes and contradictions that can be observed in the area. The magistrate who makes a career of criminal law administration will have received in law school, and will keep, the education of a privatist. This fact can be a drawback in some ways. Emile Garçon has noted that a lawyer who is used to the accepted extensive interpretation of private laws can have difficulty in adhering to the principle of strict interpretation, which, in the interest of individual freedom and security, is essential to penal law.[24] The criminalist retains the attitudes of a privatist in another respect. He feels uncomfortable and not fully justified when he is called upon to supervise the activities of the agents of the executive branch, i.e., police officers. Criminal procedure in France is hamstrung by this approach.

On the other hand, the French attitude toward criminal law can be understood only if one remembers that it is, in the final analysis, a branch of public law. Criminal law may be administered by the regular courts and thus in some ways be similar to private law. But basically it is public law and when one says public law, a Frenchman knows that it is not and cannot be law in the strict sense.

Law in the strict sense can only develop in the area of relations

23. An exception was the *Code pénal annoté* (1952) by E. Garçon; the revised edition of this, however, was prepared by magistrates. Another exception is Robert Vouin, *Précis de droit pénal spécial* (1953).

24. Emile Garçon, "De la méthode du droit criminel," in *Les méthodes juridiques,* lectures given at the Collège Libre des Sciences Sociales in 1910 (1911), 202 ff.

between individuals, where the state is an impartial arbiter. In criminal as in administrative law, the government is required to play a more active role. Society's interest is obviously and directly involved. A Frenchman will allow the government a degree of discretion, and even arbitrariness, that is hard to reconcile with the certainty characteristic of legal principles. The assumption predominates that society's interest requires that one trust the police. Individual liberty will be guaranteed by the traditions and sense of duty of this organization, rather than by the formal provisions of codes. Of course the courts supervise the police, but the result of such supervision is slight, since the judiciary shares the public feeling and sometimes overlooks an apparent abuse. One wonders whether the abuses in question would not be better repressed if supervision had been entrusted to an administrative court similar to the Council of State, instead of to the regular judiciary, which in France is always hesitant to look into the legality and propriety of government action.

In comparing criminal law with public law and contrasting it to private law, one should also note the discretion that the government has in many cases whether or not to prosecute someone who has committed a crime. Although the person who is injured by an offense can initiate criminal action that would ordinarily lead to conviction, the prosecutor and certain other government administrators make the decision as to whether or not the prosecution should go forward.[25] It is self-evident that ordinarily the prosecuting officer will initiate and pursue the action when he has been informed of the commission of an offense. Nevertheless in France there does exist what is known as the system of discretionary prosecution.[26] The prosecutor has the choice of prosecuting or not prosecuting when an offense has come to his knowledge or suspicion: he will prosecute only if this action seems opportune, in conformity with society's interest, properly understood. This principle illustrates the gulf between private and criminal law. French jurists raise no general objection to the system of discretionary prosecution. What they consider important is that the authorities' action must be inspired by a spirit that respects the liberty and equality of citizens. As long

25. *Code de Procédure Pénale,* art. 1; see also G. Stefani and G. Levasseur, *Procédure pénale* (1959), nos. 104–105.
26. *Code de Procédure Pénale,* art. 40; see also Stefani and Levasseur, *op. cit.,* nos. 578–80.

as this spirit governs, they do not mind if the law is not strictly followed. After all, criminal law is public, and public law is different from private law.

Criminal law belongs to public law, and this fact also explains the "autonomy of penal law." [27] Penal law is not intended to be simply a sanctioning law, automatically applying substantive concepts of private law. Its purpose is very different from the purpose of private law, and this difference justifies criminalists who, in various circumstances, employ these concepts in an original manner. They convict of theft the person who, having bought an object, takes it away without paying for it. (In civil law terms, he has not taken something belonging to someone else, because ownership was transferred by agreement.) They convict as a receiver of stolen goods a person holding goods of which he has a legally acquired ownership or a lesser real right in conformity with article 2279 of the Civil Code.

Which will predominate, the traditional private law aspect or the functional public law aspect of penal law? Or will this problem be solved in the future by the triumph of a third solution, with criminal behavior ceasing to be regarded primarily as a legal problem? According to certain modern authors, the criminal is sick, a misfit, rather than a sinner whose act requires punishment. The idea that crime requires chastisement, that the penalty has a role of retribution and atonement, corresponds to a world-view based on the Christian morality of atonement for faults and of salvation. But society need not take this individualistic position. The criminologist ought to look at things from the society's point of view and also take into consideration the basic principles of modern psychiatry and medicine. The idea of prevention, reform, social defense, and security measures ought to replace the old ideas of deterrence, retribution, and punishment.[28]

It is important to point out these new tendencies here, since, without trying to predict the future, one can state that they have already partially triumphed in French law. Juvenile crime is seen today increasingly from a medical point of view instead of a strictly legal

27. See *Quelques aspects de l'autonomie du droit pénal, Etudes de droit criminel,* compiled and with a preface by G. Stefani (a publication of the Institut de criminologie, Faculté de droit, l'Université de Paris, 1956).

28. See Marc Ancel, *La défense sociale nouvelle* (1954), particularly pp. 113–30, concerning the relation between the new and the classic conceptions.

point of view.[29] In addition, the development of security measures and the individualization of sentencing give today's penal law an appearance increasingly like administrative law and unlike private law.

French criminal law is codified. During the Napoleonic period, a penal code and a code of criminal procedure were enacted. The Penal Code of 1810, although profoundly modified, remains in force today. But in 1959 a new criminal procedure code replaced the original code of procedure, which is the only one of the five Napoleonic codes to have been repealed.

We should also note that there are several special codes in the area of military justice. There are individual codes for the army (law of March 9, 1928) and the navy (law of January 13, 1938). In addition there is a disciplinary and penal code for the merchant marine (law of December 17, 1926, amended several times).

The existence of codes in the penal law area seems essential to Frenchmen because of the principle of the legality of offenses and penalties. This principle is accepted in French law, and Frenchmen can hardly imagine how individual liberty could be guaranteed without it. It is only by virtue of a statute that an offense can be defined or a penalty pronounced: *nullum crimen sine lege, nulla poena sine lege*. The Constitution of 1958 impinged upon this principle, but only in a very minor respect. Henceforth, simple police regulations are within the jurisdiction of the executive; it is they who establish their existence and fix the sanction for their violation.

V   Constitutional Law

France has had written constitutions since 1791 and today lives under the Constitution of the Fifth Republic, promulgated on October 4, 1958. One would expect, then, that the category of constitutional law would be clearly defined within the French legal system: it ought to denote the exposition of the Consti-

29. In France, unlike various other European countries (Nordic countries and Portugal), a juvenile is still judged, however, by a court; his fate is not decided simply by an administrative body.

tution's rules, as stated in the document itself and applied in practice.

Nevertheless several comments are essential to clarify the French notion of constitutional law, and in particular to show how completely it differs from both English and American constitutional law, with which one might otherwise tend to identify it. Two particular points must be emphasized. First, French constitutional law differs in scope from the constitutional law of many other countries. And second, it does not have the same overriding importance.

As constitutional law is conceived in France, it differs in content from the constitutional law of other countries. In some respects it is broader; in others it is more restricted. To illustrate this, we need only consider any French constitutional law treatise or manual. It is significant that none of them is entitled a treatise or manual of *French* constitutional law. The contents show that they are not books on French constitutional law, but rather political science textbooks setting forth the various modern political systems, including those of France since 1791 and today's French constitutional law. This latter is only dealt with toward the end of each book and in little more detail than other constitutions.

What constitutional law gains in the direction of political science, however, it loses in several other directions. First, the content of French constitutional law is limited by our distinction between constitutional and administrative law. French writers distinguish between *Government* and *administration,* the superior and inferior organs of the state. Although French writers recognize readily that this distinction is illogical and arbitrary, it exists and has the effect of splitting off from constitutional law several topics that in other countries form part of it.

Another restriction on the scope of French constitutional law is that fundamental human rights are studied under the special title of general public law or public liberties, outside of constitutional law in the strict sense. There are two explanations for this. Although human rights have sometimes been listed in and guaranteed by French constitutions, they have at other times been omitted from constitutions, which make no reference at all to such rights. This was the case under the constitutional laws of 1875, so that during the Third Republic the constitutional character of these rights was legally disputable. In addition, one can argue that by studying human rights under a special heading, we are, rather than keeping them apart from the constitution, setting them above it as unchanging principles of public law and as a kind of natural law that remains in spite of the amendment or repeal of constitutions. The notion of a supraconstitutional law has always had some appeal in France, precisely because the distinction between constitutional law and other law lacks the strength and vitality that it has in other countries.

A third and final restriction on the content of constitutional law is that, because France is a unitary state, the problems posed by federal structures of government in other countries are not of concern to French constitutional law specialists. Above the French Republic, there has been indeed, as a successor to the French Colonial Empire, the "Community," which is provided for by title XII of the 1958 constitution.[30] But the structure of the Community is not studied in constitutional law treatises in France, but rather in separate works, the old treatises of "colonial law," rechristened today "overseas law" (*droit d'outre mer*).

Different in scope, French constitutional law also differs from various foreign constitutional laws in its role in legal life and its relationship with other branches of French law.

A fundamental principle of French law denies judges the power to declare a statute unconstitutional or the right to refuse to apply it on the basis of its violation of the Constitution. No one questions this principle. It is so well established that successive French constitutions have seen no need even to state it. Moreover, not only are regular judges without jurisdiction over such questions, but there is no special constitutional court with jurisdiction to declare a law unconstitutional once it has been promulgated.[31]

The absence of any organized supervision of the constitutionality of laws deprives French constitutional law of much of the interest

30. The term *Communauté* was substituted by the Constitution of 1958 for the term *Union française,* which was used by the preceding constitution. And the term *Union française* itself was coined only in 1946. Before that time, people simply spoke of colonies and protectorates, and sometimes of the French Colonial Empire.

31. The Constitutional Council exercises its supervision only prior to the promulgation of the statute. The conditions under which it can take jurisdiction also restrict this supervision considerably.

that it has in other countries. How the President of the Republic is chosen, how the government is formed, how Parliament is elected and functions, how the responsibilities of the ministers can be invoked: these are the topics discussed by the French constitutional law specialist. And generally these topics raise few problems; it may be said that the French constitutional law specialist seeks interest for his subject by escaping from it in the direction of political science. Attracted and absorbed by political science, the French constitutional law specialist has even neglected certain legal problems which do seem to fall within his domain. Thus, the question of whether a judge can inquire into the formal regularity of a law published in the *Official Journal* is examined, somewhat unexpectedly, by French private law scholars.[32] Whether a law violating an international treaty should be applied by a judge is examined in connection with private or public international law.[33] And the question of the circumstances in which an executive act violating the Constitution may be invalidated or refused enforcement is regarded as a question of administrative law.

In other countries, the study of constitutional law is the very basis of legal studies, and a study that is paramount by the breadth of problems raised. But for a French jurist it is not a major interest. The private law jurist, in particular, need know nothing, or very little, of the various constitutions that have come and gone in France since 1791. Only the Charter of 1814, reestablishing Catholicism as the state religion, necessitated an amendment to the Civil Code; divorce had to be abolished. Aside from this, the Civil Code promulgated in 1804 has remained in force, intact despite many revolutions and changes of government during the nineteenth and twentieth centuries. Of course it has often been amended, but *never* as a direct consequence of a change of government or a new constitution.

If one compares the role of constitutional law in France with the American experience, noting the influence throughout American law of the United States Supreme Court's interpretation of the fed-

32. See, however, M. Laferrière's discussion in "Rôle du juge dans l'appréciation de l'authenticité des textes de lois publiés au *Journal officiel*," *Travaux de l'association Henri-Capitant pour la culture juridique française*, V (1949), 36 ff.

33. J. Basdevant, "Le rôle du juge national dans l'interprétation des traités diplomatiques," *ibid.*, 107 ff.; J. P. Niboyet, "La récente constitution française et le droit international," *Travaux du Comité français de droit international privé* (8th year, 1946–47), 17 ff.

eral Constitution at various points in history, it becomes obvious that constitutional law to a French lawyer and constitutional law to an American lawyer are two entirely different things.

In France, unlike other countries, constitutional law is regarded as almost pure public law, concerned primarily with the state and its organization and of only minimal relevance to private individuals. Still, we must be careful not to underestimate the importance of the relationship between constitutional and private law. In fact, French constitutions do more than describe the governmental organization. They often contain declarations of rights and preambles that proclaim general principles and state policies that can seriously alter the foundations of private law.

For example, when the state undertakes new public services or nationalizes certain enterprises in execution of a policy stated in the constitution, various previously pure private law relationships come within the domain of public law. The private law relationships created by contracts of employment give way to the status of civil servant governed by public law. The private law rules of property are replaced by administrative law rules concerning the public and private domain of the state. Particular contracts become subject to rules of public law rather than being regulated by private law rules. In short, the domain of private law can be limited by the development of the state's functions.

These considerations, however, do not lead the French lawyer to grant constitutional law a place of much importance. In practice, laws often provide that nationalized institutions shall continue to be governed by the rules of civil and commercial law, thus concealing the shift of the relationship from private to public law. In addition, the Constitution is only the very distant source of the measures mentioned above, and the study of statutes implementing the Constitution's guidelines is all that has any practical significance and does not belong to French constitutional law. In France, one will denounce the invasion of private law by public law and the encroachment of administrative law on civil law. But constitutional law will not be blamed, because jurists basically regard its dispositions as political rather than legal.[34]

34. Constitutional law understood in this manner is called by Spanish lawyers "political law" (*derecho politico*).

VI Administrative Law

To define administrative law imposes a real strain on French writers, and their attempts in this direction often fail. First, administrative law is hard to keep distinct from constitutional law, which provides its structure and basic principles. And, like constitutional law, it tends to fuse with political science, and particularly with the subcategory called public administration.

Defining administrative law is further complicated by the existence of administrative courts and the resulting natural tendency to define in terms of court jurisdiction; administrative law is sometimes equated with the jurisdiction of administrative courts. In these conditions, one approach would be simply to look at what existing manuals and treatises on administrative law contain, rather than attempting an abstract definition. This, however, is not completely satisfactory, since such manuals and treatises often state explicitly that they cover only the "general part" of administrative law. They tell us that there is also a "special part," the whole of which has not yet been dealt with in any book, with the possible exception of a few compendia of administrative law.

This confusion should be no surprise. Ancient as the notion of public law may be, we have seen that it has only recently been seriously studied in France. In many respects, it is still mixed in with political science. French constitutional law gave us a first example of this confusion. In that area, law struggles to match political science in importance, just as public international law tries to rival its master art, diplomacy. Similarly, administrative law and public administration are not clearly distinguished. Part of what writers treat as administrative law is little more than the description of French administrative practice, the way civil servants are appointed, the division of their functions, and the way they carry them out.

To a Frenchman, it seems natural for administrative law to deal with these questions. Law is not synonymous with litigation, so a necessary part of administrative law is the description of administrative officials and bodies, their capacity, and the legal means by which they carry out their functions. Common law lawyers are likely to view matters differently; the fact that most of their law is judge-made leads them to associate law closely with litigation. The continental approach is more general.

Still, much of administrative law deals with its case law, that is, with the results of litigation arising from administrative action, both between the government and private individuals and between independent government departments. Let us begin our discussion of this case law by noting a basic principle of administrative law which illustrates clearly the French view of the special position held by public law. This is the so-called principle of the preliminary decision (*décision préalable*). The procedure in a dispute between the government and an individual is not, as in private law, to go to court and ask the court for a settlement of the dispute. First, the government, by virtue of its privileged position, decides the matter as it considers proper. It imposes the tax, dismisses the civil servant, or closes the establishment that it considers illegal or unhealthy. It does not go to court for a determination that X is its debtor, that Y deserves dismissal, or that Z's business has been operated in violation of the law. Before administrative courts, the individual is always the plaintiff.[35] The government first judges its own case; the individual is limited to contesting the government's conception of the law and having the courts adjudicate it. In private law, the situation is naturally very different. Any procedure that allows parties to solve their disputes by judging their own case without going to court (such as a penalty clause, a right of unilateral termination, or a clause providing for automatic cancellation in case of nonpayment of the price) is regarded with hostility.

Administrative litigation, as we have said, is ordinarily handled by a special hierarchy of courts, called administrative courts, at the apex of which is the Council of State. The principle, which has a historical explanation, is, however, not absolute. A variety of clearly administrative litigation is placed by special legislation within the jurisdiction of the regular courts. For example, the regular courts handle litigation on indirect taxes, expropriation for public use, municipal liability in case of riots, and automobile accidents. And all penal cases automatically come to them.

More important than the dual court structure is no doubt the French acceptance of the principle that administrative law differs

35. This fact provides a partial explanation for the absence of a conflicts procedure in the administrative court system.

from private law. Different rules govern relations between private individuals, on the one hand, and relations between government departments or between a department and an individual on the other. The civil and commercial codes contain private law; they do not govern administrative law relations.

Where can we find the rules of administrative law? For many years, they were far from precise, but throughout the nineteenth and twentieth centuries things have changed gradually. Courts and legal scholars have developed French administrative law, and arbitrariness has largely disappeared, as prevailing democratic ideals require.

The development of administrative law in France has not been haphazard. At the beginning of the nineteenth century, France adopted codes that, as had been desired by natural law proponents, seemed to people then to be the embodiment of natural law. This uniform law was henceforth to be applied throughout France. The new codes were supported by the prestige of the emperor Napoleon, who hastened their preparation and spurred on the draftsmen to complete their work. It was only natural that the provisions of these codes should be taken as the basis for the creation of a new administrative law. For men of the nineteenth century, the codes precisely articulated rationality and fairness; they were the new *ratio scripta* of the universe, and thus had to be followed. Generally French administrative law follows the civil law, although judgments of the Council of State rarely cite an article of the Civil Code. The Civil Code's solutions were accepted as self-evident, since judges considered them rational.[36] A special reason is usually required before a judge will set aside such solutions. Still, special reasons often do exist and administrative law and civil law often view justice differently. These special reasons may be grouped into two categories. Sometimes a consideration peculiar to administrative law will justify a rule different from that of the civil law. The need to avoid interruption of public services thus led to the adoption, with respect to certain administrative law contracts, of the "theory of *imprévision*," which is

36. It is in this way that one must understand the citation of code articles where this is done by the Council of State: *Fauvet* decision (Council of State, March 18, 1927, art. 1166); *Ville de Mory* decision (Council of State, June 17, 1931, art. 1154). Nevertheless a "private law" text can be obligatory for the administrative courts if that is clearly the legislator's intention: *Pagès* decision (Council of State, February 19, 1943; *Code Civil*, art. 216).

rejected by civil law in all cases; the bankruptcy and eventual closing of an undertaking which provides a public service seems unacceptable. In other cases, the divergence between administrative law
and civil law results from the fact that the Civil Code, enacted in
1804, no longer corresponds to our conception of what is rational
and just. Civil Code rules are not binding on administrative courts,
and administrative judges set them aside. Sometimes, where the administrative courts have adopted a new rule, the regular courts have
even followed their example and modified their interpretation of a
Civil Code article. In this way, administrative law has become a
force for the improvement and development of the civil law itself.

There are certainly cases where the difference between administrative and civil law is hard to justify. This is inevitable as soon as
one accepts the existence of two distinct bodies of law, administered
largely by two independent judicial hierarchies. The best and most
reasonable solution will not always prevail. Nevertheless, arbitrary
inconsistency is relatively rare overall. The French ordinarily consider the existence of a separate system of administrative law as a
good thing, rather than as an added complexity.

We should note another aspect of modern French administrative
law: It is uncodified. There are statutes dealing with many aspects
of administrative law, but the principles of administrative law that
have been developed by the Council of States and scholarly writers
have never been codified. And there is no movement favoring codification of this area.

Some of the fundamental principles of administrative law are inspired entirely by public law considerations and derive from the
basic notions of French constitutional order that have prevailed
since the Revolution of 1789. Since the difficulties of the German
occupation, the Council of State has articulated these principles
carefully and denominated them expressly as general principles of
administrative law.[37] Except for these, the French administrative
courts have generally found in the Civil Code the rational principles
upon which they have based their decisions. It is understood of
course that these principles must be adapted somewhat when incorporated into administrative law. Three members of the Council of
State were appointed to the twelve-member Commission for the Re-

37. See Benoît Jeanneau, *Les principes généraux du droit dans la jurisprudence
administrative* (1954).

form of the Civil Code that was formed in 1945 and dissolved in 1965. This fact alone should indicate both the Civil Code's importance for administrative law and the absence of any movement to create a separate administrative code to rival the Civil Code. The general codification of administrative law, for which a "precodification" commission has been formed, is something completely different.[38] It is aimed only at the reorganization and systematization of specific statutes, regulations, and administrative instructions concerning various government departments and particular aspects of administrative law. No codification of the general principles of administrative law is to be included in this work.

The concept of administrative law developed in France is no doubt one of the most characteristic aspects of French law. The common law countries have no comparable concept of administrative law. The distinction between public and private law is not commonly made in these countries. It is not generally thought that legal solutions can be subject to different principles and rules depending on whether the relationship in question is between individuals or between the state (or the Crown) and a private individual. In the absence of administrative courts, no one has thought to group into a special treatise the special solutions given, through the various techniques available in the common law, to problems involving the government. The administrative law recently developed in the United States and Great Britain is not the equivalent of French administrative law. It in no way claims autonomy from the regular common law applicable between private individuals. In this new category, one simply studies the new legal problems created within the common law by the development of governmental functions and activities, without, however, seeing the legal system as divided thereby into two large parts.

The French notion of administrative law also differs from that of other Western European countries and that of the USSR and the socialist countries of Eastern Europe. In general, French administrative law is more comprehensive and more developed than administrative law in these other countries. The French Council of State is a unique institution, and its existence in the French structure has had two consequences. First, the Council of State has helped give

38. See Gabriel Ardant, "La codification permanente des lois, règlements et circulaires," *Revue du droit public et de la science politique* (1951), 35 ff.

French administrative law greater originality in comparison with private law than it has in other legal systems. But more important, it has permitted the institution of a tighter, more far-reaching, more independent supervision of administrative activities than is found in other countries.

The Council of State's creation of an administrative law over the last hundred years is impressive for lawyers. In France and abroad, legal scholars have repeatedly, and for good reason, expressed their admiration for the work and progress achieved. Simultaneously, as this admiration has grown, the Civil Code has been the subject of ever-increasing criticism. Sometimes the impression is created that French administrative law has surpassed its private law in excellence, but this is a false impression. Without minimizing the great progress in administrative law, one must recognize that technically it remains less advanced and less perfect than private law and less able than the latter to insure justice. Its doctrines are not so well established; its principles and particular rules are more flexible. In short, administrative law is less certain in France than private law, so that it is still too early to consider the drafting of a true administrative code. The fact that this uncertainty allows the equitable aspects of particular cases to be given greater attention in administrative law is sometimes advantageous. Nevertheless uncertainty in legal rules is generally undesirable, and the equity of the Council of State conceals a certain arbitrariness and is just as objectionable as the equity of the prerevolutionary supreme courts. Many Frenchmen have forgotten those old courts and are full of praise for the Council of State. Today's public law lawyers, including members of the Council of State, are less enthusiastic. While admiring the council's accomplishments, they readily acknowledge the imperfections of French administrative law and remain in awe before the monument that is private law, the work of centuries, from which they continue to draw guidance and after which they often model their own structure.[39]

39. See in particular Rivero, "Le régime des entreprises nationalisées et l'évolution du droit administratif," 147–71.

VII   Tax Law

Tax law is clearly a most important branch of administrative law, as taxation is one of the most essential and manifest relationships between individuals and the state. In today's society tax law is so important, however, that we tend to treat it as an independent branch of the law, particularly because it is too broad and complex to be dealt with in a general administrative law course. The truth is that it is one of the few specialized subdivisions of administrative law studied in law schools.

Tax law has two unusual characteristics which distinguish it from the rest of administrative law. The first is that some tax litigation is left to the regular courts. All litigation as to direct taxes is in the jurisdiction of the administrative courts. But most indirect taxes, and in particular those collected on specified transactions (stamp tax, registration tax) are within the jurisdiction of the regular courts.[40] This fact does not remove the subject from the area of administrative law, but writers frequently forget this and confuse the distinction between public and private law with the division of jurisdiction between the administrative and regular courts. For this reason, the privatists who deal with legal problems of registration frequently speak of the "particularity of tax law" when they see that private law principles are not always applied to these problems. For example, registration law sometimes ignores the legal personality of commercial partnerships; no transfer tax is collected when a partner transfers some of his property to the partnership, although in civil law this is a transfer of ownership. Conversely, tax law rejects some of the implications found by the civil law in the declarative effect of partition through the courts' interpretation of Civil Code article 883;[41] if an object from a decedent's estate is sold at public auction to one of the heirs, tax law considers this sale a transfer, rather than a simple declaration, of ownership. We should also note that tax

40. Litigation on the business turnover tax constitutes an important exception.
41. *Code Civil*, art. 883: "Each co-heir is treated as if he had inherited immediately and alone his whole share plus all items that come to him through auction and had never had an interest in the other parts of the succession."

law ignores the civil law invalidity of transactions violating morality (for example, the sale or lease of a house of prostitution); it collects a transfer tax in cases where the civil law recognizes no transfer at all. In such cases, can one properly speak of the particularity of tax law? Perhaps not. Although transfer taxes are within the jurisdiction of regular courts, they are still not part of private law. The distinctive solutions noted above seem simply to be practical applications of the accepted distinction in French law between private and public law.[42]

One thing that shows clearly the particularity of tax law even within public law is the power that tax authorities have to compromise with individuals on the penalty to be paid for tax law violations. The authorities responsible for indirect taxes and those responsible for customs can, before bringing suit or even after a judgment has been given setting the taxpayer's penalty, compromise with him. In other words, they can agree not to prosecute if the individual will pay a particular fine, or they can agree to a reduction of the fine fixed by the court.[43] "Tax fines" are considered to be both penalties and compensation, and in French law are subject to rules completely different from "penal fines," which are imposed for other penal offenses.[44]

The second important distinctive characteristic of tax law, when compared to administrative law in general, is that there are two codes of tax law in France: the general tax code (which was published in 1934 to replace five earlier codes: the codes of direct taxes, indirect taxes, transfer taxes, stocks and bonds, and business turnover taxes) and the customs code.

But one should not be deceived. In spite of a nominal similarity, the tax codes are very different from the traditional civil law codes, particularly because the same stability cannot be achieved in so rapidly changing an area as tax law. The executive is required by law to incorporate annually into the tax codes by decree new provisions required to keep the codes up-to-date. The simple fact that the tax codes are thus supplemented and changed by simple executive de-

42. See Pierre Debese, *Les déformations du droit civil par le droit de l'enregistrement* (Paris, 1945).

43. J. Laferrière and M. Waline, *Traité élémentaire de science et de législation financières* (1952), 550.

44. Pierre Bouzat, *Traité théorique et pratique de droit pénal* (1951), no. 531, p. 367; R. Vouin and J. Léauté, *Droit pénal et criminologie* (1956), 576.

cree makes evident the difference between them and the traditional codes.

Another difference which ought to be noted is that the direct tax code contains several appendices. Although taxes can be created only by legislation, the statutes often simply pose the general principles of the new tax created and delegate to administrative regulation the definition of the conditions in which these principles apply. For this reason, four appendices supplement the direct tax code: appendix I codifies the decrees in the form of regulations of public administration, appendix II the decrees of the Council of State, appendix III the simple decrees, and appendix IV the ministerial decisions supplementing the code. We should add that even with these appendices the codification of tax law is incomplete, since it does not include the many tax provisions regarded as of temporary application.

Thus, in spite of the existence of various codes, tax law in France, as in other modern countries, is a subject that is complex and difficult to master. In addition to the extreme instability of tax law, there is the fact that administrative practices are very important and often are hard to discover. Of course it is not up to the director or supervisor of direct or indirect taxes to exempt individuals from the payment of taxes they owe or to require them to pay taxes that they do not owe under the law. Nevertheless, these officials do have the right to grant extra time for payment of some taxes, for example, in the interest of the national economy, to avoid the closing of a business, or on the basis of the special facts of a particular case (such as the difficulty of submitting a declaration). They always have a considerable discretion concerning whether or not to levy an attachment on the taxpayer's property or employ other enforcement measures; and the administration can always be more or less strict in the enforcement of a tax. No matter how extensive a supervision the administrative courts may impose, they can only correct clear abuses. And their control is always unilateral in the sense that they can protect taxpayers from having to pay taxes they do not owe, but cannot compel the collection of taxes owed by a taxpaper where the administration delays its collection. Taxpayers' associations in France are not preoccupied with this latter aspect of the problem, and even if they wanted to force collection, the Council of State and other courts might well not allow them so to act.

For these various reasons, tax law shares the peculiarity of all administrative law that it is midway between administrative practice and law in the strict sense. Only its general principles are taught in the law schools. In order to solve a particular practical problem, one must consult a specialist who is up-to-date on the practices of the administration as well as on the law. Even books and journals are of dubious value here. The law is rapidly changing, as we have said, but in addition the authors of books and articles are usually heads of consulting firms and tax litigation offices, who sometimes conceal the professional secrets that insure them their clientele.

An attempt is being made currently to improve the situation by defining more precisely the limits of the tax authorities' discretion in applying tax laws and issuing directives in the exercise of this discretion. The government, however, is not eager to reveal these directives to the general public and resists all efforts to limit or define its powers in precise terms. It has good reasons for this reluctance, reasons both of general welfare and of equity in particular cases. Thus, it is doubtful whether much progress is possible in this area. No doubt tax law will retain a spirit of its own and continue to be productive of special rules, within the general framework of administrative law.

Let us conclude by noting a basic principle of tax law, that of strict interpretation of tax laws in favor of the taxpayer. According to this principle, the benefit of doubt should go to the individual in this area; he will not be taxed unless the law explicitly provides for it. Writers, nevertheless, have noted a divergence in the application of this principle between the case law of the Council of State, which applies it strictly, and that of the Court of Cassation[45] and the lower regular courts, which seem on the whole to be more sympathetic to the government's arguments. One can doubt whether the jurisdiction of the regular courts, once considered as better protecting the interests of the individual, is now advantageous to them. Here again we have evidence that the separation between the administrative and regular courts is, in the light of French tradition, something that favors the development of administrative law, rather than, as was once rather superficially thought, a threat to the rights of citizens.

45. In these areas, the Court of Cassation examines, contrary to its general practice, both questions of fact and questions of law.

VIII   Labor Law and Social Security Law

Labor law is a subject that arouses particular interest among lawyers at the present time in France, as in many other countries. The very expression *labor law* is new to France. When the Civil Code was drafted, no one thought about "labor law." There were workers and employees bound to their employers by contracts of employment. Other citizens worked independently and entered into contracts to sell their products and merchandise. It seemed sufficient if the law regulated ownership and a few essential kinds of contracts, such as sale and employment. This had been the position of Roman law and of the French Revolution. The Revolution had abolished the class structure of prerevolutionary France and intended to guarantee the triumph of individualism and exalt humanity by creating a classless society. For the future, there would be simple citizens; to set apart a class called laborers and give them a special legal status would be to continue the mistakes of the past. Thus, the law refused to recognize such a class or give it a special status. The demands of workers at the time were for legal equality through the suppression of guild-inspired restrictions of all kinds; this seemed enough.

The development of large-scale industry during the nineteenth century changed the fundamental problem. With industrialization and urbanization, a working class developed. Supported by a new class-consciousness, they attempted to organize themselves to secure an economic equality that did not follow automatically from the legal equality obtained earlier. Thanks to universal male suffrage, adopted in France in 1848, they were able to have legislation enacted gradually to satisfy their demands: recognition of the fact that legal equality was insufficient, abolition of prohibitions against workers compensating for their economic inferiority by organizing and taking collective action, establishment of a whole new body of legislation for the protection of workers. In this way a new area of law developed during the nineteenth century in response to the demands of the labor movement. It was law especially for industrial workers and was thus called industrial, or workers', legislation.

Subsequently, measures similar to those enacted for industrial workers were extended to other labor groups: commercial employees, agricultural workers, commercial representatives, artisans. The term *industrial legislation,* which had been incorporated in law school curricula, seemed unsatisfactory in two respects. As we have seen, the word *industrial* was outmoded. In addition, the word *legislation* was criticized, since a course or treatise could not be limited simply to legislation. On the one hand, one must discuss the context of the problem, such as the labor movement and the conditions and organization of labor in France, and on the other, one must go beyond legislation and discuss other factors contributing to the formation and development of labor law: for example, collective agreements, arbitral decisions, and international treaties. For these reasons, the term *labor law* replaced the term *industrial legislation.*

Now even the term *labor law* has become insufficient. The protective legislation originally developed in favor of salaried laborers has been extended to all who are, according to a current phrase, "economically weak" and has finally even gone beyond this group. Under the heading *labor law,* we now study measures that are increasingly independent of one's being salaried or even being a "worker." These measures are principally inspired by a preoccupation with social equality and the battle against poverty; they provide the citizen with some guarantees against various risks to which they are exposed and insure them compensation in particular cases. *Social law* has been proposed as a term to replace *labor law,* but the present tendency is more toward a division, so that labor law and social security law would be separately studied.

With respect to these new areas of law, we should ask the same question we did for commercial law. Are they simply areas in which both civil and administrative law have an influence and in which certain writers tend to specialize because of their complexity and inherent interest? Or are labor law and social security law today more than this? Do they have their own principles and methods and a spirit to distinguish them from the civil and administrative law from which they originally developed?

Aside from the inclusion in labor law of numerous rules of public law origin, it seems clear that labor law has a very real and considerable originality with respect to civil law, so that one can speak of the autonomy of this branch of law, or if one wishes to avoid so sharp a break, of its particularity. All labor law specialists now insist on this particularity.[46]

History supports this view. It was only in the nineteenth century, in a period of individualism, that writers began to assert the full subordination of labor law to private law. In prerevolutionary France, it was otherwise. The draftsmen of the code found only the most cursory developments in Pothier, their traditional source of inspiration. Labor law was not of particular interest to civilists and was not discussed in their treatises. The best treatment of labor law was to be found in Loyseau's treatise on feudal relationships and his emphasis is on police regulations rather than civil law principles. The personal relations created by the employment relationship were governed more by moral standards than by law, since the employer's authority over his workers, employees, and apprentices was similar to that of parents over children, a domestic authority in a sphere where the law had no role.[47]

The French Revolution, which sought to abolish all special privileges, thought it could regulate the relations between citizens without regard for the social class to which they belonged. According to the Declaration of the Rights of Man and of the Citizen, all men are born free and equal in law, and so it would have seemed illegitimate to create a special status for "laborers." To lawyers nurtured on the individualistic political ideology of the eighteenth-century philosophers, the principle of the freedom of contract seemed sufficient to guarantee the rights of laborers.

From the middle of the nineteenth century, Marxist criticism, the validity of which is indisputable on this point, denounced the theoretical nature of the political equality achieved by the French Revolution. It showed that this equality was but a trap unless it was accompanied by some economic equality. In addition, the development of industry and commerce, due to the capitalist impetus, had upset the economic and social conditions in which the working world had

46. See particularly the excellent article by Paul Durand, "Le particularisme du droit du travail," in *Droit Social* (1945), 298 ff. Also see Georges Levasseur, "Evolution, caractères et tendances du droit du travail," in *Le droit privé au milieu du XXᵉ siècle* (*Etudes offertes à Georges Ripert*) (1950), II, 444 ff.; A. Brun and H. Galland, *Droit du travail* (1958), 170 ff.

47. See the Prussian Code of 1794 (*Allgemeines Landrecht*), where the master-and-servant relationship is dealt with in the chapter on the family.

to live. As mass production became necessary, it introduced, along with industrial concentration and urbanization, the growth of the proletariat. As in prerevolutionary France, although for different reasons, it is essential today that the special context of labor law be recognized.

It is artificial to consider the relations between management and labor within the individualistic framework of the Civil Code. They cannot be seen simply as contractual relations between individuals. One cannot ignore the power of capitalism, the development of labor unions, or the large business organizations whose existence depends on the labor contracts thus concluded.

French civil law, incorporated into a code more than 150 years ago, is based on individualistic principles from which all judicial efforts have been unable to free it. But labor law requires that legal relationships be viewed from a collective point of view;[48] in this way it appears as a product of the socialist spirit. The civilist thinks in terms of individuals' rights and obligations, while the labor law specialist considers more the status of particular classes of persons.[49] The very idea of status is repugnant to the individualist spirit of the Civil Code.[50] This tension is accentuated by the fact that laborers often regard the Civil Code as a bourgeois code, interested primarily in established fortunes.[51] Such persons are little inclined to share the admiration of lawyers for this code, in which the contract of employment is sandwiched into three articles between lease and bailment. They ask if the dignity of labor and the laborer can be insured in a code that speaks disdainfully of "working men," as they are called in article 1799, which refuses to give the same credence to the word of one who sells his services as they do to his master,[52]

48. Levasseur, *op. cit.*, 462 ff.

49. Georges Scelle, *Le droit ouvrier* (2nd ed.; 1928). The statute on labor accidents applies independently of whether or not there exists a valid contract of employment. A theory of risks, distinct from that found in the civil law, is tending to become established in labor law, particularly in cases where the enterprise has ceased to function. See Durand, *op. cit.*

50. See R. Savatier, *Les métamorphoses économiques et sociales du droit civil d'aujourd'hui* (2nd ed.; 1952), *passim*, particularly 44 ff. and above all Chap. 11 ("La socialisation des contrats de travaux humains"), 227 ff.

51. *Ibid.*, 197, 228.

52. *Code Civil*, art. 1781 (repealed August 2, 1868): "The master is believed on his word concerning the security deposit given, the payment of the salary for years past, and the payments made for the current year."

and which considers manual labor, a "mechanical art," the proper destiny of an adulterine child.[53]

Other fundamental principles of labor law also contradict the spirit of the private law code. Civil law with time has been able to formulate rules that give the most equitable solution to problems in the great majority of cases and for this reason leaves little room, at least apparently, for considerations of equity. It keeps to a strict minimum the cases where equity can come in and, upsetting the security of legal relations, change the effect of a civil law rule. Labor law, on the other hand, has to solve new problems, those created by a new kind of economy based on mass production and a new kind of society, which includes an acutely class-conscious proletariat. It has not yet been able to incorporate equity into its formal rules, and thus equitable considerations are given freer play than they are in civil law.

Another, related aspect of labor law that distinguishes it from civil law is its very birth and growth processes. The civil law was formed so long ago that one no longer thinks of its formation. Although it is actively and constantly evolving, this evolution is concealed by fictions. The courts pretend that they are always interpreting the law, and legal writers speak of finding the true meaning of legal rules. Labor law is still too underdeveloped to allow such pious fictions. It is clear that here one must create, make something new. One cannot rest on a tradition that is either inexistent or rejected today. For this reason, decrees, judicial decisions, even contracts take on a different appearance. The rule set forth by article 5 of the Civil Code, forbidding judges to decide cases submitted to them as if they were stating regulations, is sometimes set aside in labor law. Collective agreements are very much like regulations issued by public authorities and sometimes look almost like legislation. Decrees and regulations of the public authorities are proclaimed within a framework of very broad powers conferred by law.

The civilist is thus shocked by various accepted labor law rules. He does not regard labor law as a branch of civil law; rather he considers it a new branch of the law that has been developed in oppo-

---

53. *Code Civil*, art. 764: "Where the father or the mother of an adulterine child has secured his training in a mechanical art, or where one of them has provided him with an annuity for life, the child can bring no claim against their succession."

sition to the principles of civil law. It is significant that the Commission for the Reform of the Civil Code had excluded labor law from its consideration.

The autonomy of labor law is also made manifest by a tendency to set up autonomous courts. Labor law requires special courts and its own procedure.[54] This evolution reached its climax in 1936 with the establishment, outside of the regular judicial hierarchy and the administrative courts, of a completely autonomous Supreme Court of Arbitration, acting as a court of last resort and giving decisions which, in addition to being judgments, were often actual regulatory decisions. This court was abolished in 1939 and has never since been reactivated. Today it is only at the lower level that there are labor courts, bearing various names, sometimes supervised by the regular courts, sometimes by the administrative courts: for example, labor boards (*conseils de prud'hommes*) and the social security court of first instance. The new Supreme Court of Arbitration created by the law of February 11, 1950, has no compulsory jurisdiction and is a very different thing from the court that existed before the war.[55]

Just as in commercial law, finally, international conventions attempt to establish certain basic principles of labor law on a worldwide basis and are a factor distinguishing labor law from civil law, which retains a more national character.[56] France has signed and ratified many of the conventions that have been proposed to the world community by the International Labor Organization.[57]

In 1901 a commission was set up to elaborate a "labor and social welfare code." [58] It adopted an organization according to which the new code would include seven parts: international labor conventions; labor regulations; professional groups; courts, conciliation,

54. Durand and Levasseur, in the articles previously cited, show that the Supreme Court of Arbitration was able, during the short period in which it functioned, to elaborate doctrines particular to labor law, accepting the solutions that the labor boards had tried to establish but that had been overruled by the Court of Cassation, which insisted on maintaining the principles of civil law. Levasseur notes in this connection (p. 467) that the judges for the Supreme Court of Arbitration were recruited primarily from among public law lawyers.

55. Concerning this court, see Brun and Galland, *op. cit.*, 942–43.

56. See *ibid.*, 87 ff.

57. Of the 104 draft conventions prepared by the ILO between 1919 and 1956, France has ratified 73. See *ibid.*, 104.

58. The present title is Labor Code (*Code de travail*). There is, in addition, a code of maritime labor (*Law of December 13, 1926*). Agricultural labor is dealt with in Book VII of the Rural Code (*Code rural, 1955*).

and arbitration; workers' insurance; welfare; and assistance. The first four parts of this plan were promulgated by the legislature in 1910 (Part I), 1912 (Part II), 1924 (Part IV), and 1927 (Part III). A proposal for the last three parts was rejected in 1929. In its present state, this code is severely criticized.[59] The limit of the mandate of the drafting commission was to organize the existing legislation without revision. Some laws were left out of the code but still remain in force even in the apparently codified areas. Many new laws, not part of the code, have been enacted, while others modifying the code have been uncomfortably accommodated within its framework. Articles appear throughout the code with awkward numeration (e.g., in Part I: articles 31a, 31x, 31vg). A decree-law of May 20, 1955, provides for the drafting of a revised labor code to include by "consolidation" all texts not at present included and to modify their form. This work has not yet been completed.

This experience with labor law tends to prove that codification is feasible only in a given area of the law at a particular point in time, when conditions are favorable, the subject in question has been developed, and it has achieved a satisfactory level of stability and cohesiveness. Labor law did not satisfy those conditions, and the attempt to codify it was doomed to failure.

Today much of labor law is public law. Although social security legislation cannot be considered part of administrative law, it does not seem that its rules could be set forth in a code of the private law type. Rather, we must consolidate all of the various texts in the area, as is projected for many of the specialized areas of administrative law.[60] In reality, administrative practice is as important to know as are the legislative dispositions, so that a code that simply collects the latter would not satisfy the public's needs.

59. See P. Durand and R. Jaussaud, *Traité de droit du travail* (1947), I, no. 98, pp. 117 ff.
60. See above, pp. 130, 134.

IX   Law of Evidence and Procedure

Procedural rules were of first importance in the development of Roman law. The history of Roman law is the history first of the actions, then of the formula with all the improvements and subtleties that were gradually incorporated in it by legal technique. Slowly, however, things changed, with the progress of legal science in the late Roman empire and in the modern legal systems of Roman inspiration. From the actions, interdicts, injunctions, and various other procedural remedies of Roman law, lawyers inferred the existence of rights and on the basis of these established new outlines for their system. The court action is no longer regarded as the most essential aspect of the problem; the possibility of going to court has come to be regarded as just one of the consequences normally attached to legal rights.

The universities have pushed this evolution even further—in our opinion, too far. For today's French lawyer, the law is something far above procedure, and procedure is but a servant of the law, useful for the practical application and implementation of the principles of justice. The work of legal scholars is primarily to discover and define legal principles. It is for the practitioner to insure their application and create the instruments necessary to this end. In the French conception law is an ideal, and we accept the risk that this ideal may be ineffective because of insufficient contact with day-to-day practice. We regard the risk as justified by the greater possibility, when procedural problems are ignored, of seeing the basic policies involved and promoting progress. Legal practice always lags somewhat behind, and sometimes even resists progress, but will finally give in to the force of principles and create the instruments necessary for their implementation. Progress will finally be accepted by the practitioners for the common good, but the way must be prepared by the thinkers of the legal profession.

This approach has its advantages. But the danger is obvious: theories can go astray and descend into idle speculation completely lacking in practical value. Theoretical lawyers are in danger of creating an ideal legal system that is of no relevance to practitioners. French law may have resisted this danger better than most, but it has not been completely saved. French procedural and evidentiary law appear relatively underdeveloped.

With respect to procedure, there are no general treatises. We study separately civil, criminal, and administrative procedure. In the area of execution of judgments, an additional distinction must be made between civil and commercial law, since bankruptcy exists in France only for businessmen. The jurisdiction of French courts in litigation involving foreign law and the enforcement of foreign judgments are studied in connection with private international law.

Treatises dealing exclusively with procedure exist only for civil procedure. Criminal and administrative procedure are dealt with, more or less adequately, in the general criminal and administrative law treatises. And even the manuals or treatises on civil procedure are not devoted exclusively to this subject.[61] They describe the whole French court structure, and include the rules defining the jurisdiction of various courts. They also present the general theory of court actions, describe the procedure to be followed before various courts, and finally discuss the possible appeals that can be taken against judicial decisions. Sometimes they deal also with the enforcement of judgments, but more often this is left to specialized works.[62]

In the law schools, civil procedure is studied in a single one-semester third-year course; criminal procedure is dealt with in another one-semester course; and administrative procedure is almost totally ignored. Law students do not really expect to learn procedure in the university. It is implicitly agreed that the subject can only be learned in practice. Efforts are seldom made to present legal questions from the procedural point of view.

In this area, practitioners do not use the works written by theoreticians, which are few and always out of date. Rather there are compilations especially prepared for them: repertories, formularies, *jurisclasseurs*, and practice manuals written by legal practitioners. These works are little known in the law schools, where it is even unusual for the libraries to purchase them. Procedure is an area

61. The professor of civil procedure at the Faculty of Law in Paris, M. Solus, has properly entitled his course *Droit judiciaire privé* ("private law procedure").

62. Unlike Swiss law, execution of judgments is dealt with in France as part of the study of procedure and not as part of administrative law. See, however, the differences noted in the preceding paragraph.

where there is a clear divorce in France between the law schools and practice.

This divorce is clearly undesirable. The specific disposition of a case is often explained by its procedural context, and one cannot properly evaluate judicial decisions without understanding this context. Thus scholars sometimes express surprise that a court, in a particular case, did not invoke a particular theory or argue in a particular way that would have led to a better solution to the case than was given by the court. In such criticism, they often forget that the court is not free to consider the case just as it likes. It is bound by the positions of the parties and cannot give a remedy not requested by them, even though it may think this would be a better solution. Much criticism of the courts is misplaced; it should be addressed rather to the representatives or advocates of the parties. The judge does his best, but he is not free to consider a case as teachers and scholars often do.

The law of evidence is probably even more neglected in France than that of procedure. Whereas procedure maintains a certain independence with respect to civil law and is dealt with especially within the framework of criminal and administrative law, evidence is never given more than a chapter in each area. The expression *law of evidence* does not even exist in France, and one must go back a hundred years to find a book that deals with the subject as a whole.

To make matters worse, discussions of civil law evidence are divided so that admissibility of evidence is covered in civil law treatises, while the manner and procedure for submitting evidence are dealt with in connection with civil procedure. With respect to admissibility, there are no general rules.

Unless the contrary is expressly provided, one has to be satisfied, for better or worse, to treat as the "general law of evidence," i.e., the rules generally applicable to evidentiary problems, the Civil Code articles concerning the proof of obligations (articles 1341 ff.). The situation is still worse and more confused with respect to administrative law, where the general treatises say nothing at all about evidentiary problems.[63] And in the criminal area, rules of evidence

63. See, however, Paul Pactet, *Essai d'une théorie de la preuve devant la juridiction administrative* (1952).

seem to be extraordinarily imprecise and flexible.[64] Finally, proof of foreign law is neglected and sometimes even omitted from treatises on private international law, although it could seem vain to construct theories for the application of one foreign law or another if the proof in court of foreign law is not acceptably organized.

How can we explain this underdevelopment in the law of evidence and the apparent lack of interest in France in such a fundamental area? Just as for procedure, one might blame the overly theoretical approach of French lawyers. They are less interested in the administration of justice, which raises evidentiary questions, than in the law itself, which they consider without an overriding preoccupation with its application. This explanation, however, is incomplete. The indifference of French lawyers to evidentiary questions is explained basically, without doubt, by the importance in French law of the principle of the judge's intuitive conviction (*principe d'intime conviction*).[65]

The principle of the judge's intuitive conviction, as it is understood in France, diminishes the importance of many evidentiary questions. This is particularly so in the area of obligations, the heart of the civil law. The requirement of documentary evidence that the law imposes in various circumstances is without any great practical importance, since the absence of such documentary evidence where required *ad probationem* is rarely decisive. And why discuss at length the idea of "presumption," when a judge can merely state that there are various relevant presumptions on which he has based his decision? [66] The rule of Civil Code article 2279, according to which "with respect to movables, possession is equivalent to title," similarly seems to make evidentiary questions unimportant with respect to movable property. Evidentiary questions assume real importance only where the principle of the judge's intuitive conviction is not fully accepted, as in the area of civil status.

To have a complete picture of French evidence law, two addi-

64. Twenty-eight pages (721–48) are given to this subject in Bouzat, *op. cit.* See, however, the article by J. Patarin, "Le particularisme de la théorie des preuves en droit pénal," in Stefani (comp.), *Quelques aspects de l'autonomie du droit pénal,* 7–76.
65. One should also note that, in contrast with the common law, there is in France no jury whose task needs to be defined or action directed.
66. See, however, R. Decottignies, *Les présomptions en droit privé* (1950).

tional factors must be understood. First, one must remember that French civil law imposes formal requirements for the valid conclusion of various kinds of contracts. These requirements may fulfill the same function as evidentiary rules do in other countries. And second, with respect to criminal law one must consider the French notion of the criminal trial. Foreign jurists are sometimes shocked by the way advocates and prosecutors argue in criminal cases. They introduce factors which may seem completely irrelevant to the case: for instance, background of the accused, previous criminal record, and family situation. Are these factors really irrelevant? Frenchmen, rightly or wrongly, think not. They feel that it is more just to judge the individual on the whole of his conduct than on the particular circumstances of the violation in question. This may insure a more just disposition in some cases and a less just disposition in others, but individual liberty does not seem to be endangered by the French system. The system can be criticized more for softening the penal system and allowing guilty individuals to escape a deserved punishment than for wrongly convicting innocent persons.

Thus the difference in the development or atrophy of evidence law seems to result not from a greater or lesser technical perfection of the law. Rather it reflects different policy decisions and different conceptions of the best way for the legal system to achieve justice.

Procedure and evidence have been neglected by French scholars, but it should be noted that this aspect of French law has not been completely ignored. It is the practitioners, more than the scholars, who deal with it, and one is indebted to them for real progress in the area, particularly in the last few years.[67]

French procedural law also can proudly boast of having been one of the first to solve a fundamental problem of justice by facilitating access to the courts for the poor. French legislation as early as 1851 organized legal assistance to indigents. Legal aid took further steps forward in laws enacted in 1901 and 1907. While the situation is still far from ideal, legal assistance is made available under conditions infinitely more liberal than in most other countries. In France, a greater effort has been made to realize in practice the democratic principle that the courts must be accessible to all.

67. See H. Solus, "Les réformes de procédure civile: Etapes franchies et vues d'avenir," *Le droit privé français au milieu du XXe siècle* (*Etudes offertes à Georges Ripert*) (1950), I, 193 ff.

The question preoccupying French jurists today in the procedural area is the enforcement of judgments. In many cases in France, the execution of judgments is, to an excessive degree, left up to the good faith of the person against whom the judgment was given. Over the last twenty years, the government has too often neglected its responsibility to require the unwilling to comply with court decisions. This failure causes deep concern among French jurists. It is true that the Council of State can correct it by requiring the state to pay damages in such cases, but this remedy is insufficient, both in itself and because of the delay and expense involved. This situation must be remedied if the prestige and supremacy of the law are to be maintained in France.

PART SIX

Sources and Methods
of French Law

Differences in sources and methods of research between the French and other legal systems have been emphasized by comparative law scholars. Many interesting studies have been published in this area as books, sections of books, and law review articles. But the subject has still not been as fully exhausted as one would expect. Two major criticisms can be leveled at this literature. First, it has frequently considered the subject, especially in early times, from a rather theoretical point of view. Second, with respect to French law, it has been concerned almost exclusively with private law, and has given insufficient attention to differences in methods and sources between various branches of the law within France itself.

Our primary aim here is to counter the second of these shortcomings. For many authors, the essential characteristic of French law, with respect to its sources and methods, is that it is codified. This characterization, however, is only partly true. No French law was codified until 165 years ago, and still today all of administrative law remains uncodified. And within the codified areas, methods of interpretation differ sharply, particularly as between private and criminal law. As we have already noted, labor law, too, has considerable distinctiveness in this respect. It is, therefore, by looking at the various branches of French law that we should study its sources and methods. Private law can be but a starting point, since principles accepted there are frequently inapplicable to other branches.

The other major shortcoming of the comparative legal literature is that often it is overly theoretical. During the exegetic period, the impression was often given that French judges had no creative role, that their function was simply to apply more or less automatically provisions of codes and statutes. More recently, authors have reacted against this oversimplification, which exaggerated the contrast between French law and the common law. It has indeed become fashionable to praise the creative role of the judiciary, a role which it is hard to reconcile with the once-alleged strictness of code provisions. The reason for the reversal is obvious. Over the last fifty years, the western world has undergone such upheavals that profound changes in the law were everywhere required. More or less consciously, legal scholars and judges of every country have modified their views on procedures and methods of reasoning. Flexibility of the law has come to be stressed, whereas a hundred years ago stability and certainty were generally the supreme values.

In France as in other countries, it is difficult to describe the situation precisely.[1] In fact, there are opposing tendencies. Some maintain the traditional approach and refuse to admit that times have changed. Others are more progressive and apply new methods. Methods are likely to differ from court to court, and even among individual jurists, each of whom has his own peculiar temperament. We can do no more than attempt to analyze the present situation, pointing out what appears to us, here and there, to constitute its dominant tendency. The reader must remember that mathematical precision is impossible and that the attitudes and intuition of each lawyer are of considerable significance. This latter fact is ascribable as much to differences of policy as to differences of technique. It seems that we have not yet arrived at the end of the evolution that has, since the turn of the century, profoundly transformed established principles and practices of judicial activity.

With these preliminary observations, we may now enter upon the study of our subject. We shall look at the different sources of French law one after another in order to discuss their respective importance and the role and methods of interpretation of each. Among these sources we shall first consider legislation (*la loi*), including in this expression not only statutes (in the formal sense) and codes, but also all the various executive orders. In accordance with French tradition, after legislation we shall consider custom. We shall then endeavor to define the role and characteristics of judicial decisions (*la jurisprudence*) and of scholarly writing (*la doctrine*). Finally we shall see to what extent solutions to which the sources and methods previously analyzed and described seem to lead may sometimes be set aside by fundamental principles of law. We shall examine the effects of equity, public policy, good morals, and the notion of general principles developed in administrative law.

1. For France, see the papers and discussions on statutory interpretation in *Travaux de l'Association Henri-Capitant pour la culture juridique française* (1949), V, particularly 61 ff., 85 ff.

I   Legislation

Legislation dominates French law. Its importance
is particularly great in private and criminal law and makes France
indeed a "country of written law." [2] Since the beginning of the
nineteenth century we have had the five Napoleonic codes, each of
which aspires to regulate its subject comprehensively: Civil Code
(1804), Code of Civil Procedure (1806), Commercial Code
(1807), Penal Code (1810), Code of Criminal Instruction (1811).
These codes of course no longer provide the exclusive regulation in
their several areas; special statutes have been enacted to amend and
supplement them.[3]

Judicial decisions and scholarly writing also play a considerable
role in these same fields, and the importance of custom must not be
overlooked. But these other sources remain secondary, at least in
theory. On the surface, only legislation counts as a source of French
private and criminal law. The principle is particularly clear in
criminal law, where the adage of *nullum crimen, nulla poena sine
lege* is solemnly affirmed and reaffirmed. Only a statute can define
a crime and prescribe the punishment for its perpetrator.[4] But the
principle appears to triumph almost as completely in private law;
judges in the regular courts are statutorily required to state the
grounds for their decisions and hardly ever fail to base them on
legislative texts. They seldom rely on other sources of law. In reading their opinions, one therefore gets the impression that in both
private and criminal law, legislation is the sole source of legal rules.

The situation is different in public law. Many opinions of the
Council of State rely for their justification upon no legislative pro-
vision at all. And no code exists covering all administrative law.
Nevertheless, legislation remains an important source of administra-

2. The term "country of written law" (*pays de droit écrit*) is used in another
context to describe those parts of prerevolutionary France, prior to the Napoleonic
codification, where Roman law was applied; its opposite is then "country of customary law" (*pays de coutume*).
3. The Code of Criminal Instruction was replaced in 1958 by a new Code of
Criminal Procedure.
4. Note, however, that under the Constitution of 1958 minor offenses are
within the jurisdiction of the executive branch's regulatory power.

tive law. A body of special statutes, supplemented by regulations and decrees, deals with many administrative law matters. In tax law, a principle prevails similar to that in criminal law, that no tax or duty may be levied without statutory authority. Even in areas not regulated by statute, the situation is similar to that which existed in the territories of written law of pre-Napoleonic France with respect to private law. Although there is no compilation binding as legislation, the private law codes are regarded as an expression of natural law and equity and thus play a significant role; their principles are rejected in administrative law only for good reason. Thus, it is accurate to call France a country of written law only if it is well recognized that the expression must be understood in two quite different senses, depending on whether one is considering private law and criminal law or administrative law.

France is a country of written law. The essential significance of this expression is that to a French jurist, statutes appear to be not so much an occasional manifestation of legislative omnipotence as the normal mode of expressing the law. Enacted law is not opposed to immemorial custom or reason. On the contrary, for a Frenchman legislation embodies reason. Custom, incapable of adapting itself to social change, varying without apparent justification from region to region, seems inherently irrational. The Napoleonic codes are in no way a product of governmental arbitrariness. Because they were created to satisfy the demands of the school of natural law, it was at first thought that they should incorporate the very principles of reason. Drafted by experienced practitioners, the French codes incorporated natural law theories only insofar as they could safely be admitted to correct and improve the solid tradition which remained their basis. On the morrow of the codifications, no one doubted that the codes were a step forward. The enthusiasm with which almost all continental Europe, then Latin America and the countries of the Orient, accepted or imitated them, has strengthened the French in this opinion. Even today French lawyers and students consider it obvious that codification means improvement; legislation is a source of law superior to custom. They cannot conceive how developed countries can fail to codify their law. They rarely question why French administrative law has not been codified. Where the question is considered, it is answered in terms of an inferiority in the administrative law caused by its insufficient maturity. In criminal law, particularly, codification is considered a decisive improvement in that it allowed us to establish the principle of *nullum crimen, nulla poena sine lege.* In France one has difficulty conceiving how individual freedom and security can be insured where criminal law is uncodified.

Let us now turn to the question of statutory interpretation. Here a few distinctions are essential. First there are, of course, distinctions according to the area of law considered. Principles of interpretation cannot be the same in private law, where the judge is accustomed, and feels somewhat obliged, to tie his decision to a statutory text, and in administrative law, where he does not feel the same obligation. In addition, specific principles of interpretation exist in such fields as criminal and tax law in the interests of liberty and the rights of property. Alongside this first order of distinction and in combination with it, it is necessary to make distinctions from another point of view. The word *interpretation* is sufficiently imprecise and equivocal that one applies it in reality to several types of reasoning.

Interpretation of a statutory provision means in the first place the search for what its terms literally signify or can signify in themselves, in an objective sense, apart from any quest for the intention of its author or any consideration of social utility or moral justification. This first type of interpretation is sometimes called literal interpretation. It raises no difficulties. The first job that any lawyer faces is to discover what the statutory text means or may mean by analyzing the terms used by the legislator. Literal interpretation of the statutory text can lead the lawyer to three possible conclusions: (1) here is how the text settles my case; (2) here are two solutions between which I am going to have to choose; or (3) the text does not solve my problem.

Logical interpretation, which we now reach, stands back and looks at the legislative provision in its context and in relation to the whole body of rules that forms the national legal system. Its role will vary according to which of the three possible conclusions was reached through literal interpretation.

In the first hypothesis, literal interpretation dictates one solution. Is it possible, through logical interpretation, to decide that the legislator has expressed himself poorly? The solution required by his words is so contrary to the logic of the system that this is clearly not the solution he intended. In private law, and in the more flexible administrative law, this use of logical interpretation is generally conceded, although it must be rigorously established that the legislator has misdrafted his text. Criminal and tax law exclude this possibility, because they are more rigid. The poorly drafted provision will simply not be enforced. Prosecutors will not request application of the letter of the rule, and if they did the courts would refuse it. And on the other side, except in absolutely shocking cases, judges will refuse to enforce the provision as it would have read if the legislator had correctly expressed his will.

In the second hypothesis, literal interpretation leaves a choice between several solutions, all equally acceptable literally. Here logical interpretation obviously may and must be utilized. A judge cannot refuse to render a decision under pretext of the law's ambiguity (article 4, Civil Code). He must choose between the possible meanings of the statute. Consideration of the provision's statutory context and of the whole French legal system will be a principal determinant in his choice. And this is true in all branches of the law.

In the third hypothesis, literal interpretation leads to the conclusion that the text does not solve the question at issue. The question then is whether, logically speaking, the text can still have a decisive effect. Can the interpreter use the text to argue by analogy or *a contrario*, considering the logic of the legal system as a whole?

Here, criminal and tax law are special. Logical interpretation can be used in these areas so long as it functions in favor of the accused or the taxpayer. But analogical and extensive interpretation are excluded where their use would create a new crime, tax, or duty in conditions not precisely foreseen by the statute. This principle is constantly proclaimed and has found numerous practical applications. We must, however, note that in practice it has not always been respected. Thus, the provisions punishing theft have been applied by judges to the "theft of electricity," although this involves no "carrying away of the thing of another," which in terms of Penal Code article 379 is the very essence of theft. E. Garçon has noted a considerable obstacle to the application of the principle of strict interpretation of criminal and tax statutes[5] in the administration of

5. Emile Garçon, "De la méthode du droit criminel," in *Les méthodes juridiques,* lectures given at the Collège Libre des Sciences Sociales in 1910 (1911), 202 ff.

the criminal law by magistrates who receive essentially a private law education and often judge both civil and criminal cases. It is difficult for them to reject in criminal cases the methods of reasoning with which they are familiar and which they apply daily in civil cases.

In other areas of the law, the principles accepted in France are quite different. Especially in private law, France deserves to be called a country of written law precisely because lawyers constantly utilize the varied techniques of logical interpretation. The French lawyer does not just consider texts literally. He seeks from their spirit, grouping, and combination the very principles of French law, which he then uses to settle all legal disputes. This is why judicial decisions are always attached to one or more legislative texts.

Although no codes exist for administrative law, the situation there is fundamentally the same, except that logical interpretation of statutes is guided not by rules of law formulated by the legislator, but by unwritten rules of law. Logical interpretation comes as naturally, however, to administrative law lawyers as to those of the civil law. Statutes are to be applied in the spirit as well as in the letter. They provide the jurist with principles, the bases for his reasoning, and not simply with solutions for the precise questions to which their texts formally and directly apply.

For logical interpretation, should we distinguish between codes and other statutes? It is tempting to think so when we see authors speak, as they often do, of the *droit commun* ("common law") found in the codes and when they refer to various statutes as "laws of exception." It is hard to answer simply the question thus posed. As a principle, certainly no qualitative difference exists between codes and other statutes. The designation *statutes of exception* given by writers to some laws indicates, rather than a characteristic of the laws, disapproval by the writer, or is designed to emphasize that they are temporary, applicable only in exceptional circumstances, for the duration of a crisis which the writer hopes will be brief. If writers often disapprove of these statutes, it is because their solutions and spirit are often hard to reconcile with the solutions and spirit of the traditional law expressed in the codes. Thus, apart from any ill will on their part, judges have difficulty in reconciling these statutes with the codes and developing principles from them as they have developed principles from the codes. The necessary synthesis takes time. Repeated legislative action may be necessary. A tendency may persist for years to consider new statutes as abnormal appendages to the French legal system, to restrict their scope, applicability, and effects—in short to treat them as statutes of exception. Nevertheless, this approach is ascribable solely to policy, which of course can never be dissociated from law. On the strictly legal level it has no basis. The concept of a statute of exception, which as such should receive a restrictive interpretation, is not a legal concept.

A third method of statutory interpretation is the historical method, which consists of reasoning from a statute's background and from the purpose of its sponsor. To what need was the statute supposed to respond? What reform was it intended to achieve? Use of this method and the recourse to legislative reports that it implies are considered legitimate and natural in France. It is particularly common where a judge must interpret an international treaty or a statute implementing such a treaty.[6] International conventions often are accompanied by explanatory reports discussing questions treated ambiguously or omitted from the treaty. French lawyers consult these reports as a matter of course.[7]

Recourse to legislative reports is also accepted for the interpretation of ordinary statutes. Current judicial opinions show that this method of interpretation is frequently used. Historical interpretation is subject, however, to certain limitations imposed by law and by factual circumstances. In the criminal and tax fields its use is not authorized if it would lead to unfavorable results for the accused or the taxpayer; the principle of strict interpretation of penal and tax laws opposes it. In other fields, historical interpretation is possible only where the origin of the statute in question is known, and this is not always the case. Many décrets-lois and ordonnances have been promulgated without any background materials that can be consulted. Conversely, the legislative reports on a statute that has

6. Conventions and treaties that have been signed and ratified by the French government are usually published in the *Journal officiel*. They then have the force of law by themselves. There are, however, exceptions to this practice. There are cases where, for a variety of reasons, a special French law is promulgated to give effect to an international convention or treaty. This happens when "reservations" to the convention on the part of the French government have to be incorporated into it and also when the international convention in question is the result of private initiative rather than a convention between states.

7. For the contrary position of English law, see H. C. Gutteridge, *Comparative Law* (2nd ed.; 1949), 108.

been discussed at length in Parliament may be confused. An opinion expressed by a member of Parliament is not a reliable basis upon which one can establish the purpose of a legislative provision. Judges will not feel obliged to consider it. Finally, to search for the intention of the authors in old statutes, particularly the Napoleonic codes, can be pointless. A historical argument in favor of a particular interpretation of the statute can of course have some effect. But in many cases, it will fail to convince the judge. He may prefer to disregard the historic interpretation in his decision. He will prefer to use a method of interpretation based on the idea that statutes change in their meaning over time, since they have to be applied under today's conditions and not under yesterday's. This is a fourth method of statutory interpretation used by French lawyers, called "teleological interpretation."

Teleological interpretation aims to give a statute the meaning, consistent with literal analysis and not conflicting too violently with the logic of the system, that best corresponds to a contemporary view of social welfare and justice. Proponents of this method of interpretation maintain that no statutory text has a meaning that is fixed once and for all when it is enacted.[8] Statutory meaning changes with time. Is it not the same with literary and artistic works, which people "interpret" anew from time to time? Besides, today's legislator, by maintaining an old law in force, adopts it to some extent, so that one can legitimately consider, apart from any intention its authors may have had, the way in which today's legislator would wish to see it interpreted and applied, in light of his conceptions of justice and social utility. The method of interpretation thus described is the antithesis of historical interpretation. The latter seeks to explain texts by their history and past; the former seeks their justification in the effects they will produce and, therefore, in the future. It considers essentially the social objective of the statute and has thus been called teleological interpretation.[9]

8. See H. Capitant, *Introduction à l'étude du droit civil* (5th ed.; 1929), 95 ff., particularly the passages that he cites from Regelsberger. Also see Gustav Radbruch, "Arten der Interpretation," in *Recueil d'études sur les sources du droit en l'honneur de François Geny* (1934), II, 217 ff., and H. Lévy-Bruhl, "Esquisse d'une théorie des sources du droit," *L'année sociologique* (1953).

9. See, particularly, L. Josserand, *Essais de téléologie juridique*. These essays fill two lively volumes: *De l'esprit des droits et de leur relativité (Théorie dite de l'abus des droits)* (2nd ed.; 1939); and *Les mobiles dans les actes juridiques en droit privé* (1928).

The abstract concepts of codes and statutes have always contained the seeds of an interpretation based on social objectives. The legislator has not defined public policy, good morals, equity, or fault. Judges must decide how to interpret these expressions in litigation before them, and this determination will be made when the judge pronounces judgment, taking into consideration the requirements of social welfare and justice. This is especially true since no judicial precedent can, in such an area, limit the judge's discretion and oblige him to see things today as he may have seen them yesterday. We refer here to what we said above about the notion of the rule of law prevailing in France and also to what we will say below concerning the roles of custom and judicial opinions in French law.

Even beyond these abstract concepts, the interpretation of which is openly accepted as being subject to change over time, teleological interpretation of legislative texts has without question always had some effect. This is surely so at least where historical interpretation is of no help and literal and logical interpretation leave the judge a choice of solutions. The judge, in such a case, will obviously sanction the solution he thinks best and most just. Further, one can be sure that judges have always given some subtle weight to such arguments, for example, by refusing to give full value to historical and logical arguments where they conflict with their social judgment.

Until the end of the nineteenth century, however, the process was used with prudence; it was kept in disguise. No one considered setting it up as a principle of interpretation or openly proclaiming the necessity of abandoning historical interpretation. Then suddenly at the turn of the century, a doctrinal movement began to assert the merits and insist on the legitimacy of teleological interpretation. The names of R. Saleilles, F. Geny, and L. Josserand are most commonly associated with this movement in France, but the movement was international in scope; it existed across Europe, and in Germany produced the school of free law (*Freies Recht*). E. Huber in Switzerland finally even secured legislative sanction for it in the Civil Code of 1907 and his remarkable *Exposé des motifs*.

Why this sudden explosion? Several factors account for it. First, the French codes were aging; the need to overhaul them was evident as they reached the age of a hundred, in a society whose economic structure had profoundly changed, and where democratic forces were exerting renewed pressures. Other important factors were the change of political ideas following the establishment of the Third Republic and the development of administrative law. The principle of separation of powers was still proclaimed as essential to democracy, but it was understood differently than in the past. The unpleasant memory of the prerevolutionary French courts had dimmed and there was a disposition to broaden the judiciary's role; the judges of the republic were no longer regarded as a privileged class. The idea that judges could assist legal development was less shocking than in the past. They were no longer considered simply instruments for applying a law of legislative creation. The development of administrative law, moreover, furnished an example of judge-made law. Since the Council of State was not bound by the Civil Code, it could select freely from among its provisions those it considered just and would apply and those it would refuse to apply. The new administrative law revealed weaknesses and obsolescence in the Napoleonic codes. In private law, it seemed desirable to increase the flexibility of application of these codes while maintaining their structure. Partisans of the generally venerated codes and those of necessary social reforms could be reconciled through a change in the method of code interpretation. *"Par le code civil, au-delà du code civil!"* ("Through the Civil Code, beyond the Civil Code!") exclaimed Saleilles, paraphrasing Ihering's slogan for Roman law. The technique was successful. It reassured the traditionalists and still gave hope to the progressives. Practical and theoretical legal science could evolve by taking the Civil Code for a base just as the pandectists had been able to adjust the Roman law to the necessities of modern society with the *usus modernus pandectarum*. The drafters of the Civil Code were even invoked to justify this evolution, this extension of the Civil Code. Portalis was shown to have foreseen it in his magnificent *Discours préliminaire du code civil*.[10] The highest magistrate of France, the first president of the Court of Cassation, Ballot-Beaupré, at the celebration in 1904 of the Civil Code's centenary gave his support to the new doctrine, but reassured the traditionalists that nothing would be changed

10. Fenet, *Recueil complet des travaux préparatoires du code civil*, I, 449 ff.

thereby. The Court of Cassation, he was bold enough to say, had always taken account of considerations of public welfare and justice in interpreting French legislation.[11]

Since this famous address, teleological interpretation has held an officially recognized place among the methods of interpretation of French codes and statutes. It is legitimate and even necessary for the judge to consider social welfare and justice in interpreting statutes. In the interpretation of statutes, the judge is not a slave of the past. He is not obliged to apply the statute in the spirit in which its authors viewed it. Statutes can change their meaning over time.

The frank acceptance of this new principle by scholars, and particularly by the first president of the Court of Cassation, has of course encouraged judges to use teleological interpretation more extensively than in the past. Several famous developments in French law since 1900 bear out this supposition. Foremost among these is the acceptance by the courts of the famous theory of abuse of rights, with applications throughout private law.

While the importance of this method of interpretation must not be underestimated, neither should it be overestimated. The French never approached the extremes of the German school of free law; teleological interpretation remained subject to real limitations. First, it cannot be used to contradict either literal or logical interpretation. A text will receive an interpretation dictated by concerns of public welfare and justice only where its literal meaning permits; and the cohesion of the basic principles of French law must not be violated or seriously threatened. Second, teleological interpretation has not triumphed fully over historical interpretation. What is now openly recognized in France is that the use of either of the two methods, where they conflict, is legitimate. The judge can choose between two kinds of arguments, those which show him how the authors of the statutory text considered it and those which assert that another interpretation will better serve public welfare and justice.

How is the judge to choose? This depends partly on his temperament, each being more open to one than to the other according to his political, economic, social, and religious orientation. It is possible, however, to be more specific here in several respects.

11. *Le centenaire du code civil* (lecture presented on the Civil Code's centenary, 1904).

First, we can observe that the judge's choice between the two categories of arguments will often be decisively influenced by the nature or age of the statute. The Napoleonic codes, more than one hundred years old, are the primary area for teleological interpretation, although the historical method retains some value even with them. On the other hand, no possibility exists of interpreting very recent statutes or regulations teleologically. Nor do international treaties lend themselves well to this method; historical interpretation has the great advantage of increasing the uniformity of their application.

A second point to note is that judges generally prefer historical to teleological interpretation. Very convincing arguments are required to make a judge accept the latter, since its use requires an expression of personal choice and the assumption of full responsibility for the decision at hand. When he uses historical interpretation, he appears more objective, and he takes little personal responsibility. Therefore, one can expect greater use of teleological interpretation by judges of the higher courts (Court of Cassation, Council of State), who are more prepared to assume responsibility, than by the lower echelons of the judicial hierarchy. It is interesting to note that, just as the teleological method of interpretation was being recognized, the *juges de paix* lost their power to decide cases on equitable principles, a power they had long had.[12]

A final question is whether teleological interpretation is used equally in all areas of French law. Actually, it is difficult to be very precise here, for the question is closely related to the degree of development of legislation in the various areas. For example, administrative law certainly takes more account of considerations of public interest than does private law. That is its very aim. But since its general principles are not codified, administrative tribunals have much less occasion to use teleological interpretation, as such, than do judicial tribunals. The statutes and regulations which they have to apply are generally too recent, and often too detailed, to allow much use of that method. In criminal and labor law, furthermore, it is through general formulae used in statutes that teleological interpretation usually finds its possibilities of application. The method is used differently when there is a jury that does not have to give

12. *Law of July 12, 1905.* See René Morel, *Traité élémentaire de procédure civile* (2nd ed.; 1949), no. 132, p. 130.

reasons for its verdict, or when one admits generally the notion of mitigating circumstances (as do our criminal statutes), or when it is declared in a statute regulating labor disputes that "the two arbitrators and the umpire will have the power to decide *ex aequo et bono.*" Within private law, it is sometimes even maintained that commercial law is more rigid than civil law. It is doubtful, however, that this observation ought to lead to the conclusion that teleological interpretation is less utilized in commercial than in civil law. Commercial law constitutes a whole too disparate to lend itself to such general conclusions. Parts of it that are governed by complex regulation will largely exclude our method, but other parts may offer it a suitable terrain.

From the foregoing, let us emphasize a few points. French law knows no strict canons of interpretation as do some foreign countries. French statutory interpretation is very flexible. As in all other legal systems, it begins from the literal, grammatical possibilities and from the logic of the system. But it is important to note, even with respect to logical interpretation, the necessity felt by French judges in the regular courts to base their decisions on one or more legislative text. This leads to a use of logical interpretation of legislative texts in French private law unmatched in common law countries. Finally, to literal and logical interpretation are added two contradictory methods: historical and teleological interpretation. A lawyer will not hesitate to argue before a French judge that a particular solution is the one which the drafters of the legislative text intended. Similarly, in every situation it can be argued that that solution would lead to specified good or bad results from the point of view of public welfare and justice. The judge will weigh all these arguments. His decision will result from the value judgment made between them in his mind. He will be fully satisfied only where he can reconcile the two. Where contradictory arguments are presented, the skill of an advocate's presentation and the more or less conservative or progressive approach of the judge will determine the solution which will be adopted. It is hardly possible to be more specific than this. The law's interest for lawyers consists precisely in this ambiguity and in the possibilities of evolution and progress that it implies. In France, as elsewhere, any attempt to express the processes of judicial reasoning in formulae of mathematical precision is doomed to failure.

The processes of statutory interpretation utilized in France eliminate for practical purposes the problem of so-called gaps in the law. Ask a French lawyer any question, no matter how novel, and you can rest assured that he will find, in the arsenal of legislative texts at his disposal or by an appeal to the spirit of these texts, a rationale which will permit him to answer it. In France one must be a very bad jurist, or have a very bad case or considerable self-confidence, to ask a judge to decide a case solely on the basis of a source of law other than legislation.

In 1900 a French legal philosopher, F. Geny, advocated a new approach to this problem.[13] He sought to have French jurists concede that there are gaps in statutes, and that these must be filled with the aid of reasoning other than the interpretation of texts, by what he called "free scientific research" (*libre recherche scientifique*). Geny's work did have the effect of encouraging judges to broaden their field of vision and of calling their attention to the necessity of considering more diverse factors than they had been previously. He failed, however, in his ambition to have jurists openly acknowledge that, in addition to cases where one must interpret statutes, there are cases where one must be creative and solve problems without any assistance from legislative texts.

In France, a land of written law, legislation appears to lawyers as the only source of law. In considering the techniques of interpretation utilized by lawyers, or considering the role that judicial opinions and scholarly writing actually play, one may be tempted to think that this conviction is largely illusion. One risks a serious misunderstanding of French law and lawyers, however, if one takes this view without reservation. Psychologically, without any question, the French judge always does apply a statute. Even in those cases where he most clearly rewrites the statute, he sees himself applying and interpreting it. He does not think he is making law and would be surprised to have his actions thus characterized.

It is appropriate to add a few words to this exposition on methods of interpretation in order to show the executive's role in statutory interpretation. It happens frequently in the modern state that, on their own initiative or in response to inquiries submitted to them,

13. F. Geny, *Méthodes d'interprétation et sources en droit privé positif* (2 vols., 2nd ed., 1919; English translation, West, 1954). See also, by the same author, *Science et technique en droit privé positif* (4 vols.; 1919–24).

government departments announce their interpretation of statutes. It is current practice also for government departments to issue directives and instructions to their agents indicating how they should act with respect to statutes and regulations relating to the exercise of their functions and to their relations with individuals with whom they deal. Strictly speaking, none of these is law. In particular, "answers by ministers to written inquiries," although published in the *Official Journal* of the French Republic, do not constitute authoritative statutory interpretations binding on the courts. They only indicate how the executive interprets the statute and proposes to apply it. Similarly, ministerial directives and instructions are documents of internal organization intended to guide the conduct of officials. Theoretically, they do not affect the law and hence are not generally published in the *Official Journal*. Individuals are not expected to know them.

It is obvious, however, that these interpretations, directives, instructions, and circulars are frequently of great interest to individuals since "in fact, the circular plays a major role in French administration. Officials will tend to obey a circular, even of doubtful legality, rather than the statute itself." [14] Also, circulars sometimes are published in the *Official Journal* or in special bulletins of the departments or ministries which are made available to the public. The public has an interest in knowing how the administration, for instance, interprets and proposes to apply particular tax statutes. If the interpretation is wrong and harmful to individuals, they will refuse to submit to it and will have it corrected by contesting it before the courts, administrative or regular. On the other hand, if the interpretation is marked by a certain tendency or authorizes a certain latitude and so is favorable to taxpayers, they have a great interest in knowing it. This is especially true since there is no way of legally requiring the administration strictly to respect the law in such a case. [15] The only possible remedy in France is criticism by organs such as the *Cour des comptes*, if it may be assumed that the responsible officials are inclined to pay attention to such criticism.

What has just been said is not peculiar to administrative law, but may affect any branch of the law: criminal, commercial, or civil. In

14. M. Waline, *Droit administratif* (8th ed.; 1959), no. 415, pp. 258–59.
15. Unlike the Soviet Prokuratura, the French Public Ministry does not have this power.

considering the requirements of public policy, the police authorities, for instance, may refuse to assist in the eviction of tenants or the attachment of property except under certain conditions, even if the proper court judgment has been given ordering the eviction of the tenant or declaring a person liable to pay a certain amount. The instructions addressed to police commissioners and other government agents on this subject are clearly in violation of the law. Still, individuals should be familiar with them before bringing an action in which they will incur expenses, since, even if they are victorious, their action will not permit them finally to obtain what they seek. The instructions to the commissioners of police, which the latter will obey under fear of discipline, cannot be referred to the Council of State for invalidation, since they have an internal administrative character and do not claim to establish a rule of law. In addition, it is impossible for the courts to compel a commissioner of police to help execute a judgment. The only thing which the victorious litigant can do in such a case is to bring an action against the state for damages caused by the malfunctioning of a public service. The remedy would be efficacious only if sufficient damages were awarded by the Council of State. In practice, the contrary often occurs.

Interpretations by the French government of international treaties concluded by France are authoritative. French courts consider themselves bound by these interpretations where they are more detailed and derive from a new agreement that has been adopted, promulgated, and published in the same form as the original convention. Even beyond this, the courts tend increasingly to rely on the Government's interpretation, provided only that this is given by a decree rather than by simple ministerial circular.[16]

16. On this point see H. Batiffol, *Traité élémentaire de droit international privé* (3rd ed.; 1959), no. 41; P. Lerebours-Pigeonnière, *Droit international privé* (7th ed., by Y. Loussouarn; 1959), no. 54.

II   Custom

Books on French law, particularly introductions to private law, which present the general theory of sources of law, suggest that custom has played a very limited role in French law since codification. This impression is avoided only if one considers case law as a kind of judicial custom. This position can be maintained. Edouard Lambert, in his book on the function of comparative civil law, tried to show through a historical and comparative study that the only true customary law is that formed by courts.[17] We shall not debate that question here. Rather, we shall discuss the role played in modern French law by custom, in the traditional sense of that term, i.e., the continuing behavior over a period of time of those governed by the law, with the understanding that their behavior is required by the law.

Traditional legal analysis distinguishes three categories of custom: *consuetudo secundum legem* ("custom supporting law"), *consuetudo praeter legem* ("custom preceding law"), and *consuetudo adversus legem* ("custom contrary to law"). What is the role in French law today of these three types of custom?

Consuetudo secundum legem is custom formed within the framework of legislation to facilitate and direct its application. It plays a very important role in French law, and the small attention given it by writers results from their failure to see clearly its fundamental importance. This, however, is not difficult to understand. The law often refers to ideas and uses terms of everyday life rather than relying on a special legal vocabulary. The Civil Code speaks of marriage, signature, fault, uncle and nephew, furniture, animals used in farming, acts of administration, and payment, for instance. In some cases, these terms may be used with a special legal meaning. But usually lawyers take the meaning of legislative terms from the sense that ordinary men give them, i.e., from custom.

Article 970 of the Civil Code tells us that the holograph will must be completely written, dated, and signed by the testator. What is the

17. Edouard Lambert, *La fonction du droit civil comparé* (1903); Marcel Waline, "Le pouvoir normatif de la jurisprudence dans la technique et les principes du droit public," in *Etudes en l'honneur de Georges Scelle* (1950), II, 613 ff.

meaning of the requirement of date? Of signature? It is custom *secundum legem* that answers these questions. An indication of the year, or even of the month and year, does not constitute a date; the day of the month must also be specified. The affixation of a seal is not a signature, but the signature need not be readable or include a middle initial; an X is sufficient for an illiterate. All of these details are provided by custom. For impediments to marriage, custom also tells us that a granduncle should be treated as an uncle.[18] It requires us to decide that there is no marriage when a Frenchman in a single ceremony takes two girls of an African tribe as wives.[19] It tells us what we should understand by "furniture" in a will.

Of course one must be cautious. Many words used in everyday speech have a different legal meaning or may be given a special meaning when one is interpreting a particular legal text. The words *brother-in-law* and *sister-in-law* are not used by lawyers to apply between persons whose spouses are brother and sister,[20] and the word *belle-mere* means mother-in-law, but not a stepmother,[21] although current usage is to the contrary. But one can say that the law uses the current meaning of words unless there is special reason not to do so; there must be some justification. The principle is that lawyers use the words of the French language in the same way as other people do. This is custom *secundum legem*.

One can see custom *secundum legem* even more clearly by looking at terms whose meaning cannot be defined by logic alone, but require a moral or value judgment. Consider for example the word *fault*, used by Civil Code article 1382. It is impossible to understand the meaning of this term without looking to the behavior of a reasonable man. Or take article 450, which requires the tutor to manage the property of his ward as would a responsible head of family (*bon père de famille*); here again one must look to the be-

---

18. *Cass. Req.*, November 28, 1877 (D.P.1878.1.209, S.1878.1.337, note by Renault).

19. *Cours d'appel de Nîmes*, June 7, 1929 (S.1929.2.129, note by Solus); *Cass. Req.*, March 14, 1933 (D.P.1933.1.28, with report by M. le conseiller Pilon, S.1934.1.161, note by Solus).

20. *Cass. Civ.*, April 25, 1923 (S.1923.1.301); *Cass. Crim.*, October 20, 1943 (D.A.1944.13); A. Rouast, *La Famille*, Vol. II of Planiol and Ripert, *Traité pratique de droit civil français* (2nd ed.; 1952), no. 16, p. 13.

21. See Rouast, *La Famille*, no. 28, p. 24, relying on the legislative history of the *Code Civil; Grenoble*, February 10, 1903 (D.P.1904.2.169); *Conseil d'État*, November 24, 1946 (D.P.1919.3.19).

havior of normal persons. It is clear that in order to give such expressions legal meaning, we must look to custom.

The rule of article 1382, as it is interpreted by the courts, is particularly clear in this regard. The Court of Cassation will consider on appeal the question of whether particular conduct, as described by a lower court, constitutes a fault, or even a grave fault. It will not consider, on the other hand, whether the lower court has properly evaluated the amount of damages due. Why this difference? The reason is that the Court of Cassation examines questions of law, but not questions of fact. The determination of whether specific conduct constitutes a fault is a question of law; custom, source of law, decides it. The determination of whether the damage suffered is equal to 100,000 or 600,000 francs, on the other hand, is simply a question of fact; there is no custom which can help one decide. But let us then look to the question of whether mental pain and suffering (*préjudice moral*) constitutes a damage in the sense of article 1382; here again custom helps us toward a solution, by telling us whether the pain felt by a father or husband whose child or wife is killed by someone else's fault constitutes, for a Frenchman, a compensable loss. Custom gives an answer, either positive or negative, to this question. For this reason, it is a question of law and the Court of Cassation must decide on the admissibility or the exclusion of compensation for such injury.[22]

Thus, custom *secundum legem* plays a very important role in French law. Its role is clearly greater in French law than in the common law. The reason has already been discussed; it is the broader character of the legal rule as it is understood by the French lawyer. The common law tends to define almost every word in a legal sense. The interpretation of a word in a particular case is often considered binding in the future. French law is more flexible in this regard, not because the meaning of words is not a question of law, but because lawyers deliberately leave the question of definition to custom and custom is a more flexible source of law than judicial decisions. Custom can change with time, circumstances, and the social milieu in question.

22. H. and L. Mazeaud, *Traité théorique et pratique de la responsabilité délictuelle et contractuelle* (4th ed.; 1950), III, no. 2207 ff., pp. 305 ff; R. Savatier, *Traité de la responsabilité civile en droit français civil, administratif, professionnel, procédural* (2nd ed.; 1951), I, no. 271 ff., pp. 345 ff., and II, no. 609, p. 186.

The second kind of custom, according to legal analysis, is custom *praeter legem*. Custom *praeter legem* establishes new legal rules that are independent of, but not inconsistent with, legislation. To study it we must distinguish between the various branches of French law. The question must be looked at completely differently depending on whether one is discussing codified or uncodified areas of the law.

In a codified area, such as civil law, where there is a code, the processes of code interpretation leave little room for the formation and application of custom *praeter legem*. Lawyers' skill, and in a sense their deceptiveness, is sufficiently great in attaching all solutions to a legislative text that no area seems to remain empty for custom to fill. For a long time, the commonly cited example in this area was the name of married women, since there was no text saying that the married woman, as is the custom, should take the family name of her husband. This example can no longer be invoked. Since the law specifies that the woman judicially separated from her husband keeps his family name, and that the divorced woman generally retakes her maiden name, one can now infer from the law that the married woman has the right to take the family name of her husband, without however having any obligation to do so.

To find a clear example of custom *praeter legem* in modern civil law one can look to the rules concerning heirlooms and tombs.[23] The code does not speak of them, and yet in the areas both of succession and matrimonial property the courts treat them according to special rules which no doubt have their strongest basis in custom. In other cases (juridical position of acts performed by the apparent heir, application of certain adages concerning the suppression of fraud and the inadmissibility of unjust enrichment), it is doubtful that one is dealing with custom in the true sense. It is definitely more accurate to consider these theories, applied by the courts, as being based on considerations of justice and equity and not on custom in the usual sense. The same thing can be said for the doctrine of *astreintes,* a kind of punitive damages, which the courts have built up in order to insure the efficacy of obligations to do and not to do.

23. R. Demogue, "Les souvenirs de famille et leur condition juridique," *Revue trimestrielle de droit civil,* 1928, pp. 27 ff.; R. Savatier, "La transmission des sépultures," *Répertoire pratique du notariat,* 1928, art. 21.707, p. 307.

The area of contract seems like the most normal place for the development of customs *praeter legem*. The Civil Code system for contracts consists of a set of imperative and suppletive rules that deal with contracts in general, and then special exceptional or supplementary rules for specific types of contract (such as sale, lease, agency, compromise, partnership). One can imagine that practice since the Civil Code would have created and standardized several new types of contract, for which customary rules enter to supplement or make more precise the application of the code solutions concerning contracts in general. This has in fact happened and various new types of contracts, unknown at the time of the Civil Code, have developed. Let it suffice to mention here life insurance, various kinds of terrestrial insurance, the installment-buying agreement, and certain kinds of transport contracts. Nevertheless, the role of custom even in these cases remains concealed. Sometimes the code rules for other contracts are applied to the new contracts. Sometimes, without mentioning custom, the court interprets the intention of the parties in conformity with the general rules on the interpretation of contracts. In neither case will custom, which is unpopular with French lawyers, be mentioned. Most interesting is the appeal to the notion of commercial usage. It is regarded as something different from custom, whose existence is willfully ignored, although it is hard to distinguish the two. The idea of a usage is more readily accepted by French lawyers, since it rests on the interpretation of the parties' intentions and does not aspire to the creation of legal rules of the same worth as those established by statute.

The word *custom* is avoided because it is discordant to the ears of the legislator. That this is a kind of semantic deceit becomes clear, however, when one begins to distinguish between "usages of fact" and "usages of law," which are said to be "quasi customs." [24] The legislator wants to be considered the sole source of French law. Sometimes he achieves this goal by codifying usages and thus transforming into legislative rules the requirements of custom.[25] At other times, his success is less complete, either because he delegates the right to regulate a particular trade to another body, or because he is

---

24. Jean Escarra, *Manuel de droit commercial* (1947), I, nos. 71–72, p. 40.

25. *Law of June 13, 1866*, governing commercial usages. This law codifies certain usages in the area of sale of goods.

satisfied to refer to "local, loyal, and constant usages" without trying to reproduce them.[26]

In commercial law, the origins of the law in the custom of merchants is remembered and the existence and creation of customary rules more readily accepted. This is true also because the Commercial Code is notoriously inferior in quality to the Civil Code. In addition, it lacks unity and does not include a set of general rules to which one can refer. It is true that the Civil Code to some extent fills this function, but the general rules are still found outside the Commercial Code, and this fact is psychologically important. Commercialists are always eager to assert the autonomy of their branch of the law and for this reason do not share the civilian's aversion to custom. Finally, and especially important, commercial life itself has changed completely since 1807. As the underlying conditions have changed, so have commercial practices; new techniques and new kinds of contracts have been invented, so different from those of a hundred years ago that reasoning by analogy from the code's provisions is often out of the question. New practices like current accounts and new kinds of business like terrestrial insurance and modern banking can develop only if they have some latitude. Thus their regulation must be allowed to develop largely by custom *praeter legem,* within the framework of a few basic legal principles which do not restrict their development.

The same thing can be said of labor law. Its claim to autonomy permits a considerable use of custom, as a result of which various institutions, such as collective agreements, arbitration, trade associations, and labor union activity, appeared and developed even before the law began to regulate them. But here we are already in an uncodified area in a very real sense, since the present labor code bears no comparison to the Napoleonic codes.

One area in which custom *praeter legem* is clearly excluded is criminal law, because of the principle of the legality of sanctions. On the other hand, within all of codified law the area most favorable to this kind of custom is probably procedure.[27] This has been particularly true for civil procedure, where an obsolete set of rules that

26. *Law of May 6, 1919,* governing place-names of products.
27. See Bertrand Boccon-Gibod, *De la transformation de la procédure sous l'influence de la jurisprudence et de la pratique* (1937).

actually dates largely from the civil procedure ordinance of 1667 has had to be at least somewhat adapted by lawyers to meet present needs. Another factor favoring the development of customary rules was the existence, under the supervision of the courts, of the traditional guilds.

For administrative law, it is hard to define the role of custom, because of the imprecision of the expression and the peculiar character of public law. There is no question that administrative practices exist in many areas, and it is often difficult to say whether these practices are, or are not, actually law.[28] The articulation by administrative courts of rules of public law has certainly often been preceded by such practices, just as in public international law the formation of law was preceded by practices that could be called customs. In both cases, the problem is one that is inherent in any discussion of customary law. Is a custom neither recognized nor officially imposed by the legislature or the courts a "legal rule"? The answer to the question depends on one's theories on the nature of legal rules. But since there is no point in arguing about such questions, let us take a purely descriptive, empirical position and note that the elaboration of legal rules by the legislature and the courts is very often based on practices of interested parties. Do such practices become customs that are rules of law before being recognized by the legislature or the courts, or must they await this sanction before becoming "legal" in the strict sense? The question is theoretical. It suggests the imprecision of the definition of the concepts of law and custom that precludes agreement on the importance of custom *praeter legem,* particularly in administrative law.

The final problem that we shall examine is the role of custom *adversus legem.* Can custom lead to the obsolescence of a legislative provision? Writers do not seem to have reached a consensus on this subject. If we here again limit ourselves to describing what happens in practice, the following conclusions seem justified. It is clear that in civil law a court will never admit that a law can lose its force because a custom contradicts it. This of course does not mean that in fact this very thing does not happen, but simply that the court will not acknowledge it and will explain it in some other way. If the

28. A. de Laubadère, *Traité élémentaire de droit administratif* (1953), no. 381, p. 209; P. Debelmas, *La pratique administrative comme source de droit* (Toulouse, 1932).

rule in question, against which the custom developed, is suppletive, it will be easy to avoid its application by saying, more or less artificially, that there are circumstances in the case that show that the parties intended to exclude, as they have a right to do, the application of this rule in their relations. If it is an imperative rule, a different technique will have to be used: through manipulation of the processes of statutory interpretation analyzed previously, which are very flexible, the law will be given a meaning without overt reference to custom, different from the apparent meaning of its terms and from the meaning intended by the legislature.

In commercial law, jurists recall the time when this area was entirely ruled by custom and are willing to go further and recognize frankly that a particular institution is regulated by custom. Still, they will never assert categorically that a statute has become inapplicable as the result of a contrary custom. They simply omit any reference to the law, or limit themselves to an affirmation that the provision invoked does not apply to the institution in question, which is regulated by custom alone. The clearest example of a custom *adversus legem* in commercial law is that of the current account. The current account is exempted from the rule of Civil Code article 1154 forbidding compound interest.[29] The courts never think of saying that there is an obligatory custom formed *adversus legem*. They simply declare that article 1154 does not apply to current account agreements, which are regulated by custom alone. In the commercial area, Civil Code article 1202, according to which joint and several liability is not to be presumed, is similarly set aside. The rights of allowance and replacement in commercial sales are further examples of accepted custom *adversus legem;* they are contrary to Civil Code articles 1184, 1610, and 1611.[30]

In administrative law, it seems necessary to accept custom *adversus legem* unless one is willing to consider purely and simply that the law is sometimes violated systematically. The Government states in a circular or instruction addressed to its agents, and frequently communicated to the public, that it will interpret a particular statute

29. *Code Civil*, art. 1154: "Interest on capital can produce interest either after court action or as a result of a special agreement, provided that the action or the agreement deal with interest due at least for a full year."

30. J. Martin de la Moutte, "Les sanctions de l'obligation de délivrance," in *La vente commerciale de marchandises*, studies in commercial law, ed. J. Hamel (1951), title III, Chap. 2.

in such and such a way, sometimes contrary to the interpretation given it by the Council of State. Instructions are sent to administrators or to agents of the Ministry of Justice telling them not to institute proceedings or require the payment of penalties for particular offenses committed in specified circumstances (exemptions from customs, exchange controls, and highway traffic regulations to promote tourism; assurance of immunity from prosecution given to a person in order to discover the perpetrator of another crime). It is always difficult to say whether or not such instructions constitute custom, and whether the courts ought thus to give them effect. What actually happens is that the administration does not bring the matter to the courts, and the question never arises of what the courts, either administrative or regular, should do if it did. Lawyers, partisans of "legality," can disapprove of such practices, but it would be unwise to neglect their existence. It is better to recognize frankly that administrative law, and public law as a whole, has characteristics that distinguish it from private law.[31] The role of the law and of statutes in this area is less to regulate the relations between the government and individuals than to set up guarantees in favor of individuals. Provided that the government respects these guarantees, it may relax the legal rules and exempt individuals from the strict application of the statutory provisions by creating a kind of custom *adversus legem,* obligatory until revoked prospectively by another act. If this interpretation is accepted, however, the custom of which we are speaking loses its character of custom *adversus legem* and becomes custom *secundum legem,* created to define the application of the law within the framework of governmental discretion provided by the law itself through the general principles of administrative law.

31. Thus it is current practice in criminal law for the prosecutor to prosecute a person for a lesser degree of an offense committed, such as second-degree murder instead of first-degree murder. See P. Bouzat, *Traité théorique et pratique de droit pénal* (1951), no. 117, p. 107; R. Vouin and J. Léauté, *Droit pénal et criminologie* (1956), 157–59; G. Stefani and G. Levasseur, *Droit pénal général et criminologie* (1957), nos. 196, 518.

III   Judicial Decisions

Many authors have analyzed the role of judicial decisions in France, and as a result, a number of prejudices that were common fifty years ago have been overcome. It is instructive to read French legal treatises, with their many references to court decisions. They indicate clearly the interest jurists have in the study of judicial decisions in all areas of French law.

The authoritarian temper of Napoleonic times created various illusions concerning the scope and effects of codification. It was thought that at least jurists and judges, if not all citizens, would no longer have any difficulty understanding a law that had become fully rational and was set forth in clear terms: search for and interpretation of the law were to give way to simple application of the statutes. The Court of Cassation, which was established in 1789, did not have as one of its original functions to insure the uniformity of judicial decisions, although today this is regarded as its principal task.[32] Doctrinal writers of the nineteenth century saw no need to study judicial decisions, an attitude that still prevails in some countries of the Romano-Germanic system, where codification came later or no regular case reports exist.

Experience has shown, however, that codification in no way excludes an active role for the courts. The principles posed by the codes simply provide a framework for the national legal system and must be made more precise in their practical application, adapted to new needs, interpreted in accordance with circumstances of all kinds.

Following the Napoleonic codification, case reports did not disappear; rather, they developed and took on a different appearance. Alongside the official reports, which were created for the first time in the year VII of the Republic (1799) for the civil and criminal decisions of the Court of Cassation,[33] private case reports appeared

32. See G. Marty, "Etude de droit comparé sur l'unification de la jurisprudence par le Tribunal suprême," in *Introduction à l'étude du droit comparé, Recueil d'études en l'honneur d'Edouard Lambert* (1938), II, 728 ff.

33. There is no official reporter for the decisions of the Council of State, but the *Recueil des arrêts du Conseil d'Etat,* established in 1821, has been published since 1947 "under the honored patronage of the Council of State." See Marie Laine, "L'évolution du *Recueil des arrêts du Conseil d'Etat statuant au con-*

in the first half of the nineteenth century. These reports publish those decisions of all courts, administrative and regular, that they consider significant. They rapidly came to constitute the very basis for the practicing lawyer's library and retain this importance today. Even the attitude of scholars toward them has changed: after trying to ignore them and to view the law without the benefit of court decisions, French writers have made a complete turnabout. In many cases, particularly where the legislation is cryptic, their treatises have become commentaries on court decisions.

The role of court decisions in France can be examined from two points of view. The first question is whether, as a matter of law, courts can and do create new legal rules. The second is what authority court decisions have as a matter of empirical fact.

The first question must, in all areas of French law, including administrative law, be answered in the negative. The position of French law can be expressed by saying that a judicial decision can never be justified simply by stating that the rule of law applied has been applied previously by other judges.

The decision of a regular court will be reversed for "absence of legal basis" if the only justification it gives for its decision is an earlier decision of the Court of Cassation. There is nothing to prevent reference in the opinion to earlier court decisions, and the practice of citing precedents is in fact becoming more frequent.[34] But reference to one or more prior cases does not constitute a self-sufficient legal argument and is not a valid basis for decision. The Court of Cassation in its opinions refrains rigorously from citation of earlier decisions it has made or to the existence of an established line of precedents. Judges fear that this might give the impression that they consider themselves bound by doctrines adopted in their decisions. In addition it would be an unacceptable violation of Civil Code article 5, which prohibits judges from making general or regulatory decisions in connection with the disputes submitted to them. The role of the courts is to solve disputes that are brought before them, not to make laws or regulations. The principle of separation

---

tentieux (Recueil Lebon)" in *Conseil d'Etat, Etudes et Documents,* no. 5 (1951), 153.

34. For arguments against the development of this practice, see Pierre Mimin, *Le style des jugements (Vocabulaire, construction, dialectique, formes juridiques* (3rd ed.; 1951), no. 129, p. 253.

of powers, as it is understood in France, prevents the formal creation of legal rules by the courts.

Because this principle is fundamental to French constitutional law, the same rule applies to the decisions of the Council of State, even though there are no codes in this area. The Council of State never refers in its opinions to a decision it made earlier. And other administrative courts never justify their decisions solely by referring to a decision of the Council of State.

For this reason, judicial decisions are not a source of law in France. Strictly speaking, they never create legal rules. Their role is always understood to be the application of preexisting statutes or customs. In the absence of an applicable statute or custom, decisions can be based on principles of equity, reason, justice, or tradition. It is never enough, however, simply to refer to a prior judicial decision.

There is one clear exception to this principle, which was created by the law of May 6, 1919, on the area-names of wines. According to article 7 of this law, a judgment or decision by virtue of which the products of a particular commune have or do not have the right to a particular area-name applies not only to the parties to the litigation but also to all other inhabitants of the commune.[35] The judgments or decisions in these cases are regulatory. Also, there are many cases where judgments create rights rather than merely declaring their existence. Such judgments, of which divorce is typical, create a new legal situation, which can be set up against anyone, sometimes on the condition that the decision has been publicized. But we do not have to discuss these types of decision here; they simply modify an individual relationship, without creating a new rule of law.

Another, more important exception existed at one time in the area of labor law. The Supreme Court of Arbitration, which functioned only from 1936 to 1939 and whose activity has now been suspended, was able to render regulatory decisions. The situation of the Council of State is different. Although this institution is often required to establish regulations, these are the work of a different branch of the council from that which handles administrative litigation.

No French court can create legal rules, since the principle of separation of powers prohibits it. But there is the additional question

35. *Law of May 6, 1919*, art. 7: "Final judgments and decisions are binding on all of the inhabitants and landowners of the commune or part of the commune in question."

of what authority a court's interpretation of a statute has in fact: If the same legal question that has been decided, or an analogous question, comes up in the future, will the court considering the question be inclined to follow the doctrine previously applied, or will it regard this as of little importance and reject any arguments based on the fact that courts have previously interpreted the statute in a particular way?

During most of the nineteenth century, French writers thought they could ignore court decisions. That an opinion had been given interpreting a statute in such and such a way was regarded as without importance. Questions of law were to be treated in each case as if they were coming up in court for the first time and solved in accordance with the methods of interpretation discussed above. French writers refused to admit that the fact that a judge had made a mistake once should be any reason for him systematically to make the same mistake in the future.

The courts, however, took a different view of things. No rule of French law prohibits the citation in court of judicial precedents.[36] The existence of official and private case reports where decisions are reported makes it easy to cite them. Advocates have never failed to do so. They assume that their position will be strengthened considerably if they can show that their arguments have previously convinced either the same judges or judges situated higher in the judicial hierarchy, or for that matter any judge at all. Although such arguments may not be legally binding, they cannot help but affect a court. There is a natural tendency for courts to follow precedents; it is a way to insure consistency in their decisions, for which a need is still felt in spite of the codification. Courts regard themselves as engaged in an important common endeavor, the administration of justice. They can economize their time and labor for questions that have not already been considered. They can reinforce practices that have been adopted on the basis of an earlier court's interpretation of a statute. They make it less likely that the losing party will appeal

36. A law was passed in the Soviet Union after the Revolution of 1917 forbidding citation before the courts of decisions rendered under the czars. Nothing of this sort was ever done in France; prerevolutionary decisions could be cited immediately after the Napoleonic codification. Three new editions of Guyot's *Répertoire de jurisprudence*, published before the Revolution, were published during the Restoration by Merlin under the title *Répertoire universel et raisonné de jurisprudence* (18 vols., 5th ed.; 1827).

the decision, and they accelerate the end of litigation, if they make it appear that the law is clear. There are numerous arguments to make a court follow precedents, particularly those of tribunals higher in the court hierarchy.

The citation of precedents is common in French law, before both regular and administrative courts. Its legitimacy is beyond dispute. Not only private advocates, but also agents of the Public Ministry constantly cite judicial decisions in support of their arguments and discuss the decisions that might seem contrary to their position. The written arguments of the Public Ministry and the commissioner of the Government are often presented in the case reports before the text of the opinion of the Court of Cassation (or lower courts) or the Council of State; one need only glance at these written arguments to see how common and important the practice of citing judicial decisions is in France.

The French judge is never required, legally, to follow a precedent. But to what extent will he in fact consider it? It is of course difficult to answer this question precisely, since many factors that are hard to evaluate will have their effect, such as the personality of the individual judge and the equities of the particular case. Nevertheless, various general observations can be made by considering first the Court of Cassation, then the lower regular courts, and finally the Council of State and the lower administrative courts.

With respect to the Court of Cassation, two different situations must be considered: that where its own earlier decisions are cited to it and that where one or more decisions given by lower courts are invoked.

In the first case, it is understood that the Court of Cassation can always change its mind and reverse itself, but it is equally certain that it will not do so readily. The general rule here is that the Court of Cassation will follow the precedent that it has laid down, even if it is but a single decision rendered on the question.[37] The

37. The desire of Court of Cassation judges to remain faithful to their established case law is particularly evident in the criminal chamber, where it has led to a little-known but very interesting practice. The judges of this chamber have reached an understanding that they will rely upon only those decisions of the criminal chamber that are published in the official *Bulletin des arrêts de la Cour de cassation en matière criminelle* and will regard as without precedential value those of their decisions that are published only in other case reports. When the criminal chamber of the Court of Cassation renders a decision, its members hold

Court of Cassation considers its principal role today as enforcement of the uniform application of the law. This function cannot be fulfilled if the Court of Cassation itself does not have a stable case law. There is no example of the Court of Cassation reversing a decision taken by it with all chambers sitting together. In the case where the precedents consist of one or several decisions of a single chamber of the Court of Cassation, reversals in the case law are well known. But still they are rare when compared to the number of cases where the court has remained faithful to its previous position in spite of active opposition to this position by scholarly writers.

The arguments to which the Court of Cassation is most sensitive in favor of a reversal of its precedents would seem to be the following: either the existence of inconsistencies between various decisions *or* a change in the sociological context of the problem raised before the court. Two chambers of the Court of Cassation may have taken opposing positions; a conflict of this sort will not be allowed to continue and one of the chambers will fairly quickly abandon its position and adopt the other's point of view. Or the lower courts may reject an opinion of the Court of Cassation and continue to give contrary decisions. In such a case, the Court of Cassation will reexamine, and possibly reverse, its position. Consideration of the position of the Council of State can in some cases have the same effect; although civil law and administrative law are technically independent, they obviously have a mutual attraction for each other. In exceptional cases, the Court of Cassation may be convinced by the Council of State's example to reverse an earlier position.

Actually this possibility leads us into the second reason mentioned above: The reason why the Court of Cassation will adopt the position of the Council of State rather than maintain the consistency of its own position is that the solution given by the Council of State seems to it better than its own, more in harmony with the current sociological context of the problem raised. The question of reversals in the case law of the Court of Cassation cannot be examined in-

---

a special meeting to decide whether or not the judgment should be published in the official *Bulletin*. Only about 10 percent of their decisions receive this distinction, although the law has provided since 1947 that all decisions of the Court of Cassation are to be published. The same practice is not followed in the civil chamber of the Court. About 90 percent of the decisions of this chamber are published in the *Bulletin des arrêts de la Cour de cassation en matière civile* and the judges are willing to consider decisions appearing in private case reports.

dependently of the methods of statutory interpretation in use. To the extent that the teleological method is used, the law can develop without the legislative texts changing at all. Thus, it might appear that there has been a reversal in the case law when in fact it would be more correct to say that the statute has changed and that the courts have merely recognized that this modification has taken place.

Attitudes concerning family relations (husband and wife, parents and children) and the status of illegitimate children have changed in France over the last hundred years. The need to keep private property free of all restrictions seems less clear, and we are more ready to recognize the value of some servitudes and to allow some kinds of perpetuities. The relative importance of real and personal wealth has changed, particularly because of the development of share companies of all sorts. We are less concerned with keeping property within the family, and on the other hand are more aware of the disadvantages of excessive fragmentation of land. Mechanization and urbanization have changed the context of the law of civil delicts and the law concerning certain contracts. The Court of Cassation is naturally aware of these modifications in the sociological setting of the law, that is, in the political and economic conditions and the moral and social conceptions that justify our legal rules.

An opinion it gave a hundred, or even fifty, years ago will often be of limited value. It is unimportant to the extent that it is based on conceptions that are no longer accepted or on circumstances that have since changed. Could we conceive today, as the Court of Cassation said in 1898, that an individual can be considered "in need," and could thus claim maintenance from his relatives, when he has received a considerable amount of money as a dowry? [38] The opinion of the Court of Cassation in 1898 is explained by a style of life and conceptions that have been completely abandoned since then. If the Court of Cassation were faced with a similar case today, it would certainly abandon its earlier position. In such a case, however, no one would speak of a "reversal in the case law" (*revirement de jurisprudence*).

Or the Court of Cassation may never have had occasion to decide the question brought before it. The decisions cited before it may all come from lower courts. The authority of these decisions will be rela-

38. *Cass. Req.*, February 23, 1898 (S.1902.1.307).

tively slight before the Court of Cassation. They will become important only in certain very special circumstances. One possibility is that there may be many concordant decisions indicating an established case law. Or the lower court decision may have concerned a particular category of persons, who as a result have changed their practices in reliance on the decision (practice of notaries, form contracts in the area of insurance or maritime commerce).

Let us now consider the lower regular courts. It is easy to understand the authority in fact that court decisions have for them. If the decision cited is from the Court of Cassation, the civil and commercial courts of first instance and the courts of appeal will very probably follow the position taken, even if it has been stated in a single decision. The contrary will be true only in circumstances where a reversal of position by the Court of Cassation can be expected (e.g., an old decision, which no longer seems justified). Resistance to the Court of Cassation's position is also possible if the lower courts think the court may still be unsure of the position it has taken. This has happened principally in the area of extracontractual liability, where legislation is concise in the extreme and is of little assistance in deciding particular cases. It has been clear that the Court of Cassation was searching for the best approach, from among several that were proposed by legal scholars. In certain cases where the Courts of Appeals have criticized the position taken by the Court of Cassation, the latter has changed its position.

The lower courts of course give less weight to decisions of other courts than to those of the Court of Cassation. In such a case, they are particularly sensitive to the existence of an established case law. They will also usually attach more importance to their own previous decisions: an opinion of the Court of Appeals of Poitiers will have more importance in Poitiers than in Grenoble or Toulouse. The situation of courts located in Paris (Court of Appeals of Paris, Court of Major Jurisdiction of Paris) is unique. Their decisions are accorded special weight, partly because of the higher rank in the judicial hierarchy held by judges in these courts, but particularly because these courts, divided into various chambers, have judges who specialize in certain kinds of questions, so that their opinions in these areas are sometimes more carefully thought through and better reasoned. Similar reasoning can give special importance to a few other civil and commercial courts for particular kinds of questions, where circumstances give their judges expertise (maritime commerce in Marseille or Le Havre, area names for wines in Bordeaux, customs problems in Avesnes and Lille, for example).

In the administrative courts, the same principles clearly govern the authority of judicial decisions, even though the law is judge-made. This fact might lead one to expect that more importance would be given to precedents in order to insure a solid foundation for the law, which must rest on a consistent and stable case law. On the other hand, however, because it is not as limited as regular courts by legislative texts, the Council of State is more open to a progressive interpretation of the law. It is encouraged in this by the constant and close relations its judges have, within the council itself, with those participating in the active administration of the country. Thus, on balance the case law of the Council of State is probably more flexible than that of the Court of Cassation.

This fact should be underlined, since one finds statements, sometimes coming from very eminent jurists, that give the opposite impression.[39] One must not take such statements literally. In all cases, the authority of judicial decisions in France is one of fact alone, not of law; and in this respect the decisions of the Council of State are no different from those of the Court of Cassation.

To have a correct notion of the authority of judicial decisions in France, two additional points need to be kept in mind. First, one must recall the French conception of legal rule and the distinction between law and fact; the role of judicial decisions is obviously affected by these conceptions. Second, one must consider the external form of French judicial decisions: their conciseness and formal style, particularly, affect their authoritative value.[40]

39. See the arguments of M. Romieu in the *Botta* decision (Council of State, July 8, 1904) (S.1905.3.81, note by Hauriou): "We attach the greatest importance to the decision that the Council of State will give in this dispute, since it will have a general effect and its theory with respect to invalidation will apply to all the agencies that are within its jurisdiction, both judicial agents of all sorts and even agencies in the active administration."

40. See the interesting work of Pierre Mimin, *Le style des jugements*, on the form and style of judgments and the necessity for them to obtain the "greatest possible density" (p. 92) and to maintain the "dignity of the judicial approach" (p. 215). "Verbosity is understandable when you are paid by the line, but a judicial decision must assert itself in rigorous brevity" (no. 88, p. 193). There is no doubt that the attitude expressed by President Mimin is shared by the great majority of French jurists. The higher the court the shorter its decision in France, where a very brief decision is regarded as a sign of experience and wisdom.

And finally we should mention the form of French case reports, which are very different from those published in other countries. The number of judicial decisions published in France each year is relatively limited. Also, decisions are frequently published with accompanying critical notes evaluating their worth. Finally, a French lawyer is not upset if he cannot find a decision in which he is interested, since he always has the solid rock of his codes to rely upon. There is no doubt that these practical factors, more than considerations of legal theory or principle, produce the differences between the way judicial decisions are regarded in France and the way they are regarded in other countries, particularly those of the common law.

IV   Legal Scholarship

What are the characteristics and forms of French legal scholarship, and what is its influence in contemporary French law? These questions receive almost no attention in France. All one can find on the subject in our legal literature are basic comments in the introductions to law study written for first-year law students. Beyond that we rely on lawyers' experience: they have to be familiar with what is published in France. From experience they know, a bit intuitively, what use they can make of a particular piece by a particular author. What can one say on such a subject that is not trite? Everything seems self-evident, nothing seems worth saying, and even reflection seems pointless.

Anyone who studies foreign legal systems will rapidly come to question this point of view. He will want to learn particular things about the scholarly writing in any foreign system he approaches. Too often he will find it difficult to discover them. He will appreciate the handicap caused by lack of information for the foreign lawyer who tries to study the French legal system. Moreover, the study of foreign legal systems quickly reveals the unusual aspects of our own scholarship, and sets in relief, as peculiar to it, traits and characteristics that may have seemed self-evident and not worthy of discussion.

French legal scholarship has its own characteristics, which set it off from the writing done in common law countries, socialist countries, and even from that done in most other countries of the Romano-Germanic system.

The contrast between French and common law legal scholarship has been made most often, but it is often presented in generalities that actually say little about real differences. The point of departure for a comparison should be consideration of the tasks that French and English scholars, respectively, set for themselves within their systems, and the different relations that exist in France and common law countries between judicial decisions and scholarly writing. Compared to the common law scholar, the French lawyer takes great liberty with judicial decisions. The law, whether or not contained in codes, seems to him as something that precedes and stands above judicial decisions. The courts try to discover, interpret, and apply the law. There is no reason why scholars should not cooperate with the courts in this enterprise, and there is no reason why they should feel inferior to judges. Pressed by the quantity and urgency of litigation, sometimes influenced by peculiar factual circumstances, judges cannot always study thoroughly the strictly legal questions that come before them, and they are even less able to evaluate the social consequences of their decisions. Legal scholars, free of the burdens and circumstances that influence judges, must guide them and try to bring order and coherence to their decisions. Legal scholars would be failing in their job if they merely systematized, and accepted as an undisputable premise, the decisions that are often made under unfavorable conditions. One of their essential roles is criticism of judicial decisions and opinions, similar to their role, more on the policy level and less as a legal matter, as critic of legislation. Policy and law cannot and must not be dissociated; interpretation really embraces two processes, since under the guise of interpretation judges often really create new law. The courts are not simply interpreters of existing law; they are also creators of new legal rules. The role of the legal scholar is to cooperate with them in both tasks by contributing a point of view that may be more abstract, but that also is more serene because disengaged from advocates' battles, and more enlightened because elaborated under better working conditions and at greater leisure. Criticism of judicial decisions is an essential function of legal scholarship, a mission that it can fulfill the more effectively because judicial decisions, in the final analysis, are only a secondary source of law in our country. The framework established by the codes remains intact in spite of severe criticism of judicial decisions.

This approach differentiates our legal system from the common law system. In the latter, courts have greater prestige than in France. But in addition, this prestige seems to be more important to them. A stable case law is more necessary, reversals of case law are sufficiently disruptive that one tries to avoid them, and criticism of judicial decisions must be undertaken with greater moderation, since if the case law falls, or even if the prestige of the courts is only put in doubt, the whole structure of the law could crumble. English lawyers instinctively sense this danger. To guard against it, writers frankly concede the superiority of judges. They do not claim, as in France, equal status. Their criticism of judicial opinions is always expressed with deferential moderation. They limit themselves to description and analysis of what the judges in their wisdom have said. They describe the evolution that is taking place, seek to build a system and pick out tendencies through comparison with earlier judicial decisions. They do not criticize the courts, in the strict sense of the term.[41]

Since the function of legal scholarship differs in France and England, it is easy to understand that the methods of expression are different as well. Certain kinds of works, in which writers are content to classify judicial decisions and present them in summary form, are more popular in England than in France. This is the pattern not only of "books of practice," but also of "digests," for which the nearest parallel in France would be the summary tables that appear in the principal case reports every five or ten years. The more typically American pattern of dictionaries, which are restricted to the interpretation that courts have given to particular terms and expressions used in public and private acts, is equally foreign to the French. On the other hand, case notes written with the freedom typical of French writers are unimaginable in England, and even

41. It is only in a different sort of work, which is more in the area of philosophy, general theory of law, and sociology, that critical attitudes are expressed. And even there, the criticism is directed toward the policies of the courts and legislature; it is seldom, if ever, addressed to the manner in which the present law is being applied.

the chronicles of judicial decisions that appear in French reviews will often shock the common lawyer. This is a particularly important observation, since it is through this type of writing that French scholars have their greatest practical influence, elementary treatises aside. The very format of our case reports shows that French judges in no way resent scholarly criticism as an attack on their dignity. Quite to the contrary, they regard it as assistance to them and do not hesitate to patronize the reports and reviews in which they are censured. One must read the written arguments of the Public Ministry before the Court of Cassation and other regular courts, and the arguments of the commissioners of the Government before the Council of State, to understand the importance in France of scholarly criticism, as it relates to judicial practice and decisions.

We have seen that scholarly writing has a very different function and takes different forms in France than it does in common law countries, particularly England. French legal scholarship is also very different from legal scholarship in the other countries with Romano-Germanic legal systems, and also from that in the Soviet Union and the Eastern European socialist countries.

French writers study the questions that, rightly or wrongly, interest them. They publish the books they want and set forth their personal opinions, tied to their personal conceptions of justice and social utility. They freely criticize existing law, both statutory and judge-made. They suggest improvements. They try to keep and strengthen a contact with practical reality by analyzing carefully judicial decisions and by inquiring into the way practitioners view, apply, and try to bend or twist existing rules of law.

The situation is different in the Soviet Union and the Eastern European countries. The works that are published in these countries, in conformity with a plan and by publishing houses that are all state-owned, are given the same essential function as is the law itself, to cooperate with the government in its pursuit of particular policies. Treatises have to stay within the prevailing ideological line. They contain many citations to political leaders to prove their orthodoxy. They are generally discussed by study groups prior to publication. After publication it is from the point of view of their orthodoxy that they are evaluated—and often severely criticized. Since books published in the Soviet Union are intended to publicize and defend government policy, writers have little concern with judicial decisions. It is not the courts that make government policy. There is no point in reporting good decisions, since commentary on the statutes will serve accepted goals better. And it is better to ignore bad decisions, which simply deserve to be reversed or modified by higher courts. Some degree of change has to be noted, however, in recent years in the USSR as well as in the popular democracies, where problems are now sometimes approached by legal writers from a sociological, rather than a purely legal, point of view. This is particularly true of the fields of criminal and family law.

That French legal scholarship should have characteristics that set it off from English and Russian legal scholarship should not surprise us. It may seem more strange, however, to find that French scholarship is also very different from the scholarship of other Latin and Germanic countries. Nevertheless, there are great differences in the legal scholarship of the various countries with Romano-Germanic systems. Certainly there is a tendency in some of these countries to lean toward conceptions and forms that are prevalent in France. But even then legal scholarship can conceive of its task differently, or it may lack the opportunities it has in France. In many countries, probably most, the relations between judicial decisions and scholarly writing are on a different basis than they are in France.

Probably the strongest contrast at the present time is with the scholarship of the other Latin countries. Italian scholarship, in particular, is extremely dogmatic when compared with French.[42] In Italy, the law is regarded as the science of rights and duties of men living in society; this science is founded on the analysis of legal concepts and is as fully as possible divorced from political science and sociology. Even judicial decisions are seen as purely factual data, uninteresting for those who seek through study to define a dogmatic science. Scholars ignore judicial decisions and seldom cite them in their books or courses. In this way, Italian legal scholarship is extraordinarily theoretical in comparison with modern French scholarship. No doubt the Italian approach has its advantages. It helps to keep the law on the high plane of principles, from which practice always tends to draw away. It helps develop agility in legal analysis, increase our understanding of basic concepts, and perfect the tone and expression of rules. It risks, however, making law too theoretical

42. Cappelletti, Menzman, and Pueblo, *The Italian Legal System* (1968).

a science, losing sight of the essentially practical function of legal rules. Nineteenth-century French legal scholarship saw its role as Italian scholarship does today, but finally the gulf thus created between scholarship and policy was found unhealthy and forced French scholars at the turn of the century to reorient their thinking. Today, French civil and commercial law scholars, as well as those in administrative law, take judicial decisions as the basis of their study. It is certain that French scholarship today is further removed from the Italian position than from the English, in spite of the similarity of technique of legislative expression of legal rules and concepts in France and Italy.

Compared to French legal scholarship, German scholarship is also dogmatic, although less so than the Italian. The principal contrast between French and German legal writing, however, should be sought on a different level, in the difference in the types of works that one finds in the two countries. The German jurist still keeps distinct the two activities that he considers proper for legal scholarship: exposition of the law applied by the courts, and systematization and criticism of the existing law. The exposition of the rules actually applied, involving an analysis of judicial decisions, is done in annotated codes (*Kommentar*) as objectively as possible, with a minimum of criticism. Legal theory, on the other hand, including the exposition of the system with its concepts, the function of the rules, and their advantages and disadvantages is done in a completely different type of book, manuals (*Lehrbuch*) and monographs, in which judicial decisions are largely ignored. The fusion in a single book of *Kommentar* and *Lehrbuch* scholarship is characteristic, on the contrary, of today's French legal scholarship. The French lawyer, in his manuals and treatises, tries to combine the two roles. He explains how the law is actually applied and at the same time tries to criticize or defend it and show how it has evolved and is evolving. Increasingly, this approach dominates even those works in France intended primarily for the use of practitioners rather than students, such as legal encyclopedias and repertories.

V   Supereminent Principles

Having spoken of legislation, custom, judicial decisions, and legal scholarship, we might seem to have exhausted the
sources of French law. Certain supereminent principles, however,
must also be considered. Such principles have a double role. First,
they help fill any gaps which exist in legislation in that limited area
of French law where, to borrow Geny's term, one can use "free scientific research." And second, in exceptional circumstances these
supereminent principles can help correct existing legislation. The
law serves a particular ideal; its goal is the realization of our conception of social order and justice. Whatever the applicable rule of law
might seem to be, we would not apply it if its application directly
and indisputably contradicted the requirements of social order and
justice, as those notions are understood in our society. In such a
case, supereminent principles are used to correct the poorly conceived rule and avoid its application. In both roles, such supereminent
nent principles would seem essential to any legal system. They are
necessary if one is to realize the system's full potential and avoid
making it too formal. They insure that the system serves effectively
the goals we set for it.

Let us first examine the problem of gaps in the law. According to
article 4 of the Civil Code, a judge cannot refuse to decide a case
because of the silence, insufficiency, or ambiguity of the law. And
article 185 of the Penal Code sets a modest fine and five to twenty
years' prohibition from holding public office for any judge, court,
or administrative authority who, for any reason whatsoever, including silence or ambiguity of the law, fails to settle the parties' dispute.[43] The judge, whether civil, penal, or administrative, thus must
always give a decision when a case is brought before him. He can
decide that he lacks jurisdiction, but if he accepts jurisdiction, he
must settle the substance of the matter by his decision.

Legislation and custom, however, may be insufficient and not tell
him how to solve the problem. Moreover, since prior judicial decisions and writings by legal scholars are not true sources of law, a
case cannot be decided simply by citing their authority. If the judge

43. Robert Vouin, *Précis de droit pénal spécial* (1953), no. 403, p. 415.

finds that there is a gap in the legislation that is not filled by custom, how can he settle the dispute? In truth this problem is usually avoided in French law. In both private and public law, although through two different techniques, judges seldom (if ever) see any need to call upon these supereminent principles, because the legal system that the judge is applying never has any gaps.

In the branches of French law that are codified, we have already discussed the technique that is used: it is that of a somewhat forced interpretation of legislative texts.[44] In the arsenal of code articles at his disposal, the judge can always find a rule to cite in support of his decision. The existence in the codes of very general formulae, such as Civil Code article 1134 for contracts, article 1382 for delicts, and article 544 for property, practically guarantee the judge a basis for his decision. Only very exceptionally will he base his decisions on an equitable principle, such as the one that prohibits unjustified enrichment.

The situation is different for the administrative judge. He has no code and so will often give decisions without citing any legislative text in his support. In such a case, he ordinarily simply asserts the existence in French law of the legal rule he applies; he does not think he needs to justify his assertion by invoking a supereminent principle of law. Writers, in their commentaries, have been less circumspect and have argued that the decisions of the administrative courts are in fact based on certain supereminent principles.

Moreover since 1940 the Council of State has changed its approach and has abandoned its reluctance to be bound by principles, no matter how general and consequently ambiguous, and has repeatedly asserted in its opinions the existence in French law of supereminent principles, that dominate its decisions. It has required that the government, in its regulations and conduct, conform to the general principles thus stated, so that these principles, independent of any legislation or custom, seem to dominate modern French administrative law.[45]

Supereminent principles thus do come into play and have a definite role in supplementing and thus perfecting the French legal

44. See Georges Ripert, *Travaux de l'Association Henri-Capitant pour la culture juridique française* (1950), VI, 68.

45. On these principles, see Benoît Jeanneau, *Les principes généraux du droit dans la jurisprudence administrative* (1954).

system. But by the use of two different techniques—forced interpretation of private law legislative texts and in public law the more elementary technique of simply asserting the existence of a legal rule —their role remains somewhat disguised. Except for the general principles of law that are recognized by administrative court opinions, reading French judicial opinions will not reveal their importance or content.

A different question is whether supereminent principles can go beyond the filling out of the legal system and also act to correct a rule that, at first sight, seems to be part of the legal system but whose application in the case at hand would contradict the requirements of public policy and justice. The judge, whether civil or administrative, may follow the usual reasoning processes using legislation and custom and decide how a particular dispute should be solved. Is this solution absolutely obligatory or can the judge change or set aside the application of this rule by invoking supereminent principles?

This question will immediately suggest to lawyers the distinction in Roman law between civil law and praetorian law, or that in England between common law and equity. Let us state at the outset that there is not, and never has been, in French law anything comparable to these distinctions.[46] Nevertheless, techniques do exist by which French courts can avoid a solution that seems to be required by legal rules, but is unjust or seems to have serious inconveniences for the society.

A first supereminent principle that one might think of is resort to the concept of equity. At first glance, this technique seems to be ill-regarded in France. The word *equity* has a bad press in France; French lawyers immediately associate it with the idea of arbitrary action. "God save us from the equity of the *parlements* [prerevolutionary courts]" is a formula that is often cited and continues to influence the minds of lawyers and judges. Aside from the few exceptional cases where the legislator himself has referred to equity, a litigant has no chance of success if he simply argues the equity of his position to the judge. The French judge decides in law, not in equity.

46. See John P. Dawson, "Remedies of the French Chancery before 1789," in *Festschrift für Ernst Rabel* (1954), I, 99–140.

Still, it is clear that French courts are not, and cannot be, indifferent to the equitable posture of litigation before them. To use these equitable factors effectively, however, one must present the argument in a different way and rely upon a principle that the judge will be inclined to utilize. Wherever the teleological method of statutory interpretation is required in order to interpret a particularly broad concept used by the legislator, or even where it is just authorized, parties can make considerable use of equitable arguments. The judge who has to decide whether the cause for a contract is immoral (article 1133, Civil Code), or whether a testator was of sound mind (article 901, Civil Code), or whether an expense of an emancipated minor is excessive (article 484, Civil Code), or whether a condition in a donation is immoral (article 900, Civil Code), or whether there are extenuating circumstances in the case of a penal offense (articles 463 and 485, Penal Code) can give very considerable weight, in fact, to equitable considerations. This will also happen where he must evaluate certain kinds of conduct and their consequences in order to decide a case. To decide that a person has committed a fault or to evaluate damages caused, particularly exemplary damages, in the situation envisioned by Civil Code article 1382 certainly requires a judge to weigh equitable factors carefully.

In public law, we should recall the government's discretionary power to enforce or not enforce the rights of society or of a particular government agency against individuals. We have already discussed the system of "discretionary prosecution," which is part of French criminal law. Tax authorities, too, can grant taxpayers extra time for the payment of their taxes; in some cases the government can even compromise on the amount of penalty owed by a person. Such rules and administrative practices allow equity to play a role in French law that is not apparent if one considers only the legislative texts.

There are other approaches that can make a judge consider the equitable posture of a case, in addition to those mentioned above. Some of these are based upon ancient tradition, as in cases where there has been fraud. Ordinarily it is a poor argument to tell a judge that equity is on your side, but the contrary can be true if you argue that you have been defrauded. The Latin adage *fraus omnia corrum-*

pit ("fraud spoils everything") has continuing validity in France. French judges readily apply it in certain types of situations, even though no general code text articulates it.[47] The effective scope of the adage, the conditions in which it can be invoked, and its effects are in fact quite imprecise. There are cases where its application is traditionally excluded. This is true of marriage, where, according to Loisel's picturesque phrase, "One deceives if he can" (*Il trompe qui peut*). Other rules prevent its application because they are recognized as being eminently formalistic, such as rules establishing formal requirements, fixing time limits, and establishing particular required procedures.[48] But there is not total agreement on the scope of this exclusion. The adage *fraus omnia corrumpit* seems to be available against statements in public registers like the commercial register and the registry of mortgages.[49] According to a recent decision, it is there to protect the victim of the fraud and not to punish its author.[50] Unlike rules of equity, it acts *in rem* rather than *in personam* and thus can even be invoked against third persons in good faith. It has been applied in the areas of persons (invalidation of acts performed by an interdicted person prior to his interdiction), succession (invalidation of an ill-considered partition of a succession), obligations (liability of the person who helps a debtor violate his contractual obligation), matrimonial relations (invalidation of acts performed by the husband in fraud of his wife's rights, particularly pending a divorce hearing), and private international law (the so-called theory of fraud on the law).

Another way to make a judge consider equitable factors in reaching his decision is to invoke the doctrine of unjustified enrichment.[51] Here again the courts hide behind a Latin maxim: *Jure naturae aequum est neminem cum alterius detrimento et injuria fieri locupletiorem* ("By the law of nature it is not just that anyone should be

47. Georges Ripert, *La règle morale dans les obligations civiles* (4th ed.; 1949), 287 ff., particularly 314 ff.

48. See the general report of Paul Roubier on legal technique and method since the Civil Code of 1804, in *Travaux de l'Association Henri-Capitant pour la culture juridique française* (1950), tome VI, 48–49.

49. M. Picard, *Les Biens*, Vol. III of Planiol and Ripert, *Traité pratique de droit civil français*, no. 650.

50. Cass. Civ., May 10, 1949 (D.1949.277, note by Lenoan; S.1949.1.189, note by Bulté; J.C.P.1949.4972, note by Becqué).

51. John P. Dawson, *Unjust Enrichment* (1951).

enriched by the detriment or injury to another").[52] This adage comes from the *Digest* and has always been the basis for several doctrines and rules of French law: unauthorized management of another's affairs, undue payments, expenses incurred on the property of another, the idea that one who fights to avoid a loss should be preferred over one who fights to hold a gain (particularly with respect to the creditor's action to invalidate transactions in fraud of his right). It is only recently, however, that the doctrine has been held to state a general equitable principle that can justify recovery by an impoverished person in cases not specified by the code. The doctrine of abuse of rights is certainly the most important tool available. It has completely changed the relationship between law and equity in France in recent years.

Nowhere do the French codes state that persons' rights have limits that their holders cannot exceed. The idea seems to have been foreign to the codes' drafters. Eighteenth-century legal philosophy was the source of inspiration for these codes, and it exalted the role of the individual, the independence of his will, and the natural rights of men. Both the Declaration of the Rights of Man and of the Citizen and the Civil Code are based on these ideas and seem to consider a person's rights as his absolute prerogatives. *Neminem laedit, qui suo jure utitur* ("He who exercises his right injures no one").

Since the beginning of the twentieth century, French private law has been influenced by Ihering's ideas and by doctrines developed in French public law to the effect that the government and its agents have functions to fulfill rather than, in the strict sense, rights to assert. Civil, commercial, and procedural law all have reacted against the idea that a person's rights are absolute. The principle has been proposed that an individual must not abuse his rights. Because French courts always feel that they must have a legislative text on which to base a new doctrine, they used Civil Code article 1382 in this case. A person commits a fault and becomes liable for damages if he abuses his rights. The doctrine of abuse of rights, for this reason, is covered by French writers in books on delictual liability, although the principle is in fact a general one. Because it dominates

52. Pomponius, *Digest,* L. 17, *De regulis juris,* 206.

all French law and is applied throughout the legal system, some people think it should be placed at the very beginning of the Civil Code with the other general principles that are presented as being applicable to all French private law.[53]

Sometimes it has been argued that the doctrine of abuse of rights is the private law equivalent of the doctrine of abuse of power in French administrative law. Such an analysis makes it seem that the doctrine has completely revolutionized the French legal system. Individuals could no longer act freely in their own interest; they would simply have social functions and "rights" granted to help them fulfill these functions. In other words, personal rights would exist essentially for the good of society and not for the benefit of their holders; their use would be conditioned and limited by the social interest that they are designed to serve. An individual could not abuse his right, in the sense that he could not divert it from the social goal that defines its scope and justifies it.

This socialist conception of rights prevailed in the civil code of Soviet Russia.[54] In France it was articulated by the illustrious public law lawyer Léon Duguit and has also had its private law advocates, the most important of whom was L. Josserand. But there have always been reservations. Even its most fervent supporters have always admitted that in addition to "functional rights," which must be used in conformity with certain social goals, French law also recognized "power rights," over the exercise of which no supervision is allowed.

The socialist conception has had a very considerable legislative effect. Individual freedom has been restricted in order to prevent the exercise of rights in specific ways thought contrary to society's interest. This legislative initiative has been particularly important in

53. Examples of this approach are found in the *Swiss Civil Code* (art. 2) and the German *B.G.B.* (sec. 226). Ripert, *La règle morale dans les obligations civiles*, 158–66, recalls that Saleilles proposed embodying the theory of abuse of rights in the Civil Code by inserting a new article in the preliminary book of the code immediately after the present article 6. The Commission for the Reform of the Civil Code expressly recommended that this be done: *Travaux de la commission* (1950–51), VI, 14–26, and article 147 of the proposed new Civil Code.

54. *Russian Civil Code*, art. 1: "The rights of citizens are protected by the law, except for situations where they are exercised in contradiction with their social-economic function." Also see article 1 of the *Law of July 18, 1950* in the Polish Democratic Republic: "The provisions of the law are to be interpreted and applied in conformity with the basic structure and goals of the people's state," and article 3 of the same law: "No one should use his rights in contradiction with the principles of communal social life in the people's state."

labor law (limitations on the freedom of contract in order to benefit workers, limitation on property rights in order to benefit the national economy), but they have also profoundly affected civil and commercial law.[55] Except for these legislative steps, however, French private law has remained faithful to the Civil Code conception of personal rights.

The theory of abuse of rights that the French courts have developed is only apparently analogous to the administrative law theory of abuse of power. Abuse of power has nothing to do with morality or equity. Rather, it is one aspect of the idea of exceeding one's power: the question asked is whether the government agent, acting as he did, can be objectively considered to have acted in the public interest that limits his power. The French doctrine of abuse of rights, on the other hand, has a definite moral basis. To know whether a person has abused his rights, one asks whether he has used them so as to constitute a fault, i.e., wrongful behavior. The fault can consist in having acted with the sole intention of injuring someone else; or it can, and increasingly does, consist in having acted in disregard of the interest of society or of another person. But in the doctrine of abuse of rights, it is always personal conduct that must be evaluated, and the approach is always subjective: the question is never what are the objective limits of a right and have they been exceeded, as it is in the doctrine of abuse of power.

Because of this basis, the doctrine of abuse of rights introduces an equitable evaluation into litigation. To decide whether or not a person has abused his right is to decide whether or not he has committed a fault, and no matter how one may try to define the notion of fault in objective terms, it remains essentially a moral concept to which the law gives legal effects. Equity has a similar moral basis, with the difference that it leads one to consider the relationship as a whole, with special attention to the person injured, whereas the search for and evaluation of fault center principally on the person causing the injury. The theory of the abuse of rights, because of its moral basis, is frequently used to satisfy equitable needs.

A judge may be tempted to depart from legal rules or avoid their strict application by other than equitable factors. He may feel the same need where a solution dictated by the strict application of the

55. R. Savatier, *Du droit privé au droit public à travers les personnes, les biens, et la responsabilité civile* (2nd ed.; 1950).

law seems to him to violate society's interests. In such a case, he
will use the notions of public order (*l'ordre public*) and good morals (*les bonnes moeurs*).[56] The two concepts are generally tied together and are used by the French codes in several articles, the
most general, and therefore important, being Civil Code article 6,
which states that "one may not, by private agreement, depart from
laws based on public order or good morals."

When a judge must decide whether or not an agreement violates
public order and, if so, whether the consequence should be invalidity of the agreement, he will decide the case be applying legislation, i.e., articles 6 and 1131. Thanks to the general formulae used
by the code, he can satisfy the requirements of public order and
good morals as they appear and as he understands them at the moment of his decision. Public order and good morals can be invoked
at any time, even beyond the already broad scope of these articles.
The judge can use these notions to avoid deciding a case in a way
that he finds unacceptable.

This use of the notion of public order varies according to the
branch of law in question.[57] It is used most frequently, and probably excessively, in private international law, where it is divorced
from the concept of social morality. The principles of private international law may lead to the conclusion that a particular foreign
statute is applicable to a case. Courts frequently, however, refuse to
apply the statute and apply French law in its place by deciding that
the foreign law rule violates French public order.[58]

In internal law, the notions of public order and good morals are
used to invalidate objectionable agreements by invoking Civil Code
articles 6 and 1133.[59] Here public order and good morals are simply

56. On these two concepts and the relationship between them, see Philippe
Malaurie, *Les contrats et l'ordre public: Etude de droit civil comparé* (France,
England, USSR) (1953).

57. Léon Julliot de la Morandière, "Cours de doctorat sur 'l'ordre public,'"
1930–31, 1931–32, 1950–51 (mimeographed); "L'ordre public en droit privé
interne," *Etudes de droit civil à la mémoire d'Henri-Capitant* (1937), 381.

58. Lerebours-Pigeonnière, *Droit international privé*, no. 379, has shown that
the notion of public order is utilized in private international law in two series of
cases: (1) to avoid rules of foreign law regarded in France as being contrary to
morality or natural justice; (2) to defend and impose solutions of French law
that are in fact disputed within France itself.

59. *L'ordre public* in internal law is very different from *l'ordre public* in private

general provisions that supplement other legislative rules. Where an agreement violates a statute, it would suffice to call it illegal and invalidate it as such. Even in such cases it is common to invoke articles 6 and 1133 in addition to the particular provision violated and to assert that the agreement violates public order and good morals. This characterization places an additional stigma on the agreement in question, as it insists that the invalidity is not just a matter of legal technique, but that it is required and justified by society's interest. Even in the absence of a special statutory rule to which one can refer, an agreement can be invalidated simply by invoking the general formulae of articles 6 and 1133.

Public order and good morals, moreover, are general concepts, overriding principles, that can be invoked to exclude the application of a particular legal rule, even beyond the framework of articles 6 and 1133, which deal only with the invalidation of private agreements. In internal law, however, the courts, aware that abuse of these concepts would destroy all legal security, use them with moderation. As with equity, an advocate who wants to convince a judge to utilize the concepts of public order or good morals should try to articulate more precisely the principle whose protection is being invoked and to cite an established line of judicial decisions that has accepted the role and efficacy of these concepts in such cases.

In this connection, we should mention again the cases discussed above where equity may be relevant: both the importance of equity and the idea of good morals can be invoked to support particular applications of the adage *fraus omnia corrumpit* and use of the doctrines of unjustified enrichment and abuse of rights. Other adages that are unrelated to equity can be used in connection with the concept of good morals. This is true of *in pari causa turpitudinis cessat repetitio* ("he who is an equal cause of the evil loses his remedy"), by virtue of which invalidation of an agreement may not lead to restitution of performance already made where the invalidation is based on a violation of social morality. The concept of public policy, separated from social morality, is relevant to article 645 of the Civil Code, which provides, "In a dispute between landowners

---

international law. Moreover, there is not even a single concept of *"loi d'ordre public"* in French internal law. It is necessary to distinguish between the various consequences that follow from use of the concept. See pp. 91–92, above.

for whom [running water may be useful], the court decides the case by reconciling the interest of agriculture with the respect due to ownership." [60]

In all these areas, French law may give an impression of being imprecise. The theories of abuse of rights, public order, and good morals may seem imprecise, in danger of compromising the security of legal relationships. The French lawyer, however, will share neither this impression nor this fear. His conception of legal rules allows for some flexibility both in their application and in their expression. His own intuition and a study of judicial decisions will give him a feeling for the cases where he may be able to convince a judge to consider equitable factors, public order, or good morals. Except for a few established doctrines, of which we have discussed the most important, there are few cases where these considerations can have any effect. Tradition and judicial decisions provide important guidance and points of reference with respect to such cases.

There are in fact certain "equitable rules" and "rules of public order" in French law that could, and perhaps should, be defined with greater precision than is done in the codes.[61] If this were done, we would see that only a very narrow area remains where the general notions of equity, public order, and good morals have any role and where ambiguity is, consequently, greater than usual.

The way the courts use the concept of public order does not create much uncertainty. Foreign lawyers are likely to get a false impression if they study, as they often do, the concept of public order as it is used in private international law. For example, in the French law of contracts public order is quite a stable and precise concept. Only in the last few years has it been invoked alone without the support of an additional text justifying its use in the particular case in question. Good morals, certainly, is a concept traditionally more independent of statutory law, but here too the courts

60. See also, concerning partition of successions, *Code Civil,* art. 832 (June 17, 1938, revision): "In the formation and composition of the shares, the separation of immovables into small parcels and the division of [industrial and commercial] establishments must be avoided." "Insofar as it is possible to avoid fragmentation of objects of the estate and division of enterprises, each lot should, as much as possible, be composed . . . of movables and immovables, and assets and liabilities of equal value."

61. Ripert advocates more precise definition in his *La règle morale dans les obligations civiles,* 181.

have developed a number of doctrines that guide the jurist. The uncertainty that remains cannot be avoided in any country. The French courts have often rejected pleas, sometimes urgently pressed, that equity be allowed to prevail over law, or that considerations of public order should determine a decision. Thus in civil and commercial law, they have refused to invalidate or modify contracts on the grounds of changed circumstances. And the administrative courts have been able to develop an administrative law that guarantees individual rights and freedoms without succumbing to the argument that public order requires that the claims of the government must always prevail.

To this list of supereminent principles, composed of equity, public order, and good morals, we must add certain general legal principles that have been articulated by the administrative courts since 1940. We have already discussed these eminent general principles, which the Council of State has affirmed are part of our legal system.[62] In some cases, however, these principles have a role that goes beyond filling in legislative gaps and compensating for the absence of an administrative code. Sometimes they fulfill a function much like that of equity, public order, and good morals. Let us read how an eminent member of the Council of State explains why that court has found it necessary, since 1940, to elaborate these principles. The principles were not mentioned before 1940 primarily because it was unnecessary

> to mention principles directly inspired by and tied to the democratic system in a country where this system was neither disputed nor endangered by those who governed, principles whose existence was so obvious that the courts had no reason to restate them and had only to apply them. . . . But in 1940 the Vichy government was formed and immediately sought to undermine the system upon which French life had been based for so many years. Then came the liberation, which was accompanied, as could be expected, by sufficient public unrest to be a matter of legal concern. Most important, the liberation left intact some of the newly created organisms, strongly imbued with the ideas of the preceding system that created them. Now,

62. See pp. 130, 195, above.

faced with this "setback to public liberties," this threat
to the very foundation of the traditional French system, the Council of State changed its approach completely and set about developing its theory of the "general legal principles," which it had previously refused
to do even though its decisions had been impregnated
with them.[63]

The quoted passage is clear: the Council of State utilized the
idea of general legal principles not simply or even principally in
order to systematize its case law, something that it has always been
somewhat reluctant to do, but in order to limit the application of
legal rules emanating from other parts of the government and to
correct these rules. Certain opinions handed down by the Council of
State using general legal principles confirm this conclusion. Thus,
the Council of State has affirmed the possibility of appeal for exceeding powers (*excès de pouvoir*), in conformity with general legal principles, against an administrative decree that the law declared "could not be appealed in either the administrative or regular
courts." [64] It proclaims principles such as equality of individuals in
the eyes of public officials in order to limit the apparently discretionary powers given to prefects by legislation. It fixes the limits for the
exercise of the executive branch's regulatory power.[65]

The members of the Council of State who have written on this
question have endeavored to show that these general legal principles are only a broad interpretation of the written law and in no
way endanger the supremacy of the written law. The truth seems
to be that, since the Council of State has the wisdom to limit its
use of these concepts, the general legal principles do not threaten
the supremacy of the written law in the administrative law area any
more than the use by the regular courts of the principles of public
policy and equity threaten the supremacy of legislation in the civil
law area. Nevertheless it seems to us, as it does to the majority of

63. Maxime Letourneur, "Les principes généraux du droit dans la jurisprudence
du Conseil d'Etat," in *Conseil d'Etat, Etudes et documents, no. 5* (1951), 19,
21–22; see also René Cassin, "Le Conseil d'Etat gardien des principes de la
Révolution française," *Revue internationale d'histoire politique et constitutionelle*,
1951, p. 54.

64. Council of State, February 17, 1950, *Ministre de l'Agriculture v. dame
Lamotte.*

65. On all these points, see Jeanneau, *op. cit., passim*, but particularly 52–53,
59–60, 63, 160.

writers,[66] that alongside the general principles that constitute an expansion and systematization of principles posed by the legislator, there is another category of general principles, whose character is reforming rather than conforming. These principles aim at insuring the supremacy in French law of those conceptions of order and justice, as opposed to purely formal law, that we regard as the foundation of our society. The general principles, when seen with this function, can be used to "neutralize some legislation," to "rank legislative law beneath judicial law." [67] The law is not an end in itself; it serves the conception that we have of our social life and of justice. An attachment to formalism must not lead us to sacrifice the means to the end. The strictness of the law must be relaxed if its strict application violates what we believe justice requires. The appeal to general legal principles by the administrative courts and the use of concepts such as equity, public order, and good morals by the regular courts are required by our very conception of law. The use of these general principles and broad concepts is based in itself on an awareness that positive law is not an end in itself and is not sufficient to accomplish the final goal of the legal system— justice. This technique provides a means of incorporating into the legal system broad value-oriented norms, which some will call basic concepts of the society and others will call natural law.[68]

66. See *ibid.*, 218 ff.
67. These terms are borrowed from MM. Rivero and Vedel; see Jeanneau, *op. cit.*, 11, 146.
68. See *ibid.*, 220, 233, 254, analyzing the approaches taken by M. Hauriou, J. Rivero, and L. Duguit.

APPENDIX A

The Teaching of Law in France

Admission Requirements

The admission requirements for French faculties of law are simple. Basically, a particular level of prior academic achievement is required. Students wishing to study for the license in law (*licence en droit*) must have passed the baccalaureate, a comprehensive examination given at the end of French secondary school studies (or hold an equivalent French or foreign diploma). For the doctoral program, one must already hold the license in law (or an equivalent French or foreign diploma). No prior diploma is required for students who want to study for the certificate of capacity in law; the only requirement is that one be at least seventeen years old.

The diplomas required of foreign students who want to register as license in law or doctoral students are specified in equivalency lists prepared by the Minister of National Education. These lists, however, are not exhaustive, and one can request admission on the basis of other diplomas or other qualifications. The decision in such cases is up to the dean of the faculty of law and a request should be submitted to him.

Admission, registration, and examination fees in a faculty of law are insignificant—less than 100 new francs per year ($20.00).

Curriculum

I. License in Law
Studies for a license in law last four years, which are divided into two two-year cycles.

After the first cycle, one receives a Bachelor of Laws degree. The courses in this program, all of which are required, are the following:

FIRST YEAR
Legal institutions and civil law (persons, family law)
History of society and social institutions
Economics
Constitutional law and political institutions
International institutions (one-semester course)
Financial institutions (one-semester course)

SECOND YEAR
Civil law (obligations, principal real rights)
History of society and social institutions
Administrative law
Economics
Labor law (one-semester course)
General penal law and criminology (one-semester course)

The second cycle is divided into two sections for law students; they must decide whether they want to study private law or public law and political science.

The required courses for students in the private law section are the following:

THIRD YEAR
Civil law (principal contracts, securities, land registration)
Commercial law (commercial acts, businesses, partnerships and share companies)
Roman law and prerevolutionary French law (obligations) (one-semester course)
Social security (one-semester course)
Civil procedure (one-semester course)
Criminal procedure (one-semester course)
General penal law (one-semester course)
Roman law and prerevolutionary French law (property) (one-semester course) ⎫
Economic fluctuations (one-semester course) ⎭ students choose one of two

FOURTH YEAR
Civil law (matrimonial property law, successions, gifts, and wills)

Commercial law (contracts, commercial paper, bankruptcy)

Roman law and prerevolutionary French law (matrimonial property law, successions, gifts, and wills) (one-semester course)

Private international law (one-semester course)

Two one-semester courses or a single year-long course, elected from among the other subjects taught in the faculty

The required courses for students in the public law and political science section are the following:

THIRD YEAR

Commercial law (commercial acts, businesses, partnerships, and share companies)

Social security (one-semester course)

Civil procedure (one-semester course)

Criminal procedure (one-semester course)

Advanced public international law (one-semester course)

Tax (one-semester course)

History of political thought (one-semester course)

Economic fluctuations (one-semester course)

FOURTH YEAR

Major national services and enterprises

Law of the French overseas Community (one-semester course)

Civil rights (one-semester course)

Private international law (one-semester course)

Money and banking (one-semester courses)

Two one-semester courses or a single year-long course, elected from among the other subjects taught at the faculty

In addition to the courses already mentioned, students can choose their electives from the following list of offerings:

Maritime law

Execution of judgments

Literary, artistic, and industrial property

Registration

Comparative civil law

Insurance law

Special penal law
Historical sociology of law
Land and air transport
European organizations
Major contemporary political problems
Islamic law
Various economics courses

All these courses last one semester, except for the one dealing with major contemporary political problems. At the present time, legal philosophy and sociology of law are taught in the Paris Faculty of Law only at the doctoral level.

II. Doctorate

There are two kinds of doctorate, the State Doctorate (*Doctorat d'Etat*) and the Doctorate of the University (*Doctorat de l'Université*). The latter is exclusively for foreign students.

The State Doctorate requires that the student receive a Diploma of Higher Studies, or DES (*Diplôme d'études supérieures*) and that he write and defend a doctoral thesis. The Diplomas of Higher Studies in law available at the Faculty of Law in Paris are the following: DES in legal history and Roman law, DES in private law, DES in criminal science, DES in public law. There are also Diplomas of Higher Studies in political science and in economics. For every DES, there are both required and optional courses.

For the Doctorate of the University of Paris, a student must pass an examination and write and defend a doctoral thesis. The differences between it and the State Doctorate have lessened since a reform of the latter in 1959. Candidates for the Doctorate of the University are simply given a wider variety of options than those for the State Doctorate. They can choose from among the following areas: private law, commercial law, penal law, Roman law, legal history, international law, public international law, private international law, constitutional law and political science, administrative law, labor law, and comparative law. In whatever area he chooses, the student must take four courses. Some courses are required, and the student's program is then filled out by optional courses that are fairly strictly regulated.

Connected Institutes

Various institutes have been created and function as appendages to the faculty of law or to the University of Paris. Several of them are teaching institutions and award diplomas. One of their great advantages is that they permit professors in the faculties of law to associate with lawyers (foreign professors, judges, administrators, and practitioners) who are not necessarily members of a university and bring to their teaching the fresh air of experience.

Those institutes in Paris to be particularly noted are the Institute of Business Law (*Institut de droit des affaires*), which offers a two-year program of studies, the Institute of Criminology, the Institute of Advanced International Studies, and the Institute of Comparative Law.

Teaching Methods

The principal method of instruction in France is still the magistral lecture, delivered without discussion. Courses are held three hours a week in the license in law program and one hour per week in the doctoral program. License courses actually begin at the end of October and continue to the end of May. Doctoral courses begin in mid-November and run until the end of April. The first semester closes and the second begins on February 15, although this fact is of importance only for one-semester courses. The only vacations within the academic year worth mentioning are for Christmas (fourteen days) and Easter (fourteen days).

It is increasingly regarded as desirable to supplement the lecture method by the use of other teaching methods. Attendance at two one-and-a-half-hour sessions of "practical exercises" per week has been required for license in law students in each of two areas they select. One and a half hours of directed research is also provided for each subject studied in the doctoral program.

One can legitimately deplore the insufficiency of our present system regarding personal contacts between professors and students. Nevertheless, it should be noted that in Paris there is one or more adviser for the students of each foreign country. The list of these professor-advisers is posted and can be obtained from the secretariat of the faculty. It is also true that there are fewer students in the doctoral courses and in the various institutes than in the license in law program. Students attending these other courses can easily establish contact with professors if they really want to. The French professor takes little initiative to meet his students, but he meets them willingly if they indicate that they desire such contact.

Examinations

License examinations are given in June and again in October. A student cannot enter the second year of the license in law program until he has passed the first, and so on. Written examinations are given in the two subjects in which the student has chosen to take the "practical exercises." In the other subjects, examinations are oral.

Doctoral examinations are given in May and again in November for the Doctorate of the University and in November and February for the State Doctorate. They also include both written and oral examinations.

The examinations are difficult and the percentage of failures in the written and oral examinations is very high. The extraordinary number of students registered in French faculties should not be misconstrued. Many are called, but few graduate. The doctoral thesis must represent an original and serious piece of work, and many doctoral theses—those that receive the notation *Très bien* (very good) and represent about 50 percent of the total—truly satisfy this requirement.

Statistics

Many misconceptions are held abroad, and even in France, concerning the number of law students and lawyers in France, and particularly in Paris. To interpret properly the statistics one must remember that French faculties actually include nearly all the social sciences; law is not the only subject taught. It should also be remembered that students can easily, and with little expense, enroll in the university. And finally, the difficulty of the examinations should be kept in mind.

In interpreting the statistics on the doctorate, it should be borne in mind that many students seek and obtain the Diploma of Higher Studies (DES) after their license in law, but never submit a thesis and thus never are awarded the doctor's degree in law.

Bibliography and Supplementary Information

Additional information on all the subjects discussed in this appendix can be found by consulting the following works, which appear annually:

Livret de l'étudiant (official publication, not restricted to law studies).

L'indicateur de l'étudiant en droit (Librairie générale de droit et de jurisprudence, 20 rue Soufflot, Paris V, France).

Guide Sirey de l'étudiant en droit (Librairie Sirey, 22 rue Soufflot, Paris V, France).

Guide du doctorat en droit (Librairie Joly, 19 rue Cujas, Paris V, France).

It is also possible to write directly to the secretariat of the Faculty of Law (12 place du Pantheon, Paris V, France) or to the various institutes attached to this faculty (same address, except for the Institute of Comparative Law, which is 28 rue Saint-Guillaume, Paris VII, France).

APPENDIX B

General Bibliographical Information

A *Bibliographie du droit français* was published in 1964 as a supplement to the present book, under the auspices of the International Association of Legal Science. The best way to bring this bibliography up-to-date is to consult either the treatises and other books dealing with the area of law or the particular question involved, with the bibliographical notes that they include, or the bibliographic chronicles that appear from time to time in various legal periodicals. An advantage of this method is that it allows one to find not only the books, but the notes and articles as well, on the question at hand. As for articles, reference must also be made to the *Index of Foreign Legal Periodicals*, published since 1960.

Another possibility is to consult the catalogues published by the various law publishers. In fact lawbooks in France are published by a small number of specialized publishers. Among the most important are the following:

> Librairie générale de droit et de jurisprudence (Pichon et Durand-Auzias), 20 rue Soufflot, Paris V, France.
> Librairie Dalloz, 9 rue Soufflot, Paris V, France.
> Librairie Pedone, 13 rue Soufflot, Paris V, France.
> Librairie Rousseau, 14 rue Soufflot, Paris V, France.
> Librairie Sirey, 22 rue Soufflot, Paris V, France.
> Librairie Doma-Montchrestien, 160 rue Saint-Jacques, Paris V, France.
> Editions techniques et Librairie des jurisclasseurs, 27 place Dauphine, Paris IV, France.
> Presses universitaires de France, 108 boulevard Saint-Germain, Paris VI, France.

Catalogues are also published by specialized bookstores, which sell both new and secondhand lawbooks. The main bookstores of this sort are:

> Librairie Duchemin (Chauny et Quinsac), 16 rue Soufflot, Paris V, France.
> Librairie Joly, 19 rue Cujas, Paris V, France.

Index

Abuse of rights, 199–201

Administration: in general, 31–38; distinguished from "Government," 21n; organization, 31–34; operation through private law entities, 31, 34; deconcentration and decentralization, 32–33; role and sense of responsibility, 34–35; *See also* Administrative courts, Administrative Law, Council of State, Public law

Administrative courts: role, 24, 28, 30, 128; independence, 25; importance to independence of regular judiciary, 58; lack of criminal jurisdiction, 117; principle of preliminary administrative decision, 128; *See also* Administration, Administrative law, Council of State, Court of Conflicts

Administrative law: in general, 127–132, 205–207; created by Council of State, 36; relation to private law 102n, 129–32 *passim;* separate from constitutional law, 123; structure provided by constitutional law, 127; systematic study relatively recent, 127; definition, 127; role of administrative courts, 128; role of regular courts, 128; importance of judicial decisions, 128; principle of preliminary administrative decision, 128; particularity of, 128–29; fundamental principles of, 128–30, 195; historical development, 129; uncodified, 130; French concept and development unique, 131–32; tax law a special part, 133; evidentiary problems neglected, 146–47; role of legislation, 155–56; custom *praeter*

legem, role unclear, 176; custom *adversus legem* important, 177–78; *See also* Administration, Administrative courts, Council of State, Public law

Advocate: in general, 62–65, 67; élite of legal profession, 62; public servant, 62–63; heir to Roman orator, 64–65; partially merged with *avoué* in 1971, p. 67

Agréé, 49, 67

Alarician Breviary, 3, 6

Arbitration, 46, 116, 138, 166, 175

Avoué, 49, 64, 65, 67

Bar associations, 63–64

Bibliography: on legal education, 214; general, 215–16

Burgundian Law, 4

Case reports, 188

Categorization: importance of, 95

Civil law: in general, 108–12; preeminence in French law, 108, 111; definition, 108; content, 109, 110; commercial law not part, 109; model for development of other branches, 110, 130, 156; stability, 110–11; attempts at revision and amendment, 111–12; effect on administrative law, 129–31; little room for custom *praeter legem,* 173–74; *See also* Codification, Private law

Civil service. *See* Administration

Codification: in general, 11–16; scope, ix, 13–14; impact on global influence of French law, viii; role in French legal system, xiv; reasons for, 7; im-